A POLITICIAN THINKING

THE JULIAN J. ROTHBAUM DISTINGUISHED LECTURE SERIES

A POLITICIAN THINKING

The Creative Mind of James Madison

JACK N. RAKOVE

UNIVERSITY OF OKLAHOMA PRESS : NORMAN

Library of Congress Cataloging-in-Publication Data

Names: Rakove, Jack N., 1947– author.
Title: A politician thinking : the creative mind of James Madison / Jack N. Rakove.
Description: Norman : University of Oklahoma Press, [2017] | Series: The Julian J.
    Rothbaum distinguished lecture series ; volume 14 | Includes bibliographical
    references and index.
Identifiers: LCCN 2016057068 | ISBN 978-0-8061-5737-5 (hardcover : alk. paper)
Subjects: LCSH: Madison, James, 1751–1836—Political and social views. | United
    States—Politics and government—Philosophy. | Republicanism—United
    States—History—18th century. | Constitutional history—United States.
Classification: LCC E342 .R353 2017 | DDC 320.51/20973—dc23
LC record available at https://lccn.loc.gov/2016057068

A Politician Thinking: The Creative Mind of James Madison is Volume 14 in The
Julian J. Rothbaum Distinguished Lecture Series.

The paper in this book meets the guidelines for permanence and durability of
the Committee on Production Guidelines for Book Longevity of the Council on
Library Resources, Inc. ∞

1 2 3 4 5 6 7 8 9 10

For Roberta, Michael, and Max,
who kept the hope that springs eternal in the human breast

And for
The 2016 Chicago Cubs, who fulfilled that same hope

CONTENTS

FOREWORD

Among the many good things that have happened to me in my life, there is none in which I take more pride than the establishment of the Carl Albert Congressional Research and Studies Center at the University of Oklahoma, and none in which I take more satisfaction than the Center's presentation of the Julian J. Rothbaum Distinguished Lecture Series. The series is a perpetually endowed program of the University of Oklahoma, created in honor of Julian J. Rothbaum by his wife, Irene, and son, Joel Jankowsky.

Julian J. Rothbaum, my close friend since our childhood days in southeastern Oklahoma, was a longtime leader in Oklahoma in civic affairs. He served as a regent of the University of Oklahoma for two terms and as a state regent for higher education. In 1974 he was awarded the university's highest honor, the Distinguished Service Citation, and in 1986 he was inducted into the Oklahoma Hall of Fame.

The Rothbaum Lecture Series is devoted to the themes of representative government, democracy and education, and citizen participation in public affairs, values to which Julian J. Rothbaum was committed throughout his life. His lifelong dedication to the University of Oklahoma, the state, and his country is a tribute to the ideals to which the Rothbaum Lecture Series is dedicated. The books in the series make an enduring contribution to an understanding of American democracy.

Carl B. Albert
Forty-Sixth Speaker of the
United States House of Representatives

PREFACE

Back in the 2000s, I thought I had written pretty much everything I could about the political life and ideas of James Madison. I did have one Madison chapter planned for the book I spent that decade writing. But I had been working on Madison, in one way or another, since the early 1970s, when he became a major figure in the concluding chapters of my first book, on the Continental Congress. In 1990 I published a short life of Madison as part of the Library of American Biography, edited by my former professor Oscar Handlin. Madison was a dominant presence in my efforts to explain how a historically grounded approach to the problem of constitutional originalism would operate. In 1999 the Library of America published my one-volume edition of his writings. And I had written a number of other essays on particular aspects of his political ideas. What more did I have to say?

Yet when the invitation came to deliver the 2009 Julian J. Rothbaum Lectures at the University of Oklahoma, the idea of doing another Madison book became strangely attractive. It would allow me to bring together in one short volume a variety of ideas and positions I had presented in discrete places. Because I was the first historian to be asked to present the Rothbaum lectures, the invitation also opened an interesting venue to explain why a historian's approach to explaining the substance of Madison's thought could not be limited to critical renderings of the arguments of *Federalist* 10 and 51, complemented by a handful of other essays and documents.

More important, though, was my concern with exploring two other facets of Madison's life and career. One involved my desire to discuss and analyze the qualities of his mind. From conversations with political science colleagues like John Ferejohn and Barry Weingast I had come to realize (or at least hypothesize) that the empirical and theorizing modes of Madison's mind were very well balanced. At some point after my book *Original Meanings* appeared in 1996, I concluded that there was a recognizably game-theoretic component to Madison's thinking, particularly when he was analyzing the critical "vice" of the American federal system under the Articles of Confederation—its dependence on the voluntary compliance of the states with federal measures. What difference did it make to his course of action, I wondered, that he could cast the problems of the Confederation in these terms? But perhaps that was only one example of his distinctive intellectual traits. Madison was an acute and critical observer of the events in which he participated, yet he also had the knack or capacity of stepping back from the daily tumult of political life in order to analyze what these events revealed about larger problems of governance. Other efforts to analyze Madison's way of thinking had pivoted on the influence of such writers as David Hume and Montesquieu. But I was much more interested in the ways in which Madison's thinking was an active, ongoing response to his participation in public life. To borrow a phrase coined in conversation by Pasquale Pasquino, Madison was a "constitutional engineer." Like any engineer, he needed a deep knowledge of a body of theory. But he also had to have the capacity to solve problems on the ground—to apply that learning to real questions, and perhaps even to derive some fresh observations of his own.

This perception or conviction led to a second concern. To describe Madison as America's leading constitutional thinker involves something more than reconstructing the logic and substance of his published thought. Making sense of his leading published essays, notably including his twenty-nine contributions to *The Federalist*, will always remain a duty of Madison scholars. But Madison did his best thinking not to persuade others but for his own analytical purposes. Spare sentences in his personal letters and memoranda are sometimes as revealing as the lengthier essays of Publius, with all their nice qualifications and distinctions. Madison was at his most creative while trying to plot a course of action, not while trying to sway the opinions of skeptical readers. Understanding this form of creative political thinking involves asking questions rather different from those that have dominated the approach of the Cambridge school of the history of political thinking. It is much more a matter of political analysis than of political persuasion, even when the essays of *The Federalist* still had the latter end in view.

In developing these issues, this book relies primarily on the research and writing I have done over the past four decades. The book could be more extensively annotated than it is, and doubtless there are additional secondary sources I could have cited. I plead only that the original Rothbaum lectures and the substantial additions and revisions that I have made since 2009 were meant to state ideas I have developed over an extended period. This is, however, a great time to be a Madison scholar, and in various ways I have referred and responded to the stimulating work of other colleagues, notably Jeremy Bailey, Mary Bilder, and Colleen Sheehan (with whom I am happily coediting *The Cambridge Companion to* The Federalist). Indeed, it is so great a period to be thinking about Madison that perhaps I should come up with another topic or two of my own. In the Epilogue, I suggest two significant topics that do deserve such treatment.

Like many (though not all!) of my projects, this book has taken longer to finish than I expected. I hope my hosts at the University of Oklahoma are happy with the final version. I am deeply grateful to Cindy Simon Rosenthal for the invitation to deliver the Rothbaum lectures and for the generous hospitality that she, her staff, Ronald Peters, and other colleagues at the university provided. Joel Jankowsky was a wonderful personal host in Norman.

I have reached an age when I am mostly my own editor, which may be a big error, and that is why I appreciate the helpful comments provided by the two readers for the University of Oklahoma Press, Jeremy Bailey and Tom Mason. Over the years, it has been a great boon to discuss Madison matters with my Stanford friends John Ferejohn, Larry Kramer, and Barry Weingast; to wrestle with the recent and really excellent work done by Mary Bilder and Colleen Sheehan; and now to have the young Jonathan Gienapp as a departmental colleague.

Not too long after giving the Rothbaum lectures, I joined the board of directors at James Madison's Montpelier, just outside

Orange, Virginia. Every time I go there, I wonder about the life of the mind in this isolated corner of eighteenth-century America, and how this marchland of a provincial culture at the far reaches of the British Empire produced intellects like Madison and Thomas Jefferson. I do not have a wholly satisfactory answer to that question, but it remains a lot of fun to contemplate.

The very last stages of this book were completed while our grandson Alexander was staying at our house at Stanford. I will never know the answer to this question, but perhaps one day he will become the fourth generation of academic Rakoves (with his great-grandfather Milton, his grandfather, and Uncle Robby) to write a book about American politics. Or perhaps, like his diplomat father, Dan, he will become his own kind of cultural emissary to an ever-changing world. Whatever he does, my wife Helen and I count it as a great blessing that Alex and his mother Hyesun have joined our family.

A POLITICIAN THINKING

INTRODUCTION

Thinking about Madison's Mind

Some time around the year 2030, should the smiles of literary providence permit it, the publication of the modern letterpress edition of *The Papers of James Madison* will come to a close. Fifty-some carefully edited volumes will then be available, in four series covering the first half century of Madison's life, his tenure as secretary of state and president, and his two-decade retirement. These volumes form part of the "big six" sets of founders papers that also include those of George Washington, Thomas Jefferson, Benjamin Franklin, John Adams, and Alexander Hamilton. Other revolutionaries have also been honored: Nathanael Greene of Rhode Island, Henry Laurens of South Carolina, James Iredell of North Carolina, Robert Morris of Pennsylvania, and George Mason of Virginia. Beyond these personal papers, there are hefty sets of volumes devoted to institutions and events, including the correspondence and records of the Continental Congress, the Federal Convention of 1787, the ratification debates of 1787–88, the first federal elections, and the First Federal Congress of 1789–90.

The energy and devotion required for these publications are truly remarkable. No other nation has gone so far in preserving and publishing the record of its political birth. There is nothing comparable for the great upheavals that have transformed the histories of other nations, no similar effort to make so massively available not only documents of obvious public importance but the private papers that enable scholars to write the lives of the revolutionary generation. Unlike earlier editions of their papers, these volumes contain not only the letters the revolutionaries wrote but those they received as well. When, for example, James Madison first analyzed the defects of the constitutions that individual states had written in 1776, we read not only his August 23, 1785, letter to his college friend Caleb Wallace but Wallace's original request of July 12, describing how he had made his way from Virginia to Kentucky, rejoiced in becoming the father of two sons and a daughter who "are the great amusements of my leisure as well as the Objects of my most serious Cares," while twitting Madison over "the Taunts to which old Bachelors are justly exposed," before finally broaching the public questions on which Madison's diffident Princeton classmate now sought advice.[1]

The defining characteristic of these projects is that they present a whole-life approach to the leading members of the revolutionary generation. Personal papers appear in every volume—if not always correspondence between spouses, of which the letters of Abigail and John Adams are the exception that proves the rule, then at least to other family members, friends, acquaintances, and political connections. Within the borders of a single letter, comments on major public issues intermingle with miscellaneous news items and personal observations. Letters received count as well as autograph letters going out. These volumes present the American Revolution as it was lived, by active participants in one of the great transformations of modern history.

This observation is especially important for the subject of this book. Among all the revolutionary leaders, James Madison may be the one whose private personal life least engages biographers.[2] That is certainly the case in any comparison to his close friend and political ally Thomas Jefferson, but the comparison works equally well with the other members of the "big six." Madison's late age of marriage, complete devotion to public life, lack of a private vocation until he succeeded his father as the owner of Montpelier—these and other factors all suggest that his life was solely his public career. That indeed was how he imagined his biography should be written, as a record of his political projects, commitments, and reflections.

Foremost among these was his role in the formation of an effective national government, beginning with his efforts to ratify and reform the Articles of Confederation in the early and mid-1780s and culminating with the approval of the Constitution and its first amendments between 1787 and 1791. Madison's place in the first rank of founders depends on his status as "father of the Constitution." Although scholars still debate whether that title is fully deserved, there seems little doubt that this is the source of his hagiography. Madison is our leading constitutionalist, as both a political actor and a political theorist. No texts better express his status than his famous contributions to *The Federalist,* the eighty-five essays that he, Hamilton, and John Jay wrote in 1787–88 to support the ratification of the Constitution. Among Madison's twenty-nine essays, the most important is his first contribution, *Federalist* 10. Following closely behind the famous Tenth are the five essays that Madison wrote on the separation of powers, *Federalist* 47–51. These essays are widely regarded as the most authoritative statements of the basic theory of the Constitution. They are commonly taught in advanced placement classes in high school and in college-level introductory courses on American government. They have also generated a cottage industry of scholarship that supports the broader claim that the United States still lives under a Madisonian constitution—a claim that largely originates in the opening chapter of Robert Dahl's influential book of the mid-1950s, *A Preface to Democratic Theory.*[3] Americans inhabit a set of governing institutions that reflect the political concerns that Madison developed when he proposed a republican cure for "the mischiefs of faction" in *Federalist* 10 or used *Federalist* 51 to explain how ambition counteracting ambition would keep the three branches of government properly separated.

Yet one hardly needs fifty volumes of personal papers to establish Madison's stature as America's leading constitutional theorist. What Madison thought, the ideas that really matter as his legacy for the constitutional experiment, could presumably be reduced to a volume or two of his essential writings. Indeed, what seems most striking about our leading constitutional thinker is how little he wrote for publication and persuasion. The list of his publications is remarkably short. There are only twenty-nine essays for *The Federalist,* and Madison might have published nothing at all in support of ratification had he gone home to Virginia rather than stay in New York City to attend the Continental Congress in the fall and winter of 1787–88. After he and Jefferson moved into opposition to Hamilton's policies as secretary of the treasury, Madison drafted fifteen essays defining the core principles of the party they were about to form. These articles, which scholars refer to as the "party press" essays of 1791–92, were notably different

in tone, length, and style from his earlier writings as Publius, and
they illustrate Madison consciously experimenting with the idea
of appealing to mass public opinion.[4] The party press essays were
followed in 1793 by six far more closely reasoned articles by "Helvidius," the pen name Madison adopted after Secretary of State
Jefferson dragooned him into rebutting Hamilton's "Pacificus"
essays defending President Washington's unilateral authority to
declare effective neutrality amid the erupting wars of the French
Revolution. Madison occasionally published political essays in
succeeding years, and his 1800 "Report on the Alien and Sedition
Acts" offered a substantial defense of the ideas laid down in the
Virginia and Kentucky resolutions of 1798.

Still, for a major political or constitutional theorist, what
remains so striking about Madison is how little he wrote for
publication. Insofar as he was an essayist at all, he was responding to exigent situations. He could have left a fabulous legacy
to political theory had he used his two-decade retirement to
write either a coherent treatise on republican government or
a comprehensive history-cum-memoir of the development of
American constitutionalism covering, say, the quarter century
from independence to the presidential election of 1800–1801.
Indeed, as Colleen Sheehan has argued in a fascinating and
scrupulously annotated book, there is some evidence that in the
early 1790s Madison was actively contemplating writing a serious treatise relating ancient republicanism to the constitutional
innovations of the revolutionary era.[5] But that work, if he had it
in contemplation, never appeared. Instead, we are left with a set
of "Detached Memoranda" about men, events, and issues, drafted
shortly after he left the presidency, and "A Sketch Never Finished
Nor Applied," written around 1830, which briefly summarizes
American constitutional history from the quarrel with Britain
until the Federal Convention. In the Library of America edition
of Madison's writings that I have edited, these two documents
amount to a shadow less than forty pages.[6]

Following eighteenth-century conventions, Madison's political
writings were published either anonymously or pseudonymously.
Of course, he left numerous other public documents, both as a
member of the House of Representatives and as secretary of state
and president. But for the one founder who ranks first on the

roster of great American political thinkers, the literary pickings remain slim. Compare his oeuvre with the published works of Niccolò Machiavelli and Thomas Hobbes, the preeminent political thinkers of the sixteenth and seventeenth centuries, and Madison is very much the also-ran. He obviously remains a figure of some importance because of his association with great events, but nothing like the towering minds who reshaped the entire discourse of early modern political thought. Deconstructing the arguments of *Federalist* 10 and 51 is a less daunting task than providing a thorough interpretation of *I Discorsi* or *Leviathan*.

Yet Madison enjoyed one overwhelming opportunity that Machiavelli, Hobbes, Locke, and other notable European writers never gained. As John Adams aptly remarked in 1776, American constitutionalists had been "sent into life at a time when the greatest law-givers of antiquity would have wished to have lived."[7] That experience set them apart from the European writers whom they read, studied, and often criticized. Machiavelli wrote his great works only after the restoration of Medici rule in Florence swept him from office, never to return, much less to be in a position to apply the lessons he learned from his meditations both on the exercise of power and on the lessons of antiquity. Hobbes's long and brilliant intellectual life brought him into contact with leading members of the English ruling class, but he never occupied an office or engaged in the active conduct of public business.

By contrast, Madison's adult life began only when he joined the revolutionary movement, first as a member of the local committee of safety late in 1774, then as a militia officer in 1775, and finally as a delegate to Virginia's Fifth Provincial Convention that met in May 1776 to write the commonwealth's new constitution. In another age, the young alumnus of the College of New Jersey would have been a natural candidate for graduate school. The revolution came along instead. For the next four decades, his absences from public affairs can be numbered mostly in intervals of months. Politics became Madison's vocation—his career, really—during a period when officeholders regarded public life more as an avocation or a source of fees than a profession.[8] After Madison made his way north to join the Continental Congress in March 1780, after the snowiest winter in decades, he did not

return to Virginia until he was term-limited out of office in
October 1783—and this when most delegates served stints of
several months. He was hardly home at Montpelier before he
was elected to represent Orange County in the Virginia House
of Delegates, where he became the dominant legislator over the
next three years. Once he became eligible to return to Congress,
in 1787, he headed back to New York City, there to prepare for
the Federal Convention in Philadelphia. In truth, Madison's only
serious respite from politics came in March 1797, when he and
Dolley, his bride of three years, went back to Montpelier. For four
decades, this was a life lived within politics, and that life is best
revealed only by following its course in the way that *The Papers
of James Madison* now makes possible.

Part of that life was the life of the mind that Madison actively
pursued—a life in which knowledge of books and long hours
spent in the solitude of Montpelier, gazing west with its fabulous
front-door view of the Blue Ridge, marked one redeeming virtue
of the marchland isolation of Virginia culture. Just as Machiavelli
turned to the works of Titus Livy and other authors from antiquity
when he wanted to restore the republican government of Florence,
so Madison studied the records of ancient and modern confederacies when he began analyzing the problems of American federalism. In their own way, Madison's notes on these readings, written
in a small copybook in his very fine hand, echo Machiavelli's
famous letter to his friend Venturi, recording the metamorphosis
he felt in his study when he donned "garments regal and courtly"
to commune with his ancient teachers. Where Machiavelli drew
deep inspiration from his reading of antiquity, however, Madison
came away from his reading frustrated with how little useful
information he had gained from this line of research.[9]

The deeper truth is that Madison's political ideas were first and
foremost a response to the events in which he participated. Those
who study what Madison ostensibly *thought*—by which I mean
those who look at his published writings as the best evidence of
his ideas—will miss what is most striking and revealing about
his engagement with political ideas. For Madison, creative political *thinking*—by which I mean his ongoing efforts to analyze,
conceptualize, and explain the events in which he was participating—marked the true forum for his genius. The essays Madison

wrote for publication, including his most celebrated contributions to *The Federalist,* still remain important sources for his ideas. But they are best understood not as the conclusive statements of his thought, much less as texts that can be adequately analyzed by careful reading in isolation, but as public reflections of concerns that had already evolved in Madison's private thinking. Despite a few rhetorical flourishes meant to stir the sentiments of his readers, what seems most remarkable about Madison's essays for *The Federalist* is how well they illustrate issues and ideas with which he had previously been wrestling, and which he would continue to contemplate. It is only by identifying what those concerns were, only by tracking the course of Madison's thinking in the context of events, that we can properly understand the nature of his political intellect.

To develop this point, consider some of the questions that arise when we place too authoritative an emphasis on Madison's best-known essays. Any effort to analyze his constitutional theory has to give pride of place to *Federalist* 10 and 51.[10] There are excellent reasons for this emphasis, tied not only to the significance these texts enjoy in modern scholarship but also to the importance of the questions Madison was addressing. *Federalist* 10 marked the final statement—but also the first public one—of the argument that Madison had begun developing in the spring of 1787 as he shaped the potential agenda for the Federal Convention.[11] Madison challenged the reigning wisdom that republican governments should be limited to small, relatively homogeneous societies whose citizens share not only common traits but also a self-denying civic virtue that will lead them to subordinate private interests to public good. Rather than repudiate faction as an evil that republics must curb, *Federalist* 10 accepted it as an underlying condition of political life, rooted in differences embedded in human nature and the complexity of modern societies. An extended national republic, Madison reasoned, would offer two solutions to the "mischief of faction." First, its diversity would make it much harder for factions to coalesce into harmful majorities. Second, its extent would lead to the election of more qualified legislators who would be better prepared to deliberate on the true public good rather than simply favor the immediate interests of their constituents.

Federalist 51 marks a similar effort to reconcile the Constitution with conventional wisdom about the separation of powers. Here the challenge Madison faced was to demonstrate that the Constitution would not violate the fundamental maxim that held that legislative, executive, and judicial power needed to be kept distinct to preserve liberty. On this issue, Madison faced a somewhat different intellectual problem than the one he answered in *Federalist* 10. In the earlier essay, there was no alternative to refuting the accepted theory. But in *Federalist* 51 there was significant room to modify and manipulate the conventional wisdom rather than overturn it. The famous hypothesis of this essay confirms that each department of government must be given "the constitutional means and personal motives to resist the encroachments of the others" and, more specifically, that "ambition must be made to counteract ambition. The interest of the man must be connected to the constitutional rights of the place." If men were angels, such "controls" would not be necessary. But they were not, and so "auxiliary precautions" beyond the dependence of government on the people were necessary.

In both essays, Madison was wrestling with the intellectual legacy of "the celebrated Montesquieu," whose great work, *De l'esprit des lois,* was a dominant text for eighteenth-century political science. Montesquieu was famously associated with two orthodox propositions that supporters of the Constitution had either to refute or somehow to manipulate. One related to the optimal size of republics, the other to the idea that there were three distinct forms of power that needed to be clearly defined and distinguished. The Constitution threatened the first by suggesting that a nation-state as vast as the United States could still be governed as a republic, and the second by proposing a scheme of checks and balances among the departments that muddied rather than clarified their individual grants of power.

In his public responses to Montesquieu, Madison was entering a world of political argumentation that modern scholarship now interprets by applying the methodological concerns and approaches developed by Sir Quentin Skinner, J. G. A. Pocock, John Dunn, and other acolytes of the "Cambridge school."[12] There was a political language of republicanism and a vocabulary of the theory of separated powers that revolutionary Americans knew well, and which they incorporated in their new constitutions. Madison had to work within these settled traditions and conventions. If he did not accept these conventions, if he started from wholly new premises, his arguments would be either unintelligible or unpersuasive for most of his readers. Genuine innovation in political theory would come only when one reshaped or transformed accepted terms. But a political writer could also demonstrate his ingenuity by proving that reigning assumptions about an authority (like Montesquieu) were flawed or that the meaning of a text was more elastic than casual readers realized.

Federalist 10 and 47–51 can be treated as worthy American candidates for inclusion in the canon of political theory precisely because they raise the same issues of intention, meaning, and exposition that apply to other works. As statements of the *political theory* underlying the Constitution, they thus merit close attention as expositions of the dominant assumptions of the Madisonian constitution. But as examples of Madison's *constitutional thinking,* these essays have a more problematic status. Considering some of the questions they raise illustrates how the task of tracing Madison's thinking may diverge from reconstructing his best-known ideas.

Federalist 10 appeared in the New York *Independent Journal* on November 22, 1787. Four weeks earlier, Madison had written at length to Thomas Jefferson, offering an elaborate defense of the congressional negative on state laws that was arguably the most radical (or reactionary) proposal that he carried to Philadelphia in May 1787. Madison had promised Jefferson a fuller justification of this measure in an earlier letter, written eleven days before the Convention adjourned. The second letter more than fulfilled that promise, in terms strongly suggesting that Madison's private opinion remained unchanged by the arguments that doomed the negative at Philadelphia. There were two major uses for the negative, Madison noted. One would protect the national government against "encroachments on the General authority" by the states. The other would allow the national government to "prevent instability and injustice" by overturning state laws that violated the rights of individuals and minorities.[13] Here as elsewhere in Madison's writings, the dual criteria for judging political decisions in a republic involved asking whether they satisfied both the public good and private rights.

When *Federalist* 10 appeared a month later, Madison had no need to discuss the negative on state laws. The published version of his theory was sufficient for the task he now faced. Yet it would hardly do to accept *Federalist* 10 as a complete or even sufficient statement of Madison's ideas about the protection of liberty. The essay presented a strong hypothesis for the idea that liberty would be better protected in an extended republic than it would in the idealized model of small homogeneous societies—or, more to the point, in the smaller republics of the American states. Yet to Madison's way of thinking, the security that the Constitution promised would not effectively cover the danger to rights that would still exist within the states. That was where most laws affecting people's lives would still be enacted, by legislatures that would remain more vulnerable to the disease of faction than the new federal Congress. *Federalist* 10 constituted a powerful public response to the challenge from Montesquieu, but it did not adequately answer the problems that still troubled its author.

A different set of issues bedevils a reading of *Federalist* 51. If one examines the set of five essays that it concludes, the puzzle of Madison's restatement of the problem of separated powers becomes evident. In *Federalist* 47, Madison first took pains to define what Montesquieu and his American admirers actually meant by the idea of separated powers by working inductively from the evidence of British and American constitutional practice. The meaning of the definition had to be determined by the complex ways in which Britain and the American states allocated power among the departments, not by imposing an abstract theory or definition on practice. In the next essay, *Federalist* 48, Madison refined that point by explaining why the dangers to maintaining a proper separation were asymmetrical. Rather than assume that each branch equally threatened the other two, as the American constitution writers of 1776 seemingly supposed, Madison argued that the great danger of "encroachment" came from the "impetuous vortex" of the legislature, and especially from its lower house. Through its greater influence over the people and its authority as the rule maker, the legislature occupied the best position to weaken the authority of the other two branches. Then, in the next two essays, Madison gave his analysis a surprising twist. *Federalist* 49 and 50 turn away from the ostensible debate over the

Constitution to discuss an idea that few readers knew anything about—Jefferson's proposal to allow any two branches of a republican government to assemble a popular convention in order to monitor or reform a threat to the separation of powers. Madison used these two essays to explain why "the people themselves" could not be relied upon to act as impartial constitutional arbiters.[14]

With these stipulations clearly developed, the slate was now clean for Madison to reconcile the Constitution with the general principle of separated powers. In theory, he might well have wished to refute the leading Anti-Federalist charge on this point, which was that the worst violation of the principle of separated powers in the Constitution lay in the creation of a Senate that would improperly combine legislative, executive, and judicial (through its status as a court of impeachments) power in one small and potentially conspiratorial chamber.[15] These rhetorical options were obviously available. Yet in the end what is most striking about *Federalist* 51 is how little Madison finally says about the subject he is ostensibly addressing. Only a single paragraph of the essay explicitly addresses how the Constitution treats the separation of powers, and it does little more than endorse the principle of bicameralism and the limited veto of the president. Madison closes the discussion with a reference to the Senate, which he does not identify by name but instead describes as "the weaker branch of the stronger department." Even here Madison does not explain why he calls the Senate "the weaker branch." One could fairly object, after all, that the Senate is the stronger half of the legislature, since it enjoys the same legislative authority as the House of Representatives—other than the privilege of initiating bills "for raising Revenue," a power that Madison deemed inconsequential—as well as the power over treaties and appointments that it shares with the president. Rather than pursue the subject, however, Madison uses the concluding passages of the essay to restate the argument of *Federalist* 10—to imply that the greater security to liberty will arise not from any specific scheme of separated powers but from the existence in society of the "multiplicity of interests" that will deter the formation of "factious majorities." One could plausibly read *Federalist* 51 to suggest that the entire emphasis in public debate on the *constitutional* separation of powers was badly misplaced, and that the more fundamental issue involves understanding the *political* character of the extended republic.

Whatever his colleagues at Philadelphia or informed readers understood Madison to be saying—and some remain skeptical that they really grasped what he was saying[16]—there is no question of his attachment to the idea of an extended republic resting on a realistic assessment of human nature. At the same time, the published arguments of *Federalist* 10 and 51 were conceived to meet specific rhetorical challenges. How well they reflected the broader range of Madison's concerns or the course of his thinking remains a separate problem.

Perhaps more important, neither essay operates as a statement of constitutional ideas in the full or proper sense of the term. Constitutionalism is first and foremost a matter of how institutions of governance will work, how they will deliberate and decide or resolve conflicts over their respective realms of authority. *Federalist* 10 says almost nothing on this subject, beyond hypothesizing that federal elections will recruit a superior class of deliberative lawmakers. It operates essentially as a prolegomenon to a constitutional theory, primarily by explaining why a national republic will better resist the mischief of faction than the smaller commonwealths of the states. *Federalist* 51 and its antecedent essays do take on the task of thinking institutionally, but, again, Madison does not pursue this analysis very far.

As influential as these essays remain, they cannot capture the larger substance of Madison's ideas about constitutionalism or the prior process of political thinking that made Madison an active constitutionalist well before Hamilton asked him to coauthor *The Federalist*. To describe this Madison we need to look beyond the celebrated texts and examine how he immersed himself in the process of constitutional innovation. No one was ultimately more proud or confident about the success of that process than Madison. Yet few of his colleagues were as cautious or prudent about the idea of constitutional change. Madison thought actively about the nature of constitutional reasoning as a distinct realm of decision making, and the lessons he drew from that experience formed an essential element of his political intelligence. For Madison, constitution making was a "ticklish experiment,"[17] one that had to be conducted with due respect for what was being risked as well as what could be gained.

This book, then, is about Madison *thinking*. Its purpose is to explore how his ideas evolved out of his deep immersion in deliberations and decisions, at both the state and national levels of revolutionary governance. Indeed, one key argument is that the symmetry of Madison's involvement in the Continental Congress and the Virginia legislature during the 1780s goes far toward explaining the distinctive way in which he reassessed "the vices of the political system of the United States" (adapting the title of his April 1787 memorandum, to which we pay close attention throughout). A second argument stresses the symmetry between the empirical and theorizing components of Madison's mind—between the way in which he tried to grasp how certain decisions had been reached and his capacity to step back from those observations and ask what they reveal about the underlying structure of decision making.

These qualities of Madison's intellect were well described by Judith Shklar in her 1997 presidential address to the American Political Science Association. "He had a historian's mind, which was a great intellectual advantage," Shklar wrote. "It enabled him to penetrate to the logic of collective action, even when on the surface there seemed to be nothing but random irrationality and partisan wrangling. By reflecting upon previous occasions and experiences he was always able to see a pattern amid the confusion of men and events."[18] It is a nice aspect of this comment that Shklar, a political theorist, recognizes Madison as a tacit historian while also acknowledging that historians are not mere narrators but active seekers of "the logic of collective behavior" and "patterns" of action. Hard-nosed political scientists might scoff whether that is what historians do, but Shklar captures the dual facets of Madison's way of thinking. Had graduate school actually been a career opportunity for Madison in 1772, it is an open question which discipline he would have preferred: the study of history or the science of politics.[19]

Madison's political thinking, then, was less about rhetoric than analysis, less about persuading the public to support his positions than on determining a course of action. His original audience was himself, though later he would turn to a circle of correspondents and colleagues whose support he hoped to recruit after he had sorted out his own views. Because Madison wrote originally as an analyst, he often felt little need to elaborate his points. In public writings, such as *Federalist* 10, he could develop his argument by detailing definitions and distinctions. It would be easy to contrast Madison's knack for drawing distinctions and alternatives with, say, the candor and directness of expression that make Jefferson and Franklin more attractive figures to quote. Yet Madison could often be remarkably concise as well. Some of his passages pack more meaning into a single paragraph than other writers can express in a whole chapter or tract. As I argue below, item 7 in the "Vices of the Political System" is one such analysis. Or again, in his revealing October 17, 1788, letter to Jefferson expressing his support for a bill of rights, Madison conveyed critical insights in a single powerful sentence or two.[20] Often a scholar wishes that Madison had indulged his analytical genius a bit more, leaving another paragraph or page where one or two sentences did the work for their author. Occasionally, though, the need to answer objections did lead him to spell his ideas out at length. His October 24, 1787, letter to Jefferson, with its sustained defense of a congressional negative on state laws, reveals Madison defending an idea he knew his friend from Monticello would never approve.[21] But that letter is more the exception to the rule. When stating propositions that became essential to his political thinking, he could be quite succinct.

Great thoughts also pop up, virtually unheralded, in private letters. Madison's first discussion of the problem of the factious majority appears in a short letter to James Monroe. Writing in October 1786, Madison was originally worried about the sharp sectional division in Congress over the navigation of the Mississippi River.[22] But when he returned to this theme in the final item in "the Vices," the problem of the factious majority had evolved into a general critique not only of the injustice of state legislation but also of "the fundamental principle of republican Government, that the majority who rule in such Governments, are the safest Guardians both of public Good and of private rights."[23]

The analysis of this problem did not stop with this remark. Madison followed this observation by asking himself this question: "To what causes is this evil to be ascribed?" The answer led him to the basic conclusions he publicized in *Federalist* 10. Earlier in "the Vices" Madison raised a similar question after asking why the "compilers" of the Articles of Confederation had neglected to give the Continental Congress coercive authority over the states and then describing "how imperfectly did the States fulfill their obligations to the Union" during the revolutionary war and afterward. "How indeed could it be otherwise?" he then wrote, and his rapid-fire answer to this question immediately provided three deeply structural "causes & pretexts which will never fail to render federal measures abortive."[24]

The answers that Madison gave to these questions were substantive, not rhetorical, and they carried his thinking to the ideas and conclusions that decisively shaped his role as the leading constitutionalist of his (or perhaps any) era. The task of explaining the sources of majority misrule led Madison to challenge the conventional wisdom that republics had to rest on the self-denying virtue of their citizens and to propose instead a political sociology that made interest, passion, and faction the working materials of republican politics. So, too, the recognition of the complete inadequacy of a system of federalism based on the voluntary compliance of the states with congressional recommendations led Madison to conclude that the union had to be reconstituted on radically different principles, with a complete national government that would operate legally on its citizens rather than having to rely on the goodwill of the states.

What "the Vices" and similar documents capture, then, is not only what Madison thought but Madison in the process of thinking. Tracking his efforts to identify problems, reflect on the history in which he had participated, identify structural problems of governance, analyze the sources of political activity among officials and citizens, and finally propose and pursue constitutional solutions to these issues: all of this was the work of political thinking in the most active sense of the term. Political thinking in this case thus becomes a creative activity, a process that historians can attempt to reconstruct just as they would try to explain other aspects of human behavior. To follow Madison through this activity is thus a way of understanding the sources and character of his intellectual creativity, leading us in turn to ask, more generally, what qualities of mind make constitutional change possible.

In presenting the Rothbaum lectures upon which this book is based, I sought to capture Madison's mind in motion, to treat him less as an authoritative commentator on the origins of the

American constitution than as an exceptionally creative politician whose success rested upon his intellectual engagement with the work of republican politics. Madison did his best thinking not to persuade others but to reason out a course of political action. But, of course, that action was taking place in a republic, where the assent of the people or their representatives was also required. His efforts to secure his goals therefore did involve the further challenge of justifying his positions to public opinion, and this at a moment when the nature of public opinion was itself emerging as an active object of inquiry on both sides of the Atlantic. Madison's published writings, the familiar texts that have been so closely studied, thus become evidence, too, of how his mind was working.

In pursuing these questions, I hope that *A Politician Thinking* contributes in its own way to the flourishing scholarship on the history of political ideas that has marked the past four decades. The preeminent voices in this field include, on the American side, Bernard Bailyn and Gordon Wood; on the British side, Peter Laslett, Quentin Skinner, and John Dunn; and that truly global figure, J. G. A. Pocock, who has done so much to trace the movement of ideas from sixteenth-century Italy to seventeenth-century England and then eighteenth-century America. All these writers have influenced the ways in which I have formulated the problems of this book. Perhaps the ideas expressed in these chapters lie closest to the agenda Dunn laid down in his 1968 essay "The Identity of the History of Ideas." Here Dunn criticized the then-dominant approaches to the subject by arguing that "few branches of the history of ideas have been written as the history of an *activity*." Traditional approaches gave their subjects—both the ideas and the thinkers—a doctrinal coherence and rational integrity that they never attained or possessed in real life. In a somewhat caustic voice that sounds so characteristic of young English academics, Dunn wondered whether this history, as it had been written, "is the history of anything which ever did actually exist in the past." The positive side of his platform demands to be quoted at some length. What "the customary approaches appear to neglect," Dunn added, is

> that thinking is an effortful activity on the part of human beings, not simply a unitary performance; that incompleteness, incoherence, instability and the effort to overcome these are its persistent

characteristics; that it is not an activity which takes its meaning from a set of finished performances which have been set up in type and preserved in libraries, but an activity which is conducted more or less incompetently for most of their waking life by a substantial proportion of the human race, which generates conflicts and which is used to resolve these, which is directed towards problem-solving and not towards the construction of closed formal games; that the works in which at a single point of time a set of problems issue in an attempt at a coherent rational ordering of the relevant experience are in some sense unintelligible except in terms of this context.[25]

For a historian who has to ask the perennial question, How can one reconcile the Madison of the late 1780s with the Madison of the late 1790s? this alone is an enormously helpful comment.

The most robust answers to the question of how one writes the history of political thinking have come, of course, from the Cambridge school that Skinner inaugurated and trained. Much of the work that these historians have produced focuses on the rhetoric and language of political argumentation. Here the history of political thinking is often described as a set of speech acts in which actors or authors necessarily work within but also attempt to manipulate an existing political language or set of linguistic or conceptual conventions in order to secure their aims. The history of political thinking thus pivots around argument and rhetoric, and its inquiries focus on—and sometimes agonize over—the relation between the intentions of an author and the meaning of his text.[26]

These concerns, too, are relevant to an inquiry about Madison thinking, particularly when he actively sought to influence public opinion, as he certainly did in *The Federalist* or in the party press essays of 1791–92. The difficulty of finding ways to use political language accurately, with "perspicuity," a favored word of the eighteenth century, was a question with which Madison continually wrestled, not only while framing the Constitution but also as a distinguished authority whose views on its language were often solicited by concerned correspondents. And of course the whole linguistic problem of constitutional interpretation—a continuing American problem for which there are few if any European antecedents—quickly evolved into a dominant facet of American politics.

Still, it is the question of describing Madison's way of thinking, more than analyzing his published thoughts, that defines the goal of this book. That ambition rests on understanding the special role that Madison played, not merely as a leading author of the Constitution but also as the one delegate who worked hardest to set its agenda and make sense of its meaning. Madison was a political entrepreneur in the broadest sense in which academics use that term, and he deployed his talents at a truly world historical moment. This is a claim that many scholars might now find tiresome. After all, the publication of so many books about the "big six" and other leaders has produced a justifiable ennui and fatigue with the very phenomenon of "founders' chic." Moreover, we live at a moment when much historical scholarship is rightly preoccupied with recovering the meaning of the experience of revolution for ordinary Americans of every class, race, and gender. Heroic scholarly energies have been expended to show that the American Revolution was not simply the work of a talented group of great white men but a series of events that affected and were affected by the concerns of a wide array of colonists.

One can sympathize with this reaction without wholly accepting the judgment on which it rests. In my perhaps old-fashioned view, the adoption of the Federal Constitution remains one of the most remarkable events in modern history.[27] The more one observes the unsteady and precarious history of transitions to constitutional government elsewhere in our contemporary world, and the more one wonders at the revival of authoritarian governments in the post-1989 world, the more one should appreciate how much the American revolutionary generation, acting without any useful precedents, accomplished in the late eighteenth century. Madison was active in every phase of that process, actively thinking about the decisions that would have to be made. That is reason enough to ask, What it was like to be a leading constitutional thinker and actor in these events, and what were the qualities of mind that allowed Madison to do so much to shape the origins of the American constitutional project?

CHAPTER 1

"HOW INDEED COULD IT BE OTHERWISE?"

Rethinking the Problem of Federalism

Seeing Like a State was the clever title that the political scientist James C. Scott gave to his critique of national development projects in the modern world. Scott details a history of massive, even bloodcurdling failures, like the collectivization of Soviet agriculture in the 1930s or Mao's Great Leap Forward in the 1950s.[1] *Thinking Like a Constitution* might be an equivalent title for the great national development project to which Americans are attached—to the proposition that a modern republic could be permanently constructed out of devotion to a political constitution and a growing, if incomplete, commitment to human equality.[2] Our dominant impulse is to treat the Constitution as a paradigm of national success. Of course, its history is not a register of one great achievement after another. After all, there was the problem of "the recent unpleasantness" that we call the Civil War, or the recurring argument, popular during the Progressive Era and again today, holding the Constitution responsible for our sometimes reactionary, sometimes intractable patterns of governance.[3] Whether these examples are marks of constitutional failure or mere political paralysis is an open subject of debate. Yet in a broader perspective the challenge of asking how Americans developed the concept of a written constitution as supreme fundamental law remains a matter of global importance.

The idea of "thinking like a constitution"—that is, of asking what a project of building and maintaining a constitutional system entails—remains an apt way to analyze James Madison's foundational role in American history. To think like a

constitution in the 1780s, when Americans had to rethink the
political experiments of the mid-1770s, required at least four
distinct exercises. The first involved asking how much *power* to
vest in the national government, and how much to retain in the
states. The second exercise was constitutional in a deeper sense
of the term. Had the delegates to the Federal Convention made
only modest additions to the authority of the central government,
the existing structure of the Confederation, with its unicameral
Congress, could have been left intact. But the more substantial
the transfer of power became, the more important it was to think
about the *institutional* aspects of a constitution—that is, about the
distribution of duties and authority among the three departments
of government. This was constitutionalism in the richest sense
of the term, for it forced the framers at Philadelphia to rethink
the essential traits of the republican constitutions Americans had
adopted a decade earlier. Third, beyond the realm of institutions,
a republican government depended on the flow of interests and
opinions through the larger body politic, and thus on the ways
in which public opinion would act and be acted upon. The swirl
of those interests and opinions might prove especially important,
Madison reasoned, to determining how the rights of citizens and
persons were to be defined and protected. Fourth, once a new
regime was established, thinking like a constitution ultimately
led to asking how the framework of government it created would
be maintained. From our vantage point, this problem is often
reduced to the realm of constitutional law. But from the perspective of 1787, and for some time thereafter, the extent of this
realm was either uncertain or contested. The greater problem
was to promote a *culture of constitutionalism* more generally by
convincing Americans that their constitutional commitments
should transcend other merely political values and preferences.

Madison did not give equal attention to each of these aspects
of constitutionalism at every moment. The problem of how much
power the national government should possess was the first item
on his agenda, a subject he began considering as soon as he joined
the Continental Congress in March 1780. By then Madison had
probably begun thinking about the proper structure of republican government, on the basis of his experience in the Virginia

assembly and council of state. But his first sustained comment on the subject appeared in his detailed letter to Caleb Wallace in August 1785. The question of how one would maintain a constitution over time, by contrast, became important only after Madison had the direct experience of constitution making. Yet valuable evidence about his thought on this process appears in several *Federalist* essays as well as his private correspondence during the struggle over ratification. That concern became all the more important during the party conflicts of the 1790s, when Madison concluded that his former coauthor of *The Federalist*, Alexander Hamilton, was bent on undermining the fixed "landmarks" of constitutional governance. It grew even more urgent during the final years of his retirement, when the escalation of states'-rights thinking in the 1820s and 1830s threatened to subvert the essential principle of federal power that Madison had formulated back in the 1780s.

To think about Madison "thinking like a constitution," then, requires paying close attention to the sequence in which his ideas developed, and the ways in which one question opened into another. The best point of departure lies with his approach to federalism in the seven years following his entrance into the Continental Congress in 1780.

Fittingly, Madison's first public experience was to serve as a delegate from Orange County in the Fifth Provincial Convention, which wrote Virginia's new state constitution in the spring of 1776. Just turned twenty-five, he was a member of the committee that drafted the constitution and its accompanying declaration of rights. There is no evidence that Madison played an important role on this committee. Its dominant figure was George Mason, the owner of Gunston Hall, a wonderful red-brick Georgian house an inlet down the Potomac from the Mount Vernon home of his friend and ally George Washington. Recently and grievously widowed, Mason was twice Madison's age, the father of nine surviving children, and a self-educated but deeply learned man who commanded great respect throughout Virginia and palpably embodied the living type of the virtuous republican gentleman. Madison respected Mason deeply. As a junior delegate from Orange County, he was content to sit quietly in his first public office. There was,

however, one issue on which silence proved impossible. That was
religious liberty, the first public cause to which the young college
graduate was most devoted. When the draft declaration of rights
framed the protection of religious liberty on tolerationist grounds,
Madison successfully proposed an amendment that broadened
the article to recognize that "all men are equally entitled to the
free exercise of religion, according to the dictates of conscience."[4]

Madison's experience of constitution making in 1776 mattered
in another way. A decade later, thinking retrospectively—or,
really, thinking like a historian—he realized how much the
prevailing sentiments of the late colonial era had shaped the
attitudes of the first American constitutionalists. Then, they had
a natural impulse to think backward, to react against the excesses
of the old colonial regime, and thus to worry more about the
problem of cabining the authority of the executive than about
how to nurture the proper conditions for deliberation in the
legislatures that dominated the new republican governments.
"The want of *fidelity* in the administration of power having been
the grievance felt under most Governments, and by the American States themselves under the British Government," Madison
observed in 1785, "it was natural for them to give too exclusive
an attention to this primary attribute."[5] It never occurred to
them to imagine, he remarked in *Federalist* 48, that "the danger
to liberty from the overgrown and all-grasping prerogative of
an hereditary magistrate" might be matched by "the danger
from legislative usurpations." The "compilers" of the Articles
of Confederation had similarly been too impressed with the
"enthusiastic virtue" of the state legislatures to recognize that a
national government lacking the power of coercion would often
see its recommendations go unenforced.[6]

Madison thus vividly recalled what it was like to have been a
constitution maker in the first flush of republican enthusiasm. To
think critically about the merits of an existing constitution, one
had to enter sympathetically into the political world from which
that constitution had emerged. Lessons learned from experience
could offset expectations expressed at an earlier time. More to
the point, one could not assume that the favorable conditions
operating at one moment could be replicated later. In fact, the
conditions that had operated so powerfully in 1776, Madison

explained at some length in *Federalist* 49, were likely to have been unique. "We are to recollect," he wrote, in one of those semicolon-laden eighteenth-century sentences that bears quoting in full,

> that all the existing constitutions were formed in the midst of a danger which repressed the passions most unfriendly to order and concord; of an enthusiastic confidence of the people in their patriotic leaders, which stifled the ordinary diversity of opinions on great national questions; of a universal ardor for new and opposite forms, produced by a universal resentment and indignation against the ancient government; and whilst no spirit of party connected with the changes to be made, or the abuses to be reformed, could mingle its leaven in the operation.[7]

Thinking constitutionally could never be a simple matter of designing a government in the abstract. It would always reflect the political circumstances in which a society was immersed. The revolutionary enthusiasm of the mid-1770s had made it easier to reach consensus on the new governments, but it also discouraged the authors of the state constitutions and the Articles of Confederation from dealing with issues they should have anticipated.

Madison's own conception of constitutional change—which required balancing what was theoretically desirable with what was politically possible—was shaped by his complementary experiences as a member of the Continental Congress (March 1780–October 1783) and the Virginia House of Delegates (1784–86). The dominant issue during this period was the problem of federalism, that is, of the relationship between the federal union and its member states. Well into 1786, that concern was addressed almost exclusively to the specific powers that the Continental Congress would exercise, and not to the institutional structure of national governance or to the relation between the states as political communities and Congress. The agenda of constitutional reform was limited to matters of revenue and commerce. The basic strategy that its advocates favored was to adopt particular amendments to the Confederation, in the hope that their individual success would make it easier for Americans to think more favorably about the purposes of national governance. By 1786 this strategy was proving bankrupt, because the rule requiring all thirteen state legislatures to approve amendments to the Confederation thwarted every attempt at reform. Only then did Madison begin to rethink the issues of federalism more analytically, not merely as a problem of how much power the existing Congress should possess but as a reason for examining the nature of political authority within the states. How Madison thought about the latter set of questions was a function primarily of his experience in the Virginia legislature, reinforced by his observations of developments in other states. By the winter of 1787, Madison had concluded that the crisis of the union transcended the perceived "imbecility" of Congress. It was, more deeply, a crisis of republicanism itself, a crisis affecting the individual republics that constituted the American confederation.

The starting point for Congressman Madison's thinking about federalism was the ratification of the Articles of Confederation. In March 1780, Maryland remained the one state still withholding its ratification until it was assured that a national domain would be created west of the Appalachians. Maryland directed its animus against its neighbor Virginia, with its vast claims on both sides of the Ohio River. Anxious to see the Confederation completed, Madison actively urged his constituents to cede claims to distant territory they could never govern on republican principles. Yet as a Virginia delegate he was equally responsible for defending the conditions his legislature imposed on its cession. Madison thus illustrated the dual nature of a delegate's responsibilities: to be both an acting member of the national government and a representative of one's provincial constituents. In the first capacity, his goal was to elevate his constituents' sentiments, to encourage them to understand the difficulties under which Congress labored. Foremost among these was the inadequate compliance of the states with the measures Congress expected them to implement. In his second capacity, Madison faced the perennial challenge of all representatives: to convince one's colleagues within a deliberative body that the concerns of one's constituents were as pressing as those of their own.

His prior two years of service on the eight-member Virginia council of state had brought Madison into direct contact with the array of pressing duties that the states had to carry out. Moving to Congress merely shifted the perspective from which Madison viewed these concerns. Just before he took his seat, Congress had radically devalued its currency by a ratio of 40:1 while giving the states new logistical duties under a system requiring them to raise fixed quantities of particular resources. In his first extant letter back to Governor Thomas Jefferson, Madison worried about this situation, with Congress "recommending plans to the several states for execution and the states separately rejudging the expediency of such plans, whereby the same distrust of concurrent exertions that has damped the ardor of patriotic individuals, must produce the same effect among the States themselves."[8]

Madison's intuition about how states might view each other's "concurrent exertions" would become a critical component of his reassessment of federalism in 1787. But this letter also captured the underlying principle of American federalism that had operated ever since the First Continental Congress of 1774. In this understanding, Congress held broad authority over essential matters of national security, exercising powers over war and diplomacy that were also recognizable badges of international sovereignty. But Congress lacked two other markers of sovereignty that any true nation-state must possess. It could not act directly upon the American population through the ordinary processes of law. In dealings with its member states, Congress would instead enact resolutions, recommendations, and requisitions, and the states in turn would do their best to implement those decisions, employing the statutory power that Congress lacked. The other critical component of the "internal police" of the states, the authority to tax, remained with them as well. Hence the financial stability of national governance depended on the willingness and capacity of the states to levy the taxes that Congress asked each to raise.

This was not, however, a system conceived to treat the states as sovereign judges of the measures Congress adopted, deciding which to implement, which to ignore. The premise of this first version of American federalism was that the states would do what Congress asked them to do, but under the legal means their legislatures deemed most appropriate within their boundaries. This system rested on the basic presumption that the states would possess far better knowledge than Congress could ever acquire about the most effective way to implement national measures. True, "Each state retains its sovereignty," as Article II of the Confederation affirmed, but so, too, Article XIII added, "Every

State shall abide by the determination of the United States in Congress assembled, on all questions which by this confederation are submitted to them."[9]

On the whole, the states did struggle as best they could to meet their responsibilities. To oversimplify a complex story—and generalize about a history that has never been completely written—the American war effort lurched from one year to the next with issues of inflation, depreciation, and logistics never adequately resolved, and with both Congress and the states overwhelmed by the dimensions of the struggle. Yet when Madison took up national office in 1780 the temptation to worry about disparities among the states in their responses to the crisis of supply was difficult to resist. Since late 1778, the British had focused their military effort on the southern states, the soft underbelly of the union, while northern states were effectively isolated from serious combat. In this situation, Madison's worry that the states might individually "rejudge" the urgency of congressional requisitions became more urgent, especially after the British invaded Virginia early in 1781.

Madison's initial response to the perceived failures of the states was generated within a three-member committee charged with considering how the Articles of Confederation, which finally took effect on March 1, 1781, should be executed. Citing Article XIII of the federal charter, the committee proposed an additional article authorizing Congress to employ military and naval forces against states that failed "to fulfill their federal engagements." While conceding the controversial nature of this proposal, Madison liked it enough to think that it offered a feasible solution to the central problem of the Confederation. In a confidential letter to Jefferson, Madison mused that a coercive policy relying on federal naval force to be deployed to limit the trade of the states would provide an "easy and efficacious mode" of execution.[10]

In the end, nothing came of this proposal, in part because the states would never have ratified it, and in part because the victory at Yorktown made the entire situation less urgent. So did the measures that Superintendent of Finance Robert Morris was now pursuing. But when in July 1782 Morris proposed a comprehensive plan to fund the national debt by granting Congress permanent revenues through land, poll, and excise taxes,

Madison became involved in the first round of constitutional discussions that seriously questioned the existing premises of the Confederation.

Morris was the veritable merchant prince of Philadelphia, a congressional veteran, a serious student of trade and finance, and in his way a potential statesman. Alexander Hamilton, now serving as a delegate from New York, was his protégé, and much of Hamilton's program as the first secretary of the treasury under the Constitution applied the same ideas Morris had earlier advanced.[11] But Morris also had a platoon of enemies, led by the brothers Richard Henry Lee and Arthur Lee of Virginia, who saw him as both a corrupt manipulator of public wealth and a threat to sound principles of republican government. At their behest, Virginia repealed its approval of the first amendment to the Articles that Congress had sent to the states, a 1781 proposal for a national impost on foreign goods. To secure his program against their criticism, Morris faced the dual challenge both of developing a consensus within Congress and of making the states receptive to such a change. To attain these ends, Morris attempted to rally public creditors to support his program. More riskily, he also tried to exploit reports of dissent among the officer corps of the Continental Army, then bivouacked at Newburgh, New York, to imply that a mutiny might well result if the soldiers' wages and the pensions promised to their officers went unpaid.

Madison played a major role in this dispute. Although he was less closely associated with Morris than his fellow delegates, Hamilton and James Wilson, he supported the general thrust of the superintendent's program and the principle that the only satisfactory way to meet the revenue needs of the union was through "the establishment of *general* funds to be collected by Congress."[12] He spoke at length on this point on January 28, 1783, in remarks that Lance Banning characterized as "possibly the most impressive speech of his congressional career."[13] Equally important, Madison's rejection of the alternatives to "general funds" strongly anticipated his later approach to the underlying flaw of the Confederation. Two of his reasons merit emphasis. First, securing public credit on a permanent basis would require demonstrating that Congress possessed the funds needed to pay either the principal or punctual interest. Yet "if reason did not sufficiently premonish" against this expectation, "experience has sufficiently demonstrated that a punctual & unfailing obedience by 13 separate & independent Govts. with periodical demands of money from Congress, can never be reckoned upon with the certainty requisite to satisfy" creditors. Second, any federal revenue system organized in this way would remain vulnerable to the state legislatures' temptation to divert these funds to their own purposes. This temptation would always be abetted by each state's doubts "that *others* will not fulfil their respective portions of the common obligations," leading to repeated interruptions in the flow of funds "until it finally stops them altogether." Once this expectation took hold, "what then w[oul]d become of the confederation" or "the authority of Congress?" Mutual suspicion rather than trust would become the currency of American federalism—but only for so long.[14]

In presenting this argument, Madison labored under one deep embarrassment. His own constituents in the Virginia assembly had just revoked their assent to the impost, indicating that they were hardly likely to support the project Madison was now endorsing. Two considerations, however, weighed in the other direction. Although individual delegates had to act from political loyalty to their states, they also "owed a fidelity to the collective interests of the whole." Even if delegates took "the declared sense of constituents" to operate as "a law" guiding their behavior, "still there were occasions on which the latter ought to hazard personal consequences from a respect to what his clear conviction determines to be the true interest of the former." That would be even more the case if one believed, as Madison now did, that the Virginia legislature would alter its position if it had "the same knowledge of public affairs which his station commanded."[15]

Madison's remarks implicated two essential constitutional values. The first, and more important, focused on the structure of the Confederation. The implementation and execution of national policy, he acknowledged, depended on the independent decisions of the state legislatures. But the states were free only to deliberate on "the *means* of supply," not the ends. A requisition from Congress "is as much a law to them; as their revenue acts when passed are laws to their respective Citizens."[16] In the realm of public credit, where so much depended on public confidence, the expectation of compliance had to be absolutely satisfied. Yet here, as on other issues, incentives aplenty would discourage the prompt and complete compliance of the states. No credible commitments could emerge from a process of decision making operating at two independent levels of governance.

A parallel problem of federalism also shaped Madison's references to his duties as a representative. Here a delegate's ostensible legal obligation was to execute the instructions of his constituents. On some issues—say, the cession of a state's western lands—that obligation was binding. But that duty did not prevent a delegate to Congress from advocating national concerns when dealing with his constituents. Nor could it prevent delegates from disdaining the actions of colleagues, such as Rhode Island's obnoxious David Howell, who thought solely of their constituents' interests and commands when discussion within Congress carried its consensus in other directions.[17]

This sensitivity to the dual nature of a delegate's obligations indicates how much Madison was already thinking about the problem of collective deliberation. So too, perhaps, was his decision to keep daily notes of its debates, a project that he began pursuing in the fall of 1782. The origin of this project was probably his desire either to compile a documentary record of the revolution or even to write its history.[18] But it also seems likely that Madison understood the political value of keeping his own record of what had been said.

In the short run, the debates within Congress had a different conclusion from the one Madison desired in late January 1783. Over the next three weeks, he realized that Morris's plan to secure general revenues for national purposes was bound to fail. It could not gain adequate support within Congress, nor could the delegates count on ratification in all thirteen states. Perhaps some pressure on both could be wielded by harping on the specter of military protest or mutiny. That was the stratagem that Hamilton deployed in February, even going so far as to urge Washington to take the lead in directing the army's discontent, and then growing more anxious by the day as Washington delayed answering his letter. But this démarche, which Washington wholly deflated in his dramatic appearance at the officers' meeting of March 4, would never have provided the basis for the political agreement that Madison judged necessary. It was one thing to speculate about using a restive military to support political change, another matter entirely to explain what the troops would do.

The crucial turning point came at a February 20 dinner held at the house of Thomas FitzSimons, a Philadelphia merchant, Pennsylvania delegate, and good friend of Morris. Madison and Hamilton were present, as were three other congressmen who supported the plan for general revenue. Much of the evening was spent discussing the news from Newburgh. But by evening's end everyone but Hamilton conceded that Congress would not adopt, nor the states approve, a general scheme of "taxes that wd. operate equally throughout the States." The most they could propose would be a new impost to replace the 1781 measure. The next day Madison introduced the substitute proposals that formed the heart of the revenue plan that Congress adopted in mid-April as a set of amendments to the Articles of Confederation.[19]

There were significant constitutional aspects to this debate. Arthur Lee—Madison's colleague in the Virginia delegation and Morris's outright enemy—argued that any effort to give Congress independent revenues would violate the "established truth that the purse ought not to be put in the same hands with the Sword." Better to "see Congress a rope of sand," Lee held, "than a rod of Iron."[20] Madison rejected this claim, which presumed that Congress, with its power over war and diplomacy, was essentially an executive body that should never possess the vital legislative power over taxation. But the political argument that the states would reject other forms of national taxation seemed impossible to refute. The changes that Madison and other delegates desired had to take place within the existing political framework of the Confederation.

The idea of holding a national convention to discuss a broader array of reforms to the Confederation was, however, also a project that some delegates were considering. Its leading advocate was Hamilton. He first conceived the idea in 1780, while writing a devastating critique of national governance for the New York delegate, James Duane.[21] He came back to the idea in the fall of 1782, when he and his father-in-law, Philip Schuyler, persuaded the New York assembly to adopt a resolution calling for a national constitutional convention. Believing that the revenue measures that Madison was shepherding through Congress were inadequate, Hamilton considered asking Congress to propose a convention and drafted resolutions to that effect. But judging the mood of Congress much as Madison had, Hamilton "abandoned" the project "for want of support." A few other delegates and a circle of Continental Army officers still favored the idea, but with peace breaking out in April 1783 any sense of urgency evaporated.[22]

Madison's final months as a delegate marked his own transition to peacetime. In June, Congress fled Philadelphia for Princeton after Pennsylvania soldiers staged a threatening protest for unpaid wages outside the statehouse and local officials refused to summon the militia to its defense. Like generations of Princeton alumni ever since, Madison never minded returning to his college town. But he was less enamored of his living circumstances. His Virginia colleague Joseph Jones "& my self are in one room scarcely ten feet square & in one bed," he complained to his father.[23] In late October 1783, as the formal congressional year was ending, Madison returned to Philadelphia. There he found the recently widowed Thomas Jefferson, who was now joining the Virginia delegation, and after spending several weeks together the two men rode to Annapolis, where Congress would reconvene. They discussed the revised version of the Virginia constitution that Jefferson had privately just been drafting. Going on alone, Madison stopped at Gunston Hall to sound George Mason, the existing constitution's principal author. Then, amid heavy rains that prolonged his trip, Madison rode the seventy miles to Montpelier, with no obvious prospects in life.

Madison's political retirement proved short-lived. Social status, reputation, political experience, and high rates of turnover in the legislature soon allowed him to gain a seat in the Virginia House of Delegates. He spent a snowy winter at Montpelier reading law, not with the intention of becoming a lawyer but rather as a serious intellectual exercise.[24] Building on their conversations from Philadelphia and the ride to Annapolis, Madison treated Jefferson as his scout for book purchases. "You know tolerably well the objects of my curiosity," he wrote Jefferson on March 16, 1784, his thirty-third birthday. "I will only particularise my wish of whatever may throw light on the general Constitution & droit public of the several confederacies which have existed. . . . The operations of our own," he added, "must render all such lights of consequence."[25]

Madison's interest in the affairs of Congress and the Confederation was unabated. He began the birthday letter to Jefferson, for example, by closely analyzing the difficulties Congress currently faced in ratifying the Treaty of Paris with a bare quorum of seven states, even when an ultimate decision on the subject required the assent of nine. Letters from Jefferson kept him up to date on congressional affairs—at least until Congress, now in Annapolis, adjourned, leaving a Committee of States (one delegate from each state) nominally in charge, until they too abandoned ship, leaving the United States without a national government until it reconvened at Trenton in the fall of 1784. By then Jefferson was in France, but James Monroe took his place as Madison's congressional correspondent. Madison also resumed his habit of taking annual northward excursions, which allowed him to gather his own political intelligence.

As a state legislator, Madison set himself two main tasks—one domestic, the other federal. The domestic task related to the "internal police" of Virginia. Soon after taking his seat in Richmond in early May 1784, Madison introduced resolutions to pursue the comprehensive and thoroughly republican revision of the Virginia legal code that had been Jefferson's great project of the late 1770s.[26] Madison hesitated to support another Jefferson pet project, the revision of the state constitution, especially when Patrick Henry, the assembly's dominant personality, seemed so "adverse" to the subject. But when Richard Henry Lee, another major figure, offered his support, Madison and his allies decided to proceed—only to find their cause set back when illness kept Lee away from the debate. The measure failed, not to be seriously considered again until 1829, when the venerable statesman left Montpelier one last time to attend the convention at Richmond.[27]

No less important to Madison was the second object of his concern—to ensure that Virginia acted as a pro-federal state, able and willing to do whatever was required to sustain the Continental Congress. The entire theory of the Articles of Confederation rested upon the capacity of state legislatures to think nationally. But most state representatives were amateur legislators who served an annual term or two and then happily yielded their seat to someone else. Madison, by contrast, had three and a half years of uninterrupted congressional service behind him, an intimate knowledge of national affairs, and a deep personal commitment to political life.

There was thus never a time when concern about the underlying authority of Congress and the Articles of Confederation was absent from his thinking. No one in Virginia was better qualified to justify the need to supply Congress with adequate funds or to ratify the two sets of amendments to the Articles it had sent to the states—the revenue program of 1783 and two additional amendments relating to foreign commerce drafted in 1784. Britain's closure of its West Indian ports to American ships (but not American produce) threatened northern merchants, just as ordinary citizens' natural desire to purchase British imports hurt American artisans. Both developments justified giving Congress authority to restrict British commerce, but the grant of that power demanded the unanimous approval of the states. Other issues arose that called for the active advocacy of national concerns. For example, a clause of the Treaty of Paris required opening American courts to British creditors for the recovery of pre-revolutionary debts. Virginians had good reasons to detest this provision, and the legislature promptly closed state courts to British creditors.[28] But acts like these also legitimated Britain's refusal to surrender its forts along the American frontier, which in turn promised to frustrate congressional plans to settle the national domain.

To take a pro-federal stance in the mid-1780s, Madison realized, thus required meeting two challenges. One was political. Because Congress depended on the active cooperation of the states, every legislature needed advocates who could make the case for implementing national decisions. That was the implicit theme that ran through George Washington's parting address to the states in June 1783,[29] and it remained a basic condition of federal politics over the next four years. But even if that political condition was satisfied, a second structural obstacle remained in the rules of decision laid down in the Confederation: nine states to approve major decisions in Congress, all thirteen states to ratify amendments to the Articles. These two aspects of the Confederation overlapped when the willingness of individual

states to accede to national measures rested on their calculation
of the behavior of other states. A single state like roguish Rhode
Island could thwart the amendment of the Articles. But the effective compliance of all the states with other measures would also
depend on how they assessed what their counterparts were doing.

Working within the framework of existing rules, rather than
inventing new rules to circumvent high obstacles, is always the
default option of political life. So it was with the Confederation in
the mid-1780s. Discussion of the idea of a national constitutional
convention had not wholly ended. In late November 1784, Richard
Henry Lee wrote Madison from Trenton to note that the delegates
had been privately discussing this idea. But even "the friends to
Convention," as Lee called them, seemed skeptical. "It is proposed
to let Congress go on in the mean time as usual."[30] Answering
on Christmas day, Madison offered a cautious response. "The
perpetuity & efficacy of the present system can not be confided
on," he agreed. But the question of deciding "in what mode &
at what moment the experiment for supplying the defects ought
to be made" required "knowledge greater than I possess of the
temper & views of the different States. Virginia seems I think
to have excellent dispositions towards the Confederacy." Yet the
fate of such a proposal there would probably still "depend on the
chance of its having no opponent capable of rousing the prejudice
& jealousies of the Assembly agst. innovations, particularly such
as will derogate from their own power & importance."[31]

Substitute Patrick Henry for the unnamed "opponent," and
Madison's analysis returns to the real world of Virginia politics—
to an environment in which individual leaders could exercise
disproportionate influence. That was what Madison was trying to do on the pro-federal side, capitalizing on the enormous
respect he had gained from his service in Congress. But for all his
acknowledged ability—and his Virginia colleagues did respect his
leadership, at least until his earnestness wore them down—he was
no Henry. To assay the prospects for national reform, one would
need corresponding information about the political dynamics in
every other state. In the aftermath of a long revolutionary struggle,
with Americans exhausted by events and anxious to return to
normal life, the most sensible option was to hope that the states
would adopt the amendments Congress had already proposed.

So long as that remained the case, there was no urgent reason to rethink the underlying problems of American federalism or the strategy of constitutional reform in more ambitious terms.[32] Whether from innate prudence or expedient calculations, Madison clung to this belief into the early months of 1786. He had other preoccupations, including enacting Jefferson's revised legal code and opposing the general assessment for teachers of Christianity that the legislature was actively considering. The rhythm of eighteenth-century political life also demanded respect. State legislatures met on their own schedules, set their own agenda, and were filled with inexperienced members who learned their duties on the job. Perhaps most important, there was no obvious alternative to allowing the set procedures for amending the Articles of Confederation to run their course. Even if Rhode Island remained an intractable obstacle to reform, perhaps its opposition would collapse in the face of united action by all the other states.

The key shift in Madison's thinking began in the fall 1785 session of the Virginia assembly. Madison had returned from his annual northern visit, which included a stop in New York City (the new national capital), where he discussed the "affairs of the Confederacy" with the Virginia delegates. "Congress have kept the Vessel from sinking," he wrote Jefferson, "but it has been by standing constantly at the pump, not by stopping the leaks which have endangered her." The one possible measure that offered the best chance for success was a proposal to give Congress "a general & permanent authority to regulate trade," to be exercised with a super-majority of eleven states (not the nine reserved for important powers). Should such a proposal come to Virginia, Madison commented, its fate would "depend much on the part which may be taken by a few members of the Legislature."[33]

His own part was to advance that idea, and so, as the session opened, Madison actively supported a resolution—its exact authorship is unknown, though he may well have been involved in that—granting Congress general authority to regulate trade for twenty-five years.[34] But the ensuing debates quickly proved dissatisfying after the House of Delegates reduced the length of the proposed grant to thirteen years. In Madison's view, a "short term" grant of power would aggravate rather than resolve the underlying problem of the Confederation. "Better to trust to further experience and even distress, for an adequate remedy," he wrote Washington, "than to try a temporary measure which may stand in the way of a permanent one, and must confirm that transatlantic [i.e., British] policy which is founded on our supposed distrust of Congress and of one another." Those who saw a reduction in the term of the grant as an acceptable compromise were also mistaken, for "as to the hope of renewal, it is the most visionary one that perhaps ever deluded men of sense." So naive a hope failed to anticipate the meddling that Britain or other European powers might do in American politics. It also failed to reckon with the likely difficulty of gaining the additional votes required for the approval of amendments to the Articles that would occur as the union expanded to take in "Ultramontane States" in the interior.[35]

Madison was clearly thinking strategically about the reformation of the Articles, but in terms that argued for caution rather than adventure. Risking too much, in the form of a constitutional convention, or accepting too little, in the form of a short-term concession, seemed equally risky. The immediate calculation was to await the fate of the amendments Congress had already proposed and hope that their adoption would ease the suspicion with which so many Americans viewed the idea of enhancing the central authority of Congress.

Thus Madison had mixed emotions about the idea that arose at the close of the session—to convene a conference of the states to discuss the issue of "commercial regulations." Though historians and his own later memory made Madison responsible for the resolution that led to the Annapolis conference, he himself noted that its author was John Tyler, grandfather of the future president.[36] Writing to Monroe the day after the resolution was approved, Madison observed that "the expedient is no doubt liable to objections and will probably miscarry." But, he added, "it is better than nothing" and could "possibly lead to better consequences than at first occur."[37] By mid-March 1786 he was slightly more optimistic, but still guarded in his hopes. The process Virginia had launched was "extremely uncertain," he wrote Jefferson, and "I almost despair of success." Yet "something should be tried," and this was the best measure the legislature could be persuaded to adopt. What better circumstances would appear in the future? Two other "considerations particularly remonstrate against delay,"

Madison added. These were the same concerns he had voiced previously: One was that foreign nations could play the role of Philip of Macedon with the Greeks, bribing key individuals in one or more states to frustrate measures of national interest. The other was the expected enlargement of the union, which could only exacerbate the challenge of attaining unanimity among the states by creating a new interior region with interests different from those of "the Atlantic states."[38]

Madison's reference to Philip of Macedon was not a mere show of collegiate learning. In the early months of 1786, he was also pursuing a different approach to thinking about the problem of confederation. Taking advantage of the "literary cargo" of two hefty boxes of books that Jefferson had sent him from Paris and his existing library at Montpelier, Madison began a course of reading on the history of ancient and modern confederacies. He jotted his observations in a small notebook, written in his fine hand.[39] Thus in his summary of the "vices" of the Amphictyonic League of fourth century B.C.E. Greece, Madison recorded this note: "Greece was the victim of Philip. If her confederation had been stricter, & been persevered in, she would never have yielded to Macedon, and might have proved a Barrier to the vast projects of Rome."[40] Reasoning from past to present, thinking of history as a repository of potential lessons and applications—these were familiar elements in eighteenth-century thinking. The academic side of Madison's intellect was naturally comfortable with historical reasoning, a commitment that was fortified by his own sense that "the American history" would amount to something more than a provincial story of rustic pioneers struggling for customary liberties. Madison's notes on ancient and modern confederacies represent a significant element in his thinking, for his research project was conceived to think systematically about the fundamental flaws of confederations.

By the early spring of 1786, Madison believed that the conference now set for Annapolis in September was an experiment worth trying. The efforts of Congress to secure amendments to the Articles "have miscarried," failing to secure unanimous approval by the states. The idea of a convention limited to the specific subject of commerce should "then be tried. If it succeeds in the first instance, it can be repeated as other defects force themselves on the public attention, and as the public mind becomes prepared for further remedies." But the radical alternative of giving the deputies a "plenipotentiary commission" for other changes went too far. While confessing that he was not "an advocate for temporizing or partial remedies," Madison now worried that "if the present paroxism of our affairs be totally neglected our case may become desperate."[41]

How had Madison reached this position? One concern was that Congress was discussing a new set of potential amendments or even the idea of calling a general convention, proposals that were vigorously advanced by Charles Pinckney of South Carolina. But Madison now thought that any request emanating from Congress would be viewed as coming from a tainted source. Acting with Madison's approval, Monroe took the lead in tabling a committee report with new amendments that Pinckney's actions eventually produced.[42] "Will it not be best on the whole to suspend measures for a more thorough cure of our federal system," Madison wrote Monroe in mid-May, "till the partial experiment shall have been made"?[43] Annapolis could promote the agenda of constitutional reform without risking everything in one fateful stroke.

Yet, beyond this prudent calculation, one other worry was pushing Madison's thinking in a different direction. This was the controversy that erupted when Secretary of Foreign Affairs John Jay asked Congress to revise his instructions for negotiating a commercial treaty with Spain. Back in 1784, Spain had closed the Mississippi River to American navigation below New Orleans. Southern delegates had long held that open navigation of the Mississippi was essential to regional and ultimately national interests. Jay wanted new instructions under which the United States would relinquish its navigation claims for twenty years. This would be a boon to northern merchants and fishermen (as visions of Iberians happily eating *bacalao* danced in their heads). But southern delegates believed that access to the Mississippi was vital to the expansion of their region, and that American settlers who could not freely export their produce into the Gulf of Mexico might well transfer their political allegiance to Spain. The ensuing debate produced a stark sectional division within Congress, culminating in the revision of Jay's instructions by a vote of eight states to five—even though nine states were needed to approve a treaty.

For Madison, the Mississippi question seemed doubly ominous. Not only did it threaten southern attachment to Congress, and thus the union, it also indicated that the time available for constitutional reform might be limited. The Mississippi controversy made it easier to speculate that the union might devolve into two or three regional confederacies, a development that would make constitutional amendment impossible. It also marked the first occasion when Madison began to think about the problem of factious majorities—of majorities that had the authority to rule but lacked the requisite concern for the true public good that should be their guide. "There is no maxim in my opinion which is more liable to be misapplied, and which therefore more needs elucidation," he wrote Monroe in early October, "than the current one that the interest of the majority is the political standard of right and wrong."[44] It is, of course, easy for the critics of popular government—call it either republican or democratic—to dismiss majority rule as a false principle of government. But Madison's concerns, as they began to cohere in the fall of 1786, were devoted to thinking about how majority rule might be improved.

Madison wrote this letter three weeks after the Annapolis conference met and quickly adjourned. In accord with his habit for promptitude, Madison arrived at Mann's Tavern early, on September 5, and waited anxiously for other commissioners to appear. He quickly began worrying that "the prospect of a sufficient no. to make the Meeting respectable is not flattering." On September 11, with three delegations and three commissioners from two other states (including Hamilton) present, he still doubted that a "much more respectable number" would attend. Those present had begun discussing a plan "to break up the Meeting with a recommendation of another time & place, & an *intimation* of the expediency of extending the plan to other defects of the Confederation."[45] Madison had heard similar thoughts in his summer travels. "Many Gentlemen both with & without Congs. wish to make this Meeting subservient to a Plenipotentiary Convention for amending the Confederation," he wrote Jefferson in mid-August. "Tho' my wishes are in favor of such an event, yet I despair so much of its accomplishment at the present crisis that I do not extend my views beyond a Commercial Reform. To speak the truth *I despair almost of this.*"

His concern was less that constitutional reform might prove unacceptable—though that fear was also real enough—than that the repercussions of the Mississippi controversy would prove *"fatal I fear* to an *augmentation of the federal authority."* Given the emphasis he had placed on the value of loyalty to the union, he found this situation "particularly mortifying."[46]

When the dozen commissioners who made it to Annapolis convened on September 13–14, they took the decisive initiative of proposing that a second general convention meet in May 1787 at Philadelphia. Whether this initiative should be regarded as a political démarche or a desperate gamble is a fair question. Alexander Hamilton, who drafted the convention's official report, was no foe to political adventure, as Madison well recalled from Hamilton's involvement in the Newburgh "conspiracy" of 1783. But Madison had also been weighing alternative paths of constitutional reform carefully, with a healthy skepticism about risking too much too soon. If he now agreed that the time had come for a general convention, it could not have been because the political calculus suddenly proved that the moment was ripe for such a measure to succeed. The more compelling judgment was that the failure of the Annapolis conference to provide a platform for change had demonstrated that the time available for reform was evaporating. It was desperation more than political opportunism that made the Philadelphia convention possible.

Once that commitment was made, Madison entered wholeheartedly into the task of preparing his agenda for Philadelphia—and thus in preparing the convention itself. It would be difficult to identify a more intriguing, challenging, or consequential moment in the annals of global constitutional history than the work Madison did from the fall of 1786 through the early spring of 1787. Not that Madison was alone in ruminating about the course the convention might take; many Americans were musing about the options it might consider, and conversations on this subject could range widely. "It is therefore not uncommon to hear the principles of Government stated in common Conversation," the Massachusetts congressional delegate Samuel Osgood wrote John Adams in London. "Emperors, Kings, Stadtholders, Governors General, with a Senate, or House of Lords, & House of Commons are frequently the Topics of Conversation." There was discussion, too, Osgood added, "for abolishing all the State Governments, & for establishing some Kind of general Government, but I believe very few agree in the general Principles; much less in the details of such a Government."[47] At his Mount Vernon estate on its great bluff above the Potomac, George Washington received reports from trusted correspondents about the state of opinion in their social circles and their own ideas about the convention. John Jay and Secretary of War Henry Knox sent him their sketches of what the convention might do. Washington summarized their ideas, and Madison's, as he prepared to leave for Philadelphia.[48]

As executive members of the national government, neither Knox nor Jay would attend the convention. Both men were also skeptical about the prospects for the success of the convention. Jay thought that "the Policy of such a Convention appears questionable," and Knox seemed to imagine it as an intermediate step only. Having previously hedged his own bets about reform, Madison, by contrast, acted as if the convention would now mark the decisive step. This would be high-stakes politics in the proper sense of the term. Should the convention meet yet fail to reach agreement, or propose changes that could not be approved thereafter, what would become of any future scheme of constitutional reform? Annapolis had been a disappointment, but its failure did not close the door to future efforts. A failure at Philadelphia might prove fatal.

Thus it was that Madison undertook a comprehensive effort to prepare for Philadelphia. Part of this effort rested on his political experience. Madison understood, as only a veteran lawmaker could, the advantages of being ready to seize the initiative. Most eighteenth-century American lawmakers would have regarded the notion of having a legislative agenda or program to pursue as a novelty. But Madison had spent enough time in Congress and the Virginia assembly to grasp the advantage of being better prepared than one's colleagues. That was the impression he repeatedly conveyed to those who worked with him, moderated by a demeanor that preferred reasonable discussion to the oratorical transports of a Patrick Henry. Setting an agenda did not mean that one would secure every objective. As many commentators have noted, at the Constitutional Convention Madison lost the specific points he valued most, and he left Philadelphia disillusioned in important ways with its results. But the effort to set an agenda could still mean that the topics one wanted to discuss would get the attention they deserved. Given how much uncertainty there was about what issues the convention would consider, Madison's capacious approach to the task of constitution making was significant in itself.

One preliminary step was to ensure that Virginia would be well represented. At the fall 1786 session of the legislature, Madison drafted the bill providing for the election of seven commissioners to attend the convention.[49] Once it was approved, he placed Washington atop the list of nominated commissioners. The immediate concern was less to ensure that Washington would attend—that decision "will be best decided where it must ultimately be decided," at Mount Vernon—than in "marking the zeal of our Legislature, and its opinion of the magnitude of the occasion."[50] Washington was the nation's greatest political asset, and, though Madison knew of his personal reservations about going to Philadelphia, he could also count on the general's profoundly nationalist commitment to carry the day. If the convention would be well attended, Washington would appear. If not—well, one would not want to place the general in an embarrassing situation. The courtship of Washington's attendance was an ongoing project.

The critical preparations, though, pivoted on shaping the agenda for the convention. In pursuing that challenge, Madison no longer assumed that the stock topics of reform and revenue and commerce exhausted the questions requiring consideration. Important as those matters remained, they illustrated rather than defined the deeper problems of the American "political system." Two broader concerns now dominated Madison's thinking. The first, the one that offered the broadest framework for analyzing the ills of the Confederation, was its "imbecility," or incapacity. That involved examining the fundamental premises of American federalism as those had been set in the mid-1770s. The second set of issues carried Madison far beyond the agenda that other putative reformers of the Articles of Confederation were contemplating. This concern derived from his observations about the "multiplicity," "mutability," and finally "injustice" of legislation *within* the individual states, a set of phenomena that threatened "the fundamental principle of republican Government, that the majority who rule in such Governments, are the safest Guardians both of public Good and of private rights."[51] The first problem was thus the character of American federalism, the second (which we examine in greater detail later) was the nature of republicanism itself.

Taken together, these dual concerns represented as broad an approach to the "vices of the political system of the United States" as anyone could have feasibly imagined in the political circumstances of 1787. One could conceive a more expansive agenda only by doing away with the states entirely, or by redrawing the political map to create new states that would be relatively equal in population.[52] That would solve, at least for a time, the problem created by the equal state vote in the Continental Congress. But these notions were speculative only, for the transaction costs of such changes in terms of the existing structure of state law would be staggering. As it took shape in the early months of 1787, Madison's plan was expansive enough already. It did not simply contemplate a legislative basis for national governance that went well beyond the proposed amendments to the Articles. It also imagined the national government acting as a counterweight to the deficiencies of state legislation—a radical proposal no one had previously discussed. In his thinking, the states would retain a great deal of legal autonomy. But whether they would possess anything resembling sovereignty, in the classical Hobbesean sense of the term, was another problem. Equally important, Madison couched these concerns in language that challenged the dominant views of contemporary political theory, especially as those views had been expressed by Montesquieu in *De l'esprit des lois*.

Madison left Montpelier on January 21, 1787, spent the night of the 25th at Mount Vernon, and arrived in New York on February 9, where he was again eligible to sit in Congress. That task, however, involved little real work, since Congress "remained very thin ever since my arrival, and have done but little business of importance."[53] Without serious distractions, Madison was free to pull his thoughts together. The original results of his labors are recorded primarily in four documents—three similar letters to Jefferson, Randolph, and Washington, written between mid-March and mid-April, and the memorandum "Vices of the Political System of the United States," which carries an April 1787 date.[54] Other letters bear witness to Madison's expectations for Philadelphia, but the central ideas that embodied his approach to the substantive problems of constitution making appear in these four texts.

The excitement of these texts lies in capturing Madison in the act of thinking, compiling, and constructing ideas and arguments that not only were tied to immediate political challenges but also grappled with fundamental questions of political theory. Equally important, these texts illustrate the distinct qualities of Madison's mind, the ways in which he balanced lessons of experience and observations about recent American history with a faculty for theorizing in abstract terms about the phenomena he was analyzing. In different ways and on critical points, Madison discovered or revealed a capacity to reason in recognizably game-theoretical terms. This was of course an era when formal game theory, in the modern sense of the term, did not exist, although a few contemporary figures—notably Thomas Jefferson's friend the marquis de Condorcet—were already reasoning in such ways. Madison's ability to convert his empirical observations about the defects of the Confederation and the individual governments of the states into theoretical statements about federalism and republicanism is the essential source of his creativity.

Madison's analysis of federalism arguably provides the strongest example of this propensity, and the key place to begin is with the opening items of "the Vices." The controlling characteristic of the existing Confederation was the expectation of the voluntary compliance of the states with decisions made by Congress. This expectation did *not* rest upon a robust doctrine of state sovereignty. It was predicated instead on the understanding that the national government would lack the local knowledge and administrative capacity to implement its decisions by acting directly upon the American people. The states held the formal powers that Congress lacked to enact statutes and levy taxes as well as the discretion to adapt congressional directives to local circumstances. For this system to function, the legislatures had to recognize their duty to pursue the national interest, as set by Congress, acting within a context where their deference to the collective good had to be reconciled with their appraisal of how other states would act. How well the state legislatures complied

with these factors was also a function of the ambitions and abilities of ordinary lawmakers, few of whom regarded themselves as
career politicians, much less as veterans of national deliberations.
The opening four items of "the Vices" elaborated these concerns, respectively discussing

1. Failure of the States to comply with the Constitutional
   Requisitions
2. Encroachments by the States on the federal authority
3. Violation of the laws of nations and of treaties
4. Trespasses of the States on the rights of each other

In the accompanying observations paired with these headings,
Madison briefly commented on each vice. The first one, for
instance, not only "results so naturally from the number and
independent authority of the States" but also has been "uniformly
exemplified in every similar Confederacy"—a lesson drawn from
Madison's historical reading on that subject. The third vice, with
its implications for foreign relations, was again derived "from
the number of Legislatures, the sphere of life from which most
of their members are taken, and the circumstances under which
their legislative business is carried on." Observations like these
summed to a powerful diagnosis: federal measures would always
be vulnerable to a process in which final authority resided in
multiple institutions filled with inexperienced and parochial
decision makers. On other occasions, though, as in the fourth
item, those decisions might rest less on the ignorance of legislators
than on their avowed desire to further immediate provincial
interests at the expense of either other states or foreign nations.[55]
    The most important and revealing element in Madison's
analysis of the underlying problem of American federalism came
in item 7, which he titled "want of sanction to the laws, and of
coercion in the Government of the Confederacy." The heading
evoked concerns Madison had first discussed in the early 1780s, as
a delegate to Congress. But here it is the structure of his observations that best illustrates the breadth of Madison's political intelligence. This single item—an extended paragraph—constitutes a
mini-treatise on federalism, pivoting on five concise observations.
    Madison began his analysis by restating the problem. With-
out the authority of law or the power of "coercion," the existing

"federal system" lacked "the great vital principles of a Political Cons[ti]tution. It is in fact nothing more than a treaty of amity of commerce and of alliance, between so many independent and Sovereign States." Why was this the case? Madison's first answer explained why the framers of the Articles of Confederation had not provided this essential power a decade earlier. Then, Americans were true republicans, possessing "a mistaken confidence that the justice, the good faith, the honor, the sound policy" of the states "would render superfluous any appeal to the ordinary motives by which the laws secure the obedience of individuals: a confidence which does honor to the enthusiastic virtue of the compilers, as much as the inexperience of the crisis apologizes for their errors."[56] Madison's mode of explaining the origins of political phenomena was historical as scholars would use that term; it asked why one course of action had been taken and not another. That curiosity rested in part on Madison's experience, since he could personally recall the ethos of republicanism that permeated the Fifth Provincial Convention that drafted Virginia's constitution. But it was genuinely intellectual as well, as reflected in his reading on the history of other confederacies, which he hoped, perhaps naively, would generate applicable lessons for the American case.

Yet the "inexperience" of 1776 had given way to a decade of decisions that laid bare the inadequacy of the federal system. This offered the second basis for Madison's discussion, the simple lessons of experience. "Even during the war," Madison observed in his second point, "when external danger supplied in some degree the defect of legal & coercive sanctions, how imperfectly did the States fulfil their obligations to the Union? In time of peace, we see already what is to be expected." This was historical reasoning of a second, more popular kind. Here again Madison's experience was directly relevant to his thinking, for in both Congress and the House of Delegates he had numerous examples of how prone this system was to breakdown. Yet the same conclusion was also available to any concerned citizen who conscientiously read American newspapers. Like many of us, much of the time, Madison was thinking of recent history as a source of lessons of experience.

Here, in the lessons of history, was arguably sufficient evidence to justify replacing the existing system of American federalism, with its dependence on the voluntary compliance of the states, with a form of national governance resting on the coercive authority of law. Yet against this merely empirical form of reasoning one could still juxtapose other considerations to make the opposing case, to conclude that something less than a radical restructuring of the federal system was necessary. One could argue that the American people had just completed a long, exhausting war; that state legislatures had generally struggled as best they could to meet their obligations; indeed that the burdens of the war were manifestly greater than anything imposed on American governance over the previous century and a half. Under these conditions, allowance could be made for the slackness of the federal system, without surrendering the prevailing assumptions of the mid-1770s.

But that was not the conclusion Madison reached. After stating his two historical reasons, he posed a question that was substantive, not rhetorical: "How indeed could it be otherwise?" Suddenly his mode of analysis changed, as Madison quickly offered three further reasons why a federal system relying on the voluntary compliance of the states was fatally flawed:

> In the first place, Every general act of the Union must necessarily bear unequally hard on some particular member or members of it. Secondly the partiality of the members to their own interests and rights, a partiality which will be fostered by the Courtiers of popularity, will naturally exaggerate the inequality where it exists, and even suspect it where it has no existence. Thirdly a distrust of the voluntary compliance of each other may prevent the compliance of any, although it should be the latent disposition of all.[57]

From this analysis, one powerful conclusion emerged: "Here are causes & pretexts which will never fail to render federal measures abortive." If the winning strategy for the cooperative game of federalism was to secure the uniform compliance of the states, Madison had identified three reasons why the desired outcome was unlikely. To restate his argument: States had different interests, and thus different incentives to comply. Within each state, some legislators would naturally prefer provincial interests to the general good, and this tendency would be exploited by calculating politicians who emphasized the inequality among the states.

And even when a common interest might be perceptible, mutual doubts about the performance of others would discourage the net compliance of all.

From historical judgments, then, Madison had gone on to theorize the problem of federalism in abstract terms. His points conform to the premises of modern game theory. They examine the incentives that the states possessed to comply or to shirk, weigh the preferences of legislatures and legislators against their inclination to pursue the public good, and ask how assessments of the performances of others will affect, even distort, one's own calculation of the right course of action. Equally important, Madison's assessment combined observations about the deliberative characteristics of institutions with intuitions into the psychological facets of decision making. Legislators feeling an intuitive "partiality" toward the interests of their own states would "naturally exaggerate the inequality [of burdens among the states], and even suspect it where it has no existence." Under such conditions, skepticism rather than confidence would become the dominant traits of legislative discussions about the enforcement of congressional acts. Such acts, "tho' nominally authoritative," are "in fact recommendatory only."[58]

The insight underlying this analysis did not originate in 1787. The germ of this argument appeared in Madison's congressional speech of January 28, 1783, given after he had spent three years in Congress actively worrying about coordinating policy between the national government and the states.[59] Then, too, he had portrayed the states as rival jurisdictions innately suspicious of each other's motives. Assuming competing pressure on their treasuries from both national and state needs, why would the legislatures prefer their obligations to Congress while they remained perpetually doubtful about the compliance of other states? Four years of experience since then had confirmed his original perception. But now this insight led Madison to form a broader theory of federalism, one that actively questioned the underlying premise of the Confederation. The value of theory in this instance was that it identified conditions that would always exist, not merely contingencies that it seemed urgent to overcome. If these factors would always be present—if they would always render a system of recommendatory federalism prone to disruption—then a strategy of temporary or modest reforms lost its appeal. Madison's query—"How indeed could it be otherwise?"—was actually a conclusion, not a question. The process of envisioning a new model of federalism was not quite complete in April 1787. Madison envisioned a system "which would operate in many essential points without the intervention of the State legislatures." Under such a system, the national government would act, not through recommendations to the states but through laws imposed on the population. It would then become essential to change the structure of Congress, dividing it into two houses and replacing the rule giving each state a single vote with one allocating the states different numbers of representatives based on some proportional scale. Yet the idea that the national government would have to deal directly with the states as autonomous jurisdictions did not wholly disappear from Madison's thinking. The power of coercion that item 7 of "the Vices" justified still implied that occasions could arise when the national government would have to use some kind of force against recalcitrant states. This had been a pet idea of Madison's since 1780, and one he had not yet wholly abandoned. Still, the idea of its impracticality was growing more evident. "But the difficulty & awkwardness of operating by force on the collective will of a State," he wrote Washington, who was also an enthusiast for the idea, "render it particularly desirable that the necessity of it might be precluded."[60] The coercion of states could well prove a formula not for federal governance, but for recurring confrontations between the union and the states.

One alternative to the idea of coercion was, however, already present in Madison's thinking. This was his scheme "to arm the federal head with a negative *in all cases whatsoever* on the local Legislatures." Madison first mentioned this idea in his letter to Jefferson of March 19, 1787.[61] In subsequent letters to Randolph and Washington, he candidly compared it to the royal negative on colonial laws and described it, just as remarkably, as "the least possible abridgement of the State Sovereignties" or "the least possible encroachment on the State jurisdictions."[62] To call this an "abridgment" or an "encroachment" was a bald understatement. With such a power vested in the national government, the states would retain no plausible sovereignty at all. If sovereignty as traditionally defined meant the ultimate authority to command and make law, a jurisdiction whose legal decisions were subject to review by another institution could never claim that status. *Autonomy* would be a reasonable description of the realm of state governance; *sovereignty*, as the concept was defined in the writings of Jean Bodin, Thomas Hobbes, and William Blackstone, would not. The range of uses Madison imagined for the negative is striking. So is the fact that he first proposed these uses in his March letter to Jefferson, as he was just beginning to pull his thoughts together. "The effects of this provision," he wrote, "would be not only to guard the national rights and interests against invasion, but also to restrain the States from thwarting and molesting each other, and even from oppressing the minority within themselves by paper money and other unrighteous measures which favor the interest of the majority."

The negative would thus alter the vectors of American federalism in three respects. It would enable the national government to protect itself against interfering legislation from the states. It would further allow it to mediate conflicts among the states. Third, and arguably most important, it would enable the national government to intervene within the states individually, protecting minorities against legislation violating their rights. The negative, as Madison thought about it, was conceived to address urgent needs—so urgent that he thought the national government should be able to appoint proconsular officials within the states "to give a temporary sanction to laws of immediate necessity."[63] Here, again, Madison was contemplating a practice often employed by royal governors, much to the despair of colonists.

Later in life, Madison recognized what a radically impractical proposal this was.[64] Even in 1787 the proposal could have been disparaged, even dismissed, as being hopelessly naive on a point of crucial significance to Madison's own constituents. How could any state where slavery formed a critical object—arguably *the* crucial object—of legislative concern allow its laws to become subject to national review? But in terms of Madison's agenda in the spring of 1787, that objection mattered less than his desire to make state legislation subject to approval by the new Congress. The federalism that Madison now envisioned was no longer limited to finding ways to free national governance from its debilitating dependence on the states in areas of authority it already possessed or to modestly altering the balance of power between the union and the states. Madison's agenda was more radical (or reactionary) than anything that had been discussed previously, and it demonstrates the breadth of his rethinking of the character of American federalism on the eve of the convention.

Equally important, the negative on state laws drew on sources other than the game-theoretic model of federalism that Madison had intuited in the early 1780s. Madison's concern with the internal governance of the states rested on his absorption in the nature of legislative deliberation and, beyond that, on asking whether legislative misbehavior was driven less by the vices of lawmakers than by their fidelity to "the people themselves." Here lay a different source of Madison's political creativity, for it led him into the famous wrangle with Montesquieu that we know best from *Federalist* 10, but which again originated in the development of his agenda for the convention.

CHAPTER 2

"THE PRINCIPAL TASK OF MODERN LEGISLATION"

The Locus of Republican Governance

Had Madison ended "Vices of the Political System of the United States" with his analysis of the underlying problems of federalism, that alone would have provided a sufficient basis for a major altera- tion in the form and structure of national governance. But of course his analysis did not end with item 7 or the following entry, which called for the popular ratification of whatever alterations to the Confederation the convention produced. Instead, in item 9, Madison raised a fresh subject that had not figured prominently, if at all, in the agenda of constitutional reform in the mid-1780s. The new line of analysis opened with a typically Madisonian understatement. Opposite the heading "Multiplicity of laws in the several States," he made this observation: "In developing the evils which viciate the political system of the U.S. it is proper to include those which are found within the States individually, as well as those which affect the States collectively, since the former class have an indirect influence on the general malady and must not be overlooked in forming a compleat remedy."[1] Phrases like "indirect influence" and "must not be overlooked" hardly convey the urgency that Madison felt as he then described the "multiplicity," "mutability," and, worst, "injustice" of state legislation. In his own mind, Madison believed that "the evils arising from these sources contributed more to the uneasiness which produced the Convention, and prepared the public mind for a general reform, than those which accrued to our national character and interest from the inadequacy of the Confederation to its immediate objects."[2]

The origins of Madison's concerns with the internal legislation of the states were more recent than his concerns with federalism.

This was not an issue that had troubled him during wartime. Not that he was unaware of conflicts occurring within individual states after 1776. No one living in Philadelphia could have been oblivious to the internal tensions in the politics of Pennsylvania, whose radical constitution of 1776 remained a source of endless contention. But it is far more likely that his service in the Virginia House of Delegates in the mid-1780s provided the decisive impetus for his rethinking of problems of republican government within the states. The first serious exposition of Madison's ideas about this topic came in his August 1785 letter to Caleb Wallace, discussing the lessons that Kentucky could apply when it formed its own constitution. Madison wrote that letter while he was actively opposing the general assessment bill of 1784–85, which he viewed as a great abuse of legislative power. These incidents, along with his general experience in the Virginia assembly, provided the basis for two fundamental propositions of his constitutional thinking in 1787. One involved the problem of the "factious majority," an issue he first noticed in discussing the politics of the Mississippi issue within Congress, but which he now applied to the problem of majority misrule within the states. The other was his rejection of the classical axiom that made the civic virtue of citizens the sustaining strength of a republic. The most famous expression of this thought—the passage that every student in the introductory American government course reads—is the passage in *Federalist* 10 explaining how "the latent causes of faction are thus sown in the nature of man" and emphasizing that "the most common and durable source of faction, has been the various and unequal distribution of property."[3]

Madison closed that paragraph with a final observation that now sounds commonplace. "The regulation of these various and interfering interests," he wrote, "forms the principal task of modern Legislation, and involves the spirit of party and faction in the necessary and ordinary operations of Government." To a modern reader, who is all too aware of the ease with which economic interests capture the legislative process, this remark sounds unsurprising. Yet when Madison made it, it marked another one of his understated, concise expressions that convey far more meaning than they superficially present. It arguably represents much more of a discovery than a commonplace, for the problem

that Madison was directly engaging was the recognition that
representative assemblies existed not primarily to prevent the
executive from making or giving law without the people's assent
but as the forum within which the people themselves would
actively pursue their parochial or private interests. Drawing upon
the experience of the revolution, but also pursuing the logic of
republican politics in the expanding society that Americans were
still forming, Madison began to fashion a very modern image
of the nature and extent of legislative power. This perception
went beyond the recognition of the constitutional supremacy of
the legislature. It was more directly concerned with the nature
of legislative activity and, equally important, with the deeper
sources of legislative behavior. Some of that concern involved the
deliberative qualities of representative bodies. But Madison was
equally troubled by the interplay between society "out-of-doors"
and legislative behavior, by the ways in which interests within
society would make legislators the instruments of their ambitions.

When Madison analyzed the problems of federalism, his
original concern lay with the respective *powers* of national and
state governments. The national government needed statutory
authority equivalent to what the states already possessed, and
the legislative power of the states had to be limited in other ways.
But a redress in the power to legislate was not the sole object of
Madison's concern. It was also the basis for his deeper analysis
of the institutional and political characteristics of republican
government. Before 1787, and indeed before 1801, Madison's
primary experiences in politics were deliberative and legislative
in nature. From his tenure in both the Continental Congress and
the House of Delegates, he became fascinated with the problem
of collective deliberation, with the capacity of representatives of
diverse constituencies to reason together on the common good.
Whether representatives would act as enlightened deliberators
or simply operate as agents for parochial interests was the great
conundrum that republican constitutionalism had to address.
That concern led Madison to think actively about both the internal
and external dimensions of legislative deliberation, or with what
political scientists would call the endogenous and exogenous
dimensions of legislative activity. Indeed one of the great problems in assessing Madison's thinking involves weighing the

relative importance he placed on the institutional capacity of legislators to deliberate intelligently against the ways in which the swirl of interests in society would influence or potentially control their decisions.

Madison's interest in legislative deliberation was also tied to the legal acts this process would produce. Madison was fascinated by the technical quality of legislation—by its clarity, accuracy, and "perspicuity." He understood that legislation in a republic would always be a collective activity, the result of political deliberations, and not the imposition of the rational will of a single lawgiver. The problem within the states was not merely that laws would be drafted by amateur representatives who came and went with every term, and whose legal training, even if they were justices of the peace, owed more to hands-on experience in the county court than to a close reading of Blackstone or other treatises. It was also tied to a nagging sense that ordinary lawmakers lacked the capacity and habits needed to frame laws correctly.

The basis for these concerns lay predominantly in Madison's experience representing Orange County in the Virginia assembly in the mid-1780s. This period was not an unmitigated record of legislative frustration and failure. He became a dominant force when he entered the House of Delegates in 1784 and remained an influential figure even when his earnest leadership tired many of his colleagues. Madison enjoyed significant success in advancing the adoption of the revised Virginia legal code that Jefferson had championed. His role in defeating the general assessment bill of 1784 and his subsequent success in securing passage of the landmark Bill for Religious Freedom remain seminal achievements in enlarging the realm of religious liberty. Yet his postwar service in the assembly left Madison deeply disillusioned by the tenor of its politics. That dismay was reinforced by his observations of legislative activities in other states. These impressions account for the radical (or reactionary) enthusiasm with which Madison framed his agenda for 1787. They also illustrate the fascinating relation in his thinking between the institutional and popular dimensions of republican politics.

Respect for Madison ran high when he reentered the legislature in May 1784. As Thomas Jefferson's protégé, William Short, noticed, the members "have formed great Hopes of Mr. Madison, and

those who know him best think he will not disappoint their most
sanguine Expectations." As Edmund Randolph also observed,
"He is already resorted to, as a general, of whom much has been
preconceived to his advantage."[4] This belief rested on a profound
personal truth about Madison. He was always a legislator's legislator, ever prepared for debate, in terms of knowing both the rules
of parliamentary procedure and the substance of the issues at
hand. For his part, one of Madison's chief plans was to advance
the revised legal code that Jefferson, working with George Wythe
and Edmund Pendleton, had prepared in the late 1770s. Jefferson's
great hope in preparing that code was not only to consolidate a
century and a half of legislation but also to bring it into conformity
with republican principles and aspirations. A commonwealth that
was no longer a royal province needed a republican code of laws
for a republican people. Such a code might create, for example,
a statewide system of public education, designed to ensure the
existence of a self-governing citizenry. These citizens should
live in a society devoted not merely to religious toleration but to
freedom of religious expression, allowing every person—male and
female, and youths coming of age—to decide which convictions
best suited his or her conscience, thus exercising the fundamental
natural right of belief. And in other measures that Jefferson prepared separately, he would have committed the state to using its
resources of land to give marrying couples adequate real property
to convey the economic independence—the "competence"—that
republican citizens should possess.[5]

In drafting these measures, Jefferson was playing the American version of "the legislator" or "lawgiver," a figure beloved of
Enlightenment thinking—its "answer," the historian Harry C.
Payne has written, "to the Christian saint or the Renaissance
prince. Half-mythical, half-historical, the figure of the legislator
who shapes and unifies his society dominates the political and
historical writings of the philosophes."[6] This image would naturally appeal to Jefferson, who, along with Franklin, embodied the
apex of the American Enlightenment. Working as he did in the
isolation of his first version of Monticello, preferring the company
of his wife, Martha, to the hard-drinking planter-delegates at
Williamsburg, Jefferson could imagine himself as a latter-day
lawgiver, just as his friend John Adams had marveled at being

"sent into life at a time when the greatest lawgivers of antiquity would have wished to live." Amid the pressing demands of wartime, however, the assembly had no time for Jefferson's great project. After the experience of his governorship (1780–81) and the devastating death of Martha in 1782, Jefferson had no taste for Virginia politics. It fell instead to his younger friend Madison to pursue the project while Jefferson took up his diplomatic career in France.

The spring session of the 1784 assembly met for barely seven weeks, and Madison found his days filled with its business. Summarizing its doings for Jefferson, Madison closed his letter with an early grumble about the legislature's mode of business. "This confusion indeed runs through all our public affairs," he complained, referring to the lack of information available on the state's public credit, "and must continue as long as the present mode of legislating continues. If we cannot amend the constitution, we must at least call in the aid of accurate penmen for extending Resolutions into bills, which at present are drawn in [a] manner that must soon bring our laws & our Legislature into contempt among all orders of Citizens."[7] Here Madison was already expressing his dissatisfaction with the working habits of the institution and his colleagues and the practical difficulty of framing legislation.

Madison left this first session of the assembly with one other legislative concern on his mind. Petitions had been submitted calling for a "general assessment" to be levied on behalf of the "teachers of Christianity"—that is, all Protestant ministers regardless of their denominational ties. This measure would extend public aid for religion on a "non-preferentialist" basis, grounded in the belief that such support was essential to public morality and in the conviction that the ravages of the war had gravely damaged the welfare of churches generally. Moreover, prominent members of the Episcopalian (formerly Anglican) Church sought its legal incorporation. This bill stopped short of a full establishment of the Episcopalians, but in an era when acts of incorporation were regarded as the granting of exceptional legal privileges it implied that a special relationship persisted between the state and its historically dominant church. Both measures threatened the moral and political convictions that Madison had embraced in his youth,

as well as the enlightened constitutional principle he had successfully embedded in Article XVI of the Virginia declaration of rights.

The two bills were carried over to the fall session of the legislature, when Madison found himself acting very much on the
defensive. Only the legislature's preoccupation with enacting
the incorporation bill made possible a second postponement "of
the Genl. which would otherwise have certainly been saddled
upon us."[8] By the spring of 1785, the assessment bill was "the
only proceeding of the late Session of Assembly which makes a
noise thro' the Country."[9] Making a noise meant not only general
conversation wherever Virginians gathered but the activity of
organizing petitions for and against the bill. Madison was keenly
disappointed that the Presbyterian clergy, who originally opposed
the bill, now seemed content to take their share of the revenue it
would produce. "I do not know of a more shameful contrast" than
that between their changing positions, Madison noted. But that
behavior only confirmed his conviction of the corrupting effect
that close ties between church and state would inevitably have.

Madison's response to these developments was the drafting
of his *Memorial and Remonstrance against Religious Assessments*,
a text that joins the Bill for Religious Freedom at the leading
edge of the revolutionary-era commitment to religious liberty.
Madison's original political reaction to the assessment had *not*
been to muster public opposition to the measure. He instead
thought "that the counties opposed to the measure should be
silent." But he reconsidered his position after a correspondent
warned him that such silence would be interpreted as popular
acquiescence in the measure. There was some reason to believe
that "a great majority of the people" actually opposed it, George
Nicholas wrote; indeed, "the attempt [to carry such laws into
execution] would bring about a revolution." Circulating a petition
of protest across the counties could well "deter the majority of
the Assembly from proceeding." Madison apparently received
similar advice from George Mason and other acquaintances.
Once again his reputation revealed the high expectations that
his countrymen held for him.[10]

Although the printer Isaiah Thomas soon reported Madison's authorship of the *Memorial*, another four decades passed
before he publicly acknowledged that simple fact. In writing a

petition, however, Madison was deploying the ordinary means that constituencies or groups of individuals used to convey their concerns to the realm of legislative discussion. Legislators could similarly seek to generate petitions to enhance the perception of public support for the positions they already favored. They could, that is, act strategically to mobilize public opinion for their own purposes, treating petitions not merely as an obligation they were duty-bound to advance but as a form of political expression they could actively manipulate.

Two further considerations made the campaign against the general assessment distinctive. First, this was a measure of state-wide impact, in which the public opinion to be tapped existed in every county. Most petitions, by contrast, were parochial in origin, relating to a specific interest here, a grievance there. They were generally designed not to mobilize public opinion but to transmit local concerns to the attention of relevant officials. The assessment bill was thus one of those rare measures that linked the agenda of the assembly with an issue on which citizens everywhere could express an informed opinion or preference. Second, the idea that the general assembly might transgress the fundamental right of religious freedom by requiring Virginians to pay for the costs even of a nonpreferential establishment raised a deeper constitutional concern. In the conventional conception of the protection of rights, derived from the model of monarchical government, it was the duty of the legislature to protect the rights of the people against the arbitrary will of the executive. But in the early American republics, where the will of the executive was eviscerated, the troubling question that now vexed Madison involved asking how the people's own representatives could act in ways inimical to their rights.

The outcome of the campaign against the assessment bill should have reassured Madison. The thousands of signatures his *Memorial* and other petitions collected were taken as a decisive expression of public opinion. "The steps taken throughout the Country against the genl. Assessment had produced all the effect that could have been wished," Madison observed. "The table was loaded with petitions & remonstrances from all parts against the interposition of the Legislature in matters of Religion." After the assembly abandoned the measure, Madison attained his greatest legislative achievement—the enactment, with a few modifications, of the Bill for Religious Freedom. Madison also made significant progress with the adoption of other bills in Jefferson's revised code, at least until the bill "for proportioning crimes and punishments in cases heretofore capital" met with substantial opposition. Here Jefferson's enlightened pen had followed the arguments of Cesare Beccaria. Madison fretted that the whole revisal "might have been finished at one Session with great ease, if the time spent on motions to put it off and other dilatory artifices, had been employed on its merits." Still, Madison found it "more popular in the Assembly than I had formed any idea of" previously.[11]

So Madison, two years into his service in the assembly, might have been upbeat about its work. Yet by then he was forming skeptical opinions about the character of his lawmaking colleagues and the quality of their deliberations. Some of the evidence for this lies in his periodic reports to his Parisian correspondent, Thomas Jefferson. But a better account is his letter to Caleb Wallace, the first occasion on which Madison wrote systematically about the tenor of republican government within the states. "On this Subject I confess myself a Novice," Wallace wrote, "and apprehend we have few among us who are adepts in the Science of Government." But Madison, Wallace conceded, was just such an adept, for "Providence has given you singular opportunities for maturing your judgment on the Subject."[12]

Madison began his response with a set of observations about the three departments of government. His first comments, on the legislature, recognized its preeminence in any scheme of republican government but also drew lessons from his special interests and experiences. Wallace had wondered whether a primitive constitution for Kentucky should include a senate; Madison answered affirmatively that it should:

> *The Legislative department* ought by all means, as I think to include a Senate constituted on such principles as will give *wisdom* and steadiness to legislation. The want of these qualities is the grievance complained of in all our republics. The want of *fidelity* in the administration of power having been the grievance felt under most Governments, and by the American States themselves under the British Government. It was natural for them to give too exclusive an attention to this primary attribute.[13]

Two aspects of this opening observation merit comment. First, Madison defined the essential goal of legislation in terms of institutional qualities that he believed all the American assemblies so far lacked. Second, Madison's reasoning about this problem—his *thinking* about it—had an avowedly historical dimension. In the mid-1770s, Madison recalled, the first constitution makers were naturally preoccupied with "the want of *fidelity*"—the lack of accountability—"in the administration of power," a clear reference to the actions of the Crown and royal governors.[14] The constitutional pioneers of 1776 had looked backward, not forward. Just as item 7 of "the Vices" explained the lack of national coercive authority over the states in terms of the prevalent republican assumptions of the mid-1770s, so Madison accounted for inattention to the proper structure of a legislature in terms of the misplaced concerns of the same era.

In calling attention to the need for proper senates in the republican polity, Madison was addressing a key conceptual problem in American constitutionalism. Should a republic have an upper house at all? In the conventional British model of mixed government, the House of Lords was not, strictly speaking, a representative institution. It simply was the aristocracy meeting as a group and acting to balance the unified power of royalty against the diffuse energy of the people. In a society lacking an aristocracy, like America, what entities would the upper house represent? The French philosophes who generally admired the American constitutional experiment still criticized its decision to retain a British-style bicameralism, when logic and a clear view of their own society should have led to the creation of unicameral legislatures. Their objections on this point formed the main provocation that inspired John Adams to write his *Defence of the Constitutions of Government of the United States*, that "bulky, disordered, conglomeration of political glosses on a single theme" which marked, Gordon Wood notes, Adams's failure to grasp "what was happening to the fundamentals of political thought in the years after 1776."[15] Adams insisted that all governments needed to resolve the perpetual struggle among the one, the few, and the many. But saying exactly who those few were in the American commonwealths was a difficult, even insuperable, problem. Only one American state, Pennsylvania, opted for the unicameral option. But it did so partly in response to its own provincial history, rooted in the lawgiving visions of its own founder, William Penn, and with partisan results that hardly made it a model that other states seemed eager to follow.

Lacking any manifest markers of legal aristocracy, American constitutionalists struggled to find some other basis for distinguishing upper and lower houses. The best solution seemed to involve representing property as an independent factor worthy of expression or protection. But this posed new problems. Any attempt to delineate the ownership of a specific amount of property as the basis either for voting for the upper house or for serving in it involved creating an arbitrary line. Perhaps more important, the very idea of saying that concentrated amounts of property deserved formal or further political recognition had troubling implications for republican theory, which regarded the common right to own property as a trait of all citizens. To treat holders of larger amounts of property as an interest requiring separate recognition shattered the image of the underlying homogeneity of republican society, converting a common right vested in all citizens into potentially adversarial interests pitting one group against another.[16]

Madison was quite receptive to the idea of having two distinct electorates for a bicameral legislature, one tied to general citizenship, the other qualified by property. Yet his more pressing concern lay with the quality of lawmaking. Even a badly designed senate, like the one Virginia possessed—"a worse could hardly have been substituted," he wrote Wallace—was often pressed to act as "a useful bitt in the mouth of the house of Delegates." In the abstract, Madison also believed that "it would be helpful to define the extent of the Legislative power but the nature of it seems in many respects to be indefinite." This was a theme to which he would soon return, as he sought other ways to limit the plasticity of legislative power. Madison instead closed his initial discussion of the legislative department by discussing more pragmatic solutions to the problem of "fluctuating & indegested laws." He liked the joint executive-judicial council of revision created by the New York constitution of 1777, with its limited negative on legislation. A "still better" solution might lie in giving "a standing comm[it]tee composed of a few select & skilful individuals" the dual power "to prepare bills on all subjects which they may judge proper to be submitted to the Legislature at their meetings & to draw bills for them during their Sessions." To check the additional power its members would enjoy, these authoritative draftsmen might be barred from "holding any other Office" elsewhere in government.[17]

His ensuing comments on the other two departments in his letter to Wallace were more concise but still revealing. He had "no final opinion" whether the executive should be appointed by the legislature or the people, or whether its power should be vested in a single individual or a council. More striking, in Madison's estimation the executive did not deserve "the 2d place" it enjoyed in republican thought, "all the great powers which are properly executive being transferd to the Fœderal Government." That rank instead belonged to the judiciary, as the example of Great Britain demonstrated. There the judiciary "maintains private Right against all the corruptions of the two other departments & gives a reputation to the whole Government which it is not in itself entitled to."[18]

After these introductory remarks, Madison turned to specific queries Wallace had posed. The first dealt with basic questions of suffrage and representation: who should vote, and how should legislative districts be constituted? Madison was open to the idea of having different electorates for the two houses of the legislature, one tied to protecting "the rights of property which chiefly bears the burden of Government & is so much an object of Legislation." He invoked the stock fear that those owning only "a pittance" of property "will either abuse" their power "or sell it to the rich who will abuse it." At the same time, he recognized that such a practice would offend notions of equality and that the rich possessed other sources of "influence" beyond their vote. The suffrage, Madison insisted, should be by "the ballott," which was "the only radical cure for those arts of Electioneering which poison the very fountain of Liberty." Perhaps Madison was still rankling over his defeat in 1777 by the innkeeper Charles Porter (who had no compunctions against "swilling the planters with bumbo"), but he tied this comment to observations of other states. Mechanisms had to be found to adjust a county's share of representation to changes in population. It was also important to limit the size of the legislature. "I should suppose 150 or even 100 might safely be made the ne plus ultra for Kentuckey."[19]

Limiting the size of the legislature would promote the cause of deliberation. So would the next issue Madison discussed, terms of office. That rule should vary among the departments, he observed. "For one part of the Legislature Annual Elections will I suppose be held indispensably," he noted, but then he added this qualification: "though some of the ablest Statesmen & soundest Republicans in the U States are in favour of triennial" terms. This was a remarkable understatement. The maxim "Where annual elections end, slavery begins" was a mantra of republican orthodoxy, a norm firmly entrenched in American practice. To triple the term of service, and to ascribe that opinion to the most thoughtful observers, marked a sharp break from conventional wisdom.

Collectively these comments illustrate how much Madison was concerned with the processes of legislative determination. A concern with the impact of popular passions and interests on political decisions is absent from his comments—beyond his fear of the potential manipulation of unpropertied citizens by ambitious demagogues. But that fear could be grounded in stock historical images of how republics commonly failed. A similar concern could account for Madison's admonition not to allow individuals to serve in multiple offices, a departure from the principle of separated powers that might be justified because of the shortage of qualified leaders in an infant state. Allow such "temporary deviations," and "those who become interested in prolonging the evil will rarely be at a loss for other pretexts," Madison warned. "The first precedent too familiarizes the people to the irregularity, lessens their veneration for those fundamental principles, & makes them a more easy prey to Ambition & self Interest." All of this might be true, but it was a lesson one could learn as easily from the annals of Tacitus as the experience of latter-day American republicans. At the same time, Madison argued that the road to future constitutional revision should be left open to the people of Kentucky. Doing otherwise would be "indecent," he wrote, "because an handfull of early sett[l]ers ought not to preclude a populous Country from a choice of the Government under which they & their Posterity are to live." Limiting the prospects for future constitutional change seemed far more dangerous.[20]

Madison's letter to Wallace is a helpful point of departure in tracing the development of his thinking. It is only a letter, not a treatise. As is often the case with his writing, one wishes he had said more. The letter identifies significant themes and motifs that recur in his analyses: above all, the need to improve legislative deliberation, especially through the checking mechanism of a senate, but also the difficulty of cabining legislative authority, his uncertainty about executive power, and the balance between veneration and reason in the process of constitutional revision. Madison was already thinking critically and comparatively about other state constitutions and treating them as a source of ideas and examples from which lessons could be drawn. The task of assessing these constitutions was suitable work for "the ablest Statesmen & soundest Republicans" in the nation, a class in which Madison proudly enrolled.

Still, the critical changes that carried Madison to the head of that class came in the period to come, during the eighteen months that convinced him that he should attempt to set the agenda for the Philadelphia Convention. When he wrote the *Memorial and Remonstrance against Religious Assessments*, he closed its first item with this somewhat indeterminate observation: "True it is, that no other rule exists, by which any question which may divide a Society, can be ultimately determined, but the will of the majority; but it is also true that the majority may trespass on the rights of the minority."[21] The majority has the final right to rule, but it may also do wrong. What happens then? In the *Memorial*, Madison left this question unanswered. But by 1786 he was clearly giving the problem additional thought. Part of his concern was driven, perhaps even initiated, by the Mississippi issue.[22] But increasingly the problem seemed to apply equally well to internal legislation within the states and thus to the fundamental premise of republican government.

Had the campaign against the religious assessment bill turned out differently—had a majority of the citizenry favored the measure, as its sponsors may have expected—Madison would have had handy proof for his emerging concern readily available. Even when public opinion wound up pointing in the other direction, Madison may have surmised that it was the character of the putative majority *on this issue*, rather than the general security of

majority rule, that saved the day for religious freedom. But there
was another pressing issue about which his concerns proved even
more pessimistic. This was the great question of paper money.
"A considerable itch for paper money discovered itself" at the
fall 1785 session of the Virginia legislature, Madison reported at
its close, "though no overt attempt was made."[23]

That itch became an inflammation in 1786. A letter to Jefferson,
written in mid-August from Philadelphia, contains a virtual
state-by-state survey of the subject. Madison opened this letter with a report of his journey north, including a crossing of
the Potomac at Harper's Ferry where, through a dense fog, he
viewed "50 hands" at work on the rapids in an effort to make the
river navigable through a system of ropes to pull boats up and
down. Scenes of improvement like this inspired him to remark
that "these fruits of the Revolution do great honour to it." But
there was a ledger to balance here as well, with "too many"
items "belonging to the opposite side of the acct.," Madison
complained. "At the head of these is to be put the general rage
for paper money." The phrases Madison used in this summary
betray his agitation: "this folly," "as great an evil," "a sort of
convulsion," "symptoms of the danger," "the popular torrent,"
"the epidemic malady."[24] When Madison returned to Virginia for
the fall 1786 session of the legislature, he was pleased, perhaps
even surprised, when a motion "for a paper emission" was easily
turned back "in emphatical terms by a majority of 84 vs 17."[25] But
on the other side of the account lay Rhode Island, a textbook case
of republicanism run amok. There the reign of a popular party
making the state's depreciating paper currency legal tender for
the payment of private debts symbolized everything that could
go wrong in an American republic. Had a distant aftershock of
the Lisbon earthquake of 1755 dropped the whole tiny province
into the Atlantic, few Americans would have noticed its absence
or minded its disappearance. But as the archly anti-federal rogue
member of the union, Rhode Island remained a handy object
for scorn—and also an inspiration to rethink the premises of
republican government.[26]

Paper money, and the broader question of the discharge of the
revolutionary public debt, formed the great fault line of legislative
politics within the states after 1783. As scholars know from roll call

analysis, the positions representatives took on these issues led to the formation of relatively stable political alignments within many legislatures. Whether these voting alignments created political parties in the full sense of the term is a much more controversial proposition.[27] The high turnover in legislative membership and the absence of any political coordination across constituencies make the equation between voting alignment and party activities problematic. On the other hand, the issue resonated across the country, and thus offered a basis for appealing to—and attempting to form—a source of popular opinion that might prove capable of influencing legislative action.[28] The range of state responses to issues of paper currency and public credit also varied. No contrast was more striking than that between Rhode Island and its northern neighbor, hard-money Massachusetts, where the attempt to levy taxes to pay off the state's debt led to the turmoil of Shays's Rebellion. Then, too, the adoption of different policies among the states added one more complication to the fraying bonds of union. In Madison's view, this tendency in state policies seemed likely to provoke "the same warfare & retaliation among the States as were produced by the State regulations of commerce."[29]

Madison was something of an alarmist on the question of paper money. He evidently took seriously the suspicion that the real aims of "the discontented" extended to the "abolition of debts public & private, and a new division of property"—shades of the agrarian law that formed so intriguing a theme in republican political theory.[30] He wondered whether the conventional republican theory of majority rule, which "necessarily suppose power and right always to be on the same side," held true in times of insurrection, as was the case in Massachusetts.[31]

Together these opinions demonstrate that by early 1787 Madison was just as troubled about the internal governance of the states as he was with the "imbecility" of the Confederation. The salience of the paper money issue gave heightened urgency to his prior complaints about the quality of legislative deliberation and decision. The earlier complaints did indicate basic flaws in the existing structures of republican governance within the states, but they also operated more as targets of reform than immediate sources of crisis. That was not the case with the vices that vexed

Madison as he returned to Congress in February 1787. These raised fundamental questions about the essence of republican government itself, about the willingness of citizens to respect basic rights of property and the capacity of their representatives to deliberate properly about both the public good and private rights—the two criteria Madison regularly invoked as the basic norms against which public acts should be measured.

The coalescence of these ideas is best traced in the key documents that Madison wrote between mid-March and mid-April 1787: the personal letters to Jefferson, Randolph, and Washington and "the Vices." To say that he drafted these texts in the midst of a deep passion might seem overly dramatic, especially with an individual who is often seen to embody a lucid Enlightenment rationality opposed to the play of personal passions on politics.[32] Madison had too much experience to believe he could predict how events would turn out. Even when it seemed likely that "a pretty full" meeting would take place, he wrote Edmund Pendleton, "what the issue of it will be is among the other arcana of futurity and nearly as inscrutable as any of them." He repeated the same thought to Jefferson. "What may be the result of this political experiment cannot be foreseen," he wrote on March 19. But the sense that a crisis had been reached that Madison felt personally responsible to answer seems equally clear. "The mortal diseases of the existing constitution," he observed, "are at present marked by symptoms which are truly alarming, which have tainted the faith of the most orthodox republicans, and which challenge from the votaries of liberty every concession in favor of stable Government not infringing fundamental principles, as the only security against an opposite extreme of our present situation"—that is, a return to some form of monarchical rule.[33]

Madison followed this remark with the first outline of his agenda for Philadelphia. It had four main points. Each addressed a particular aspect of legislative power. The first required "the new system" to secure "such a ratification by the people themselves of the several States as will render it clearly paramount to their Legislative authorities."[34] This was a major theoretical point, because it would clearly distinguish the legal supremacy of a constitution from the ordinary authority of statutes. Madison's second point was arguably even more radical. In addition to the positive legislative powers that "the federal head" would possess, it should also be armed "with a *negative in all cases whatsoever*" on the local legislatures, which it could use not only for the "defensive" purpose of voiding interfering legislation from the states but also for "restrain[ing] the States from thwarting and molesting each other, and even," he continued, "from oppressing the minority within themselves by paper money and other unrighteous measures which favor the interest of the majority." Third, representation in the national legislature had to rest on some other "principle" than the equal vote of the states. Fourth, federal power had to be "exercised by separate departments," not consolidated in a single institution like the Continental Congress.

This outline evolved in the subsequent documents. The letters to Randolph and Washington expanded the agenda of actions Madison wanted the Convention to pursue, and "the Vices" developed the diagnosis on which the cure rested. The starting point for his analysis began with the understated way in which he noted, in item 9, that some thought had to be given to "the evils" that "are found within the States individually." To say that they had "an indirect influence on the general malady" hardly matched the pessimism with which Madison viewed the subject. State legislation was flawed on two counts: the "multiplicity" and resulting "mutability" of the laws the states had enacted since independence. Some of this "luxuriancy of legislation" could be tied to "the situation in which the revolution has placed us." An eight-year war of independence had required the legislatures to enact measure after measure to pursue the common cause. But that impulse alone could not explain the entire phenomenon or apologize for the unnecessary length of the states' legal codes. Nor could it satisfactorily account for the short life of too many acts. "We daily see laws repealed or superseded, before any trial can be made of their merits; and even before a knowledge of them can have reached the remoter districts within which they were to operate."

Beyond these complaints, however, lay a deeper challenge. "If the multiplicity and mutability of laws prove a want of wisdom," Madison wrote in item 11, "their injustice betrays a defect still more alarming: more alarming not merely because it is a greater evil in itself, but because it brings more into question the fundamental principle of republican Government, that the majority who rule in such Governments, are the safest Guardians both of public Good and of private rights." Here at last the initial puzzlement Madison had expressed over the misuse of majority rule in the Mississippi question and potentially on the matter of religious assessments had evolved into a specific challenge to the basic principle of republicanism. Now Madison posed the analytical question that went beyond the original observation: "To what causes is this evil to be ascribed?" When Madison wrote like this, his question was genuine, not merely rhetorical. It was a mark not of a prior agenda but of an analytical desire to resolve a problem. The ensuing answer to this query in item 11 produced the first draft of the analysis we know best from *Federalist* 10. It thus reveals how the creative dimensions of Madison's thinking emerged, not in the context of justifying a completed constitution to the American public but as part of the prior process of determining what his agenda for Philadelphia would be.

Madison began his answer by identifying two sources of legislative injustice within the states: "These causes lie," he wrote, "1. in the Representative bodies" and "2. in the people themselves." Given his prior expressed concerns over legislative deliberations, one might surmise that Madison would have given the first cause extensive treatment. In fact, he addressed this problem quite succinctly. Three motives led candidates to seek "representative appointments": "1. ambition 2. personal interest. 3. public good." Unfortunately, the first two were "the most prevalent." Those who acted on these motives, especially those driven by "personal interest," would not only prove "most industrious, and most successful in pursuing their object"; they would also be willing to take actions "contrary to the interest, and views of their Constituents." Elections would not provide adequate security against their "base and selfish measures," for their "pretexts of public good and apparent expediency" and their cultivation of rhetorical "arts and industry" would lead "unwary [voters] to misplace their confidence." Then, too, these arts would also mislead "honest but enligh[t]ened representatives" who would be too inexperienced to penetrate the real designs of "a favorite leader."[35] It is hard not to glimpse the figure of Patrick Henry, the wild independent variable of Virginia politics, lurking in this last phrase. If Henry was not quite a full-throated demagogue in the mold of antiquity, he remained a formidable if mercurial force and a continual challenge to Madison's (and Jefferson's) plans for Virginia.

But Madison did not dwell on this point. Instead his analysis quickly moved on to the second set of causes.[36] This formed the novel and more exciting part of his analysis, the part he expounded at greater length, moving beyond the realm of institutional behavior into the popular sources of republican factionalism. "A still more fatal if not more frequent cause" of legislative injustice, he began, "lies among the people themselves."[37] Here, really for the first time, Madison extended his analysis of the vices of republican politics to that wonderful concept "the people themselves."[38] In his thinking, the evils of the American political system were no longer limited to the structure of the federal union or the lack of wisdom and stability in the state legislatures. A satisfactory analysis also had to cover the political behavior of ordinary citizens. Their interests, opinions, and passions, far more than the ambitions of officeholders, were the life force of republican politics. In a republic "the majority however composed, ultimately give the law. Whenever therefore an apparent interest or common passion unites a majority," Madison asked, "what is to restrain them from unjust violations of the rights and interests of the minority, or of individuals?" There were three possible answers to this question, he continued: "a prudent regard to their own good as involved in the general and permanent good of the Community"; a "respect for character," which operated only for individuals, not collective groups; and religion. None was efficacious.

A better answer to the danger of unjust legislation promoted by the interests and passions of the majority, Madison famously concluded, lay elsewhere, in "an enlargement of the sphere" of a republican society. The same interests and passions would still operate; they would be no "less predominant in this case with the majority" than they were in "corporate towns" or "little republics" (read, Rhode Island). But as "the Society becomes broken into a greater variety of interests, of pursuits, of passions," these would begin to "check each other" and to make the "opportunity of communication and concert" more difficult. From this concise analysis a major conclusion followed: "It may be inferred that the inconveniences of popular States contrary to the prevailing Theory, are in proportion not to the extent, but to the narrowness of their limits."

The "prevailing Theory" was, of course, the idea, most prominently associated with Montesquieu but also enjoying a deep genealogy, that a stable republic had to be small in its extent, relatively homogeneous in its interests, and populated by citizens steeped in a self-denying virtue of civic restraint. Madison essentially turned this theory on its head. He argued, first, that a multiplicity of interests in an extended republic would be more conducive to republican stability than homogeneity within a constricted space; and second, that the sources of this diversity were inherent in both human nature and the development of modern commercial society that encouraged individuals to pursue their self-interest.

The sources of this discovery have now engaged several generations of scholars, ever since Douglass Adair wrote his two-part essay on the origins of *Federalist* 10.[39] In Adair's rather overdramatized rendering, Madison's agenda for Philadelphia remained uncertain because of the intellectual difficulty he faced in refuting the received wisdom about the optimal size of republics. Only an encounter with the writings of David Hume, especially his essay "Idea of a Perfect Commonwealth," gave Madison the insight he needed to answer Montesquieu. In Adair's telling, Madison's reading of Hume lit a candle in his head, revealing a pathway to political innovation that otherwise might have remained hidden.

One should certainly be wary of underestimating the impact of Hume. Although Madison was not a great compiler of scholarly footnotes, Hume's "influence"—whatever that concept means— could certainly have affected his preparations for Philadelphia. Even so, the notion that Madison was somehow stumped about what to do until a reading of Hume showed him the way seems simplistic. The more striking way to perceive the development of Madison's thinking in 1787 involves understanding where the novelty of his analysis lay. The sources of his concern with majority misrule did not depend on his reading of either Hume or the history of ancient and modern confederacies. The Mississippi controversy, the general assessment debate in Virginia, and his near obsession with the potential injustice of paper money had already raised the essential questions. What was new in Madison's thinking in 1787 was his intuition or recognition that an analysis that relied on legislative misdeeds or legislators' ambitions alone was hardly sufficient. Any issue might prove subject to demagogical abuse, and Madison's language in reacting to the agitation for paper money reflects his own bias on this point. But the turmoil in state politics in the mid-1780s was ultimately the consequence not of manipulation but of the manifest impact of the revolution on issues of public credit, finance, and taxation. His concern with the shortcomings of his Virginia legislative colleagues had led to a deeper question: whether the pressures brought to bear on legislative politics from society finally mattered more than the indifferent ways in which the representatives went about their business. Reading Hume might help Madison answer Montesquieu when the time came to explain why a national republic might outperform its provincial counterparts. But the prior task involved dealing with the problem itself, with asking how the task of constitutional reform should respond to the challenge of dealing with "the people themselves."

That task remained essentially institutional in nature. Building on his mid-March letter to Jefferson, Madison used his April 1787 letters to Randolph and Washington to convert the analysis of "the Vices" into a working agenda. Madison and Washington strongly agreed that the time for equivocal measures had passed. Madison remained amenable "to retain[ing] as much as possible of the old Confederation," he wrote Randolph, but only as elements to be incorporated "into the new System." The changes the Convention proposed would not simply be amendments to the Articles. Moreover, these changes should not be presented as a set of individual articles that the states could evaluate separately or piecemeal. The new framework would have to be adopted as a whole—as a "system."[40]

It says something about Madison's ambition that he imagined the scope of these changes in this way. That conclusive step of ratification could be taken, however, only after the substantive changes were accomplished first. Madison's first point of departure, the "ground-work" of his agenda, was "that a change be made in the principle of representation." In place of the rule of

the Confederation giving each state one equal vote,[41] a different form of equality would operate. Here Madison's analysis of
the underlying problem of federalism converged with proper
principles of representation. "Under a system which would
operate in many essential points without the intervention of the
State legislatures," there was no longer any need to represent the
states as such. With laws operating directly on the population, the
equality of citizens, rather than the legal or corporate equality of
states, would provide the foundation for a rule of representation
tied to population, wealth, or both.

To this principled argument against the representation of states,
Madison coupled a political calculus that also illustrated how he
reasoned strategically about the Convention. Why would this
radical change prove politically acceptable at Philadelphia? Just as
the northern states would approve this change because of "their
present populousness," the southern states "by their expected
advantage in this respect" would do so as well. Madison here
voiced the common expectation that the future arc of American
migration would swing southwest, making the frontier more an
extension of southern than northern society, and thus bringing the
existing regional divisions closer to parity. As for the small states,
they must eventually "yield to the predominant will."[42] Both
judgments proved badly miscalculated—the latter quite soon,
the former over the next few decades—but Madison's calculation
reflects a considered political strategy. In effect he was presuming
that one might build a winning coalition by juxtaposing blocs
with current and prospective advantages.

But the main purpose of this change, Madison concluded,
was to "obviate the principal objections of the larger States to
the necessary concessions of power." Here Madison assumed
that the size (or, more specifically, the populousness) of a state
was a legitimate factor that would shape its political behavior
only temporarily—*at the Convention*, not thereafter. When one
was designing a system of government among states with different populations, the size of one's state would *initially* matter
in determining the rules of voting. But Madison rightly assumed
that this initial commitment would not last; that is, the decisions
the new government would later take would rest on factors other
than the size of each state's population, since that distinction

would never describe the real interests it contained. Other factors—the specific interests and opinions mobilizing the political concerns of its *citizens*—would provide the basis on which the people's representatives would act. But at the outset, Madison believed, the major hurdle was to remove the reservations that the large states—with the bulk of the nation's population—would have against any substantial enlargement of national legislative powers.

How substantial would that enlargement be? Here Madison's thoughts were remarkably terse. One can read his approach in two alternative ways without resolving its ambiguities. On the one hand, Madison was amenable to the idea of limiting legislative power. In the case of the national government, its legislative authority could depend on the delegation of specific powers devoted to particular objects of policy. That would impose a limitation on national legislative authority *from below*, through an original act of popular sovereignty. In the case of the states, he advocated a negative on their laws *from above*, through a process of national legislative review that would effectively diminish, or indeed destroy, the states' claim to legal sovereignty. This need seemed so urgent that Madison contemplated allowing some form of federal consular authority acting within the states "to give a temporary sanction to laws of immediate necessity" while longer-term measures were dispatched for national review. Madison's conviction that the negative should operate "in all cases whatsoever" echoed the language of Parliament's detested Declaratory Act of 1766, and his flat comparison of the negative to "the Kingly prerogative" of suspending or vetoing colonial acts further marked the depth of his reaction. To describe a negative on state laws as "the least possible encroachment on the state Jurisdictions" was no less remarkable.

The desire to cabin legislative power was thus a dominant motif in Madison's thinking. Yet that desire has to be juxtaposed against another, equally unsettling, belief. Legislative power, he understood, was inherently expansive in its very nature. The power to make rules, to settle the initial meaning of law, gave the legislature potentially indefinite authority to manipulate its acts for its own advantage or purposes. It was no easy task to say precisely where the authority of a legislature ended. It might be feasible to proscribe legislative power in some areas of policy formally. That was part of the deep logic of Madison's position on religious freedom, which coupled broad recognition of freedom of conscience with a nearly absolute position in favor of disestablishment. But in other realms of action, formal proscription either would not work or could be easily evaded. An "infinitude of legislative expedients" were always available, Madison wrote Jefferson in October 1787, to circumvent the formal denial of power.[43]

In one sense Madison was merely responding to the principle of legislative supremacy, the great constitutional outcome of 1688, a founding tenet of Lockean theory, and a doctrine that Americans reconfirmed in their first state constitutions. If the legislature was supreme, and the other branches of government depended on its authority, of course it would be the one institution most difficult to contain. But here again Madison's grasp of the danger rested as much on experience as it ever did on reading. It was not the principle of legislative supremacy within government that Madison disputed in 1787 but the manifest consequences that he perceived in the work of popularly elected assemblies across the American republic.

Madison's ideas of national legislative power thus rested on the daunting challenge of balancing a desire to constrain legislative power with an awareness of the inherent difficulty of that attempt. His answers to this overarching problem were complex. Indeed, they were typically, perhaps profoundly, Madisonian in their diversity, and thus they illustrate the value of tracking the complex lines of his thinking.

Madison had surprisingly little to say about the positive legislative powers he would vest in the national government. In his mid-April letter to Washington, he dealt with this question in a single-sentence paragraph: "In addition to the present federal powers, the national Government should be armed with positive and compleat authority in all cases which require uniformity; such as the regulation of trade, including the right of taxing both exports & imports, the fixing the terms and forms of naturalization, &c &c."[44] No doubt the double et cetera was shorthand for a longer list, but Madison did not round the subject out. The Virginia Plan, which Governor Edmund Randolph presented at the start of the Convention, treated this issue in even more general terms. In addition to retaining the legislative powers already vested in Congress under the Articles of Confederation, the national legislature should be "impowered . . . to legislate in all cases to which the separate States are incompetent, or in which the harmony of the United States may be interrupted by the exercise of individual Legislation."[45] This was no delegation of specific powers, in the form that Article I, Section 8, of the Constitution eventually took. Instead, it offered a grant of nearly plenary power under two broad conditions, whereby state incompetence or a perceived need warranted general action.

It remains unclear whether either the Virginia delegates or Madison intended this clause to serve as their ideal statement of a national legislative power or instead to function as a temporary placeholder while other issues were discussed first. Madison's political strategy was to delay any enumeration of legislative powers until the questions of representation were resolved.[46] If the large states secured some version of proportional representation, the grant of legislative power could be quite broad. If they did not, it might be tailored narrowly. Because the case for the radical reconstitution of national government seemed so manifest, Madison thought that the small-state delegates would ultimately agree to radical alterations both in the mode of representation and in the quantum of true authority the national legislature should possess.

Rather than dwell on the enumeration of specific powers, Madison preferred other solutions to the problem of checking legislative power. The two most important institutional mechanisms involved the character of the upper house and the creation of a council of revision, modeled on the one found in New York. On both issues he suffered quick reverses that proved impossible to surmount. Yet the adverse outcomes still illuminate the characteristics of his thinking.

Madison's original idea about the upper house was that it should be regarded more as a deliberative institution than a representative one. Under the Virginia Plan, the second house should be elected by "the first, out of a proper number of persons nominated by the individual Legislatures" of the states. The proposal said nothing about requiring each state to have a seat, and to keep the body small yet somehow consistent with the idea of proportional representation it is conceivable that some states would have no senators. This proposal ran into immediate objections on May 31. A few delegates preferred election by the state legislatures, while James Wilson and Charles Pinckney favored creating electoral districts of a multistate nature and allowing the people to make the choice. Madison thought that the latter mode would disadvantage qualified candidates from the small states, because ordinary voters would prefer "local partiality" to electing "a candidate of superior merit residing out of" their own area.[47] But the crucial consideration was to keep the upper house small. In opposition to John Dickinson, who favored a numerous upper house elected by the state legislatures, Madison insisted that "the use of the Senate is to consist in its proceeding with more coolness, with more system, & with more wisdom, than the popular branch." Increase its numbers, Madison warned, and its members would "par[take] of the infirm[i]ties of their constituents."[48] If a body was truly senatorial in terms of the "political authority" it possessed, "the smaller the number the greater the weight." Nor was there any reason to believe that the desired characteristics of senators would be obtained from their election by the state legislatures, the source of so much of the mischief of American politics. Indeed, in his view, any other mechanism of election would be vastly preferable.[49]

Madison and his closest ally on this point, James Wilson, lost this argument decisively on June 7, barely a week into the Convention's debates, when all ten states present voted to have the state legislatures elect the upper house. That was their second joint setback in two days; on June 6 the Convention had also rejected the idea of an executive-judicial council of revision with a limited negative on legislative acts.[50] The alternative the Convention preferred was to give the executive alone a limited negative on legislation. Madison opposed that decision for two reasons. First, he remained highly doubtful that a single individual could withstand the political force of the legislature. Second, and more important, Madison firmly believed that the benefits to be gained by involving the judges *ex ante* in the process of lawmaking far outweighed the ostensible damage this might inflict on a rigid application of the theory of separated powers. Other delegates held with good reason that judges should act only after proper legal cases came before them in their true judicial capacity. But Madison, with the active support of Wilson, had a different view. Having federal judges involved in the exercise of this power would provide the dual benefit of enhancing the authority of the executive and ensuring that this power would be used for the right ends. "An association of the Judges in this revisionary function wd both double the advantage and diminish the danger," Madison told the Convention on June 6. But the greater benefit would come in improving the quality of legislation. It was unlikely that any given judge would have to consider a case in which he had personally been involved.[51] By contrast, "how much good on the other hand wd. proceed from the perspicuity, the conciseness, and the systematic character wch. the Code of laws wd. receive from the Judiciary talents." In this trade-off, the quality of republican governance would be improved by taking constructive steps to mitigate and prevent the enactment of too many mutable and unjust laws, whereas the real damage done to the principle of separated powers would be slight.

Although this measure was initially rejected on June 6, Madison, Wilson, and several other delegates remained strongly committed to it. They reintroduced it on July 21, shortly after the Convention had adopted the equal state vote for the Senate and rejected Madison's proposed negative on state laws. This time the debate was more extensive, and it revealed the persistent strength of Madison's and Wilson's concerns about the legislative process. It was not enough to give the judges a later "opportunity of defending their constitutional rights." That power "did not go far enough," Wilson complained. "Laws may be unjust, may be unwise, may be dangerous, may be destructive," he added, "and yet not be so unconstitutional as to justify the Judges in refusing to give them effect." Madison extended this point in his remarks. Not only would the council better enable the executive to defend itself, but it would be "useful" in three additional respects. It would aid "the Executive, by inspiring additional confidence & firmness in exerting the revisionary power." It would assist "the Legislature by the valuable assistance it would give in preserving a consistency, conciseness, perspicuity & technical propriety in the laws, qualities peculiarly necessary; & yet shamefully wanting in our republican Codes." And then, more generally, it would benefit "the Community at large as an additional check agst. a pursuit of those unwise & unjust measures which constituted so great a portion of our calamities."[52]

Madison's positions rested on three propositions that were fundamental to his political and constitutional thinking in 1787–88. The first was his underlying institutional concern, even obsession, with the misuse of legislative power and its "powerful tendency . . . to absorb all power into its vortex" (a word that reappeared, modified by "impetuous," in *Federalist* 48).[53] The second was the belief that the other two departments were simply too weak to resist that vortex, unless they were allowed to intervene in the use of legislative power *before* the damage was done. Third, this creative opportunity to redress the balance of power between the dominant institution and its weaker rivals trumped any unthinking loyalty to the abstract theory of separated powers. "Experience has taught us" that "a Constitutional discrimination of the departments on paper" (which would become the "parchment barriers" of *Federalist* 48) was inadequate. Rather than "laying down the Theory in the Constitution" as a simple, mutually exclusionary rule about the role of departments, as the state constitutions had done, it was better to erect "effectual powers for keeping them separate."[54] The task of separating the powers in order to preserve liberty was not a matter of neatly distinguishing legislative, executive, and judicial powers into hermetic categories. It was rather another problem of constitutional engineering, of directing political and deliberative forces to the right points—the actual junctures—of decision making.

To describe Madison's attachment to the council of revision in this way is to realize that his design involved something more than multiplying the number of "checkpoints" within government in the cause of slowing action or making effective decision making more difficult. True, Madison was concerned with the danger of legislative impetuosity, especially when the impulse to make law originated in fluctuating passions or calculated interests swirling through the body politic and directing their energy to a responsive lower house. Like nearly all American constitutionalists in the eighteenth century, he accepted the principle of bicameralism uncritically. But Madison's commitment to the council of revision illustrates that improved deliberation, not procedural obstruction, was the guiding principle of his constitutional project at this critical moment. The objective was not to impair lawmaking but to improve it, and then to reap further benefits once laws were enacted. Bringing the executive and the judiciary jointly into the process of legislating would not only assist amateur lawmakers in their deliberations, it would also facilitate the later execution and adjudication of laws by protecting the weaker departments in the implementation of their duties.

Regrettably for Madison, his colleagues did not accept this pragmatic conception of the separation of powers. In their view, a responsible executive was a unitary executive, the sole head of an entire department, and the veto they vested in the president would be used most safely when everyone knew who was accountable for its exercise. Similarly, judges were simply the adjudicators of legal controversies properly presented, not legal experts who could freely offer their counsel for other public purposes. Judges simply could not act politically as quasi legislators, helpful as their contributions might prove. Even so, the positions the Convention adopted were highly significant in their own right. The veto restored to the executive a prerogative that Americans in 1776 had wholly rejected. The framers also revealed their acceptance of the novel doctrine of judicial review of the constitutionality of legislation. These were hardly trivial points. Yet neither did they fully reflect Madison's concern, grounded in his own experience, that improving the quality of republican lawmaking remained a fundamental challenge.

Even after the council of revision suffered its second defeat, Madison made one last effort to secure his end. On August 15 he introduced a new motion to require submitting legislative bills separately to the executive and judiciary departments. If either of these objected, a bill would require two-thirds votes in both houses to pass. If both departments objected, a supermajority of three-fourths would be required for passage. Here again he met defeat, eight states to three. But the animus of his concern, and the belief that the separation of powers should not preclude the involvement of the weaker branches in lawmaking, remained unchanged.[55] The very fact that Madison would introduce this motion, with its exceptional requirements for the passage of

ordinary legislation, indicates his unhappiness with the critical
decisions over the Senate. With its election by the state legislatures
and the equal state vote, the Senate promised to resemble the
Continental Congress, the institution whose "imbecility" had
led to the Federal Convention. How could such a body fulfill the
functions Madison ideally ascribed to it?

Madison remained an active participant in the Convention
debate to its end. No one was more committed to its success.
He had never viewed it, as others did, as a preparatory step that
might not succeed in itself but only set the stage for later reform.
The Convention was a risky adventure in high-stakes politics. So
long as it produced a government capable of acting legally on the
American people, and one that was no longer dependent on the
states, the constitutional game was still worth the deliberative
candle. Still, his disappointments were significant. The equal state
vote in the Senate; the election of senators by the reviled state
legislatures; the defeat of the negative on state laws and the council
of revision—these were all major reverses. To say that Americans
have a Madisonian constitution, as modern scholars often do, is
not to say that all of its provisions are the ones Madison preferred.

It is the nature of political life that one can never dwell too
long on reverses. Madison was not in an upbeat mood when the
Convention adjourned on September 17, as his letters to Jefferson
attest. Yet he quickly returned to New York, where the Continental Congress marked the Constitution's first stop on its road
to the states. He did not linger at Princeton for the ceremonies
where he would receive the honorary degree of doctor of laws
that his mentor, President John Witherspoon, had arranged. It
was essential to rejoin Congress, where his Virginia colleague
Richard Henry Lee was proposing to revise the Constitution
before sending it to the states. Such a direct action, Madison
worried, would make the Constitution the act of Congress, not the
Convention, potentially triggering the requirement that changes
to the Articles receive the unanimous approval of all thirteen
legislatures.[56] In the end, the Constitution went to the states as
the Convention had planned, to take effect when ratified, in its
entirety, by popularly elected conventions in nine states.

Madison stayed on in New York. Sometime in October, Alexander Hamilton recruited Madison to join him and John Jay in

writing *The Federalist*. This, of course, is the other source of our conception of the Madisonian constitution. Hamilton wrote fifty-one essays to Madison's twenty-nine, but it is the latter's work that states most, though not quite all, of the great propositions we associate with the founders' political science. Constitutional theory and history alike have benefited from the circumstances that kept Madison in New York until he returned to Virginia in early March 1788.

In accepting this invitation, Madison was under no obligation to provide a faithful record of his political thinking—or at least to discuss those critical aspects of his agenda that failed to become part of the Constitution. In arguing that liberty would be more secure in an extended national republic than in the states, the great theme of *Federalist* 10, he had no need to discuss the negative on state laws or to explain why individual and minority rights would remain highly vulnerable to the factious majorities that could more readily form in the states. Nor, when he turned to the separation of powers, did he have any reason to describe the putative benefits of a council of revision. The arguments he had made against an equal state vote in the Senate could also disappear. It was enough to note, in *Federalist* 62, that "it is superfluous to try, by the standard of theory, a part of the Constitution which is allowed on all hands to be the result, not of theory, but 'of a spirit of amity, and that mutual deference and concession which the peculiarity of our political situation rendered indispensable.'" Residents of the larger states would thus have to agree that "the advice of prudence must be to embrace the lesser evil."[57]

So the political thinking that carried Madison into and through the Convention was only partly represented in his essays as Publius. Still, what was there was significant. One can draw a straight line from Madison's pre-Convention writings through his speeches at Philadelphia and on to *Federalist* 10. But the parts we know best, the arguments that best embody the Madisonian constitution, are those that respond to the received wisdom of his age, to the known body of political thought that Anti-Federalists evoked to fashion their leading objections. What makes Madison's most famous pronouncements the leading American contribution to the canon of Western political ideas is that they explicitly address key propositions of conventional wisdom. Much of that wisdom is ascribed to Montesquieu, author of that great work of eighteenth-century political science, *The Spirit of the Laws*. On the crucial questions that Madison confronted—the optimal size of republics and the separation of powers—Montesquieu was either the best known or most influential authority. Federalist writers had to find ways to coopt, neutralize, rebut, or diminish his positions.

The core elements of this response are easily stated. The most famous proposition is Madison's insistence that the sources of faction are simply part of human nature, or at least human nature as it is manifested in modern societies. A polity predicated on the republican ideal of pervasive civic virtue, the dominant assumption of 1776, would be infeasible. Men had to be taken as they are, and their vices exploited rather than repressed. In a democracy, where the people govern directly, these vices would dominate both discussion and decision. But Americans erred in "confounding" the evils ascribed to democracies with the nature of a representative republic, where the people could act only through "their representatives and agents." With the greater extent and diversity that representative government made possible, two advantages could secure republicanism from the factious evils for which it was commonly blamed. First, although these same passions, interests, and opinions would still exist among the people, their capacity to converge and collaborate for harmful ends would be reduced. Second, the larger electoral districts of an extended national republic should encourage the election of a superior class of lawmakers. If these representatives occupied a deliberative space where the play of faction out-of-doors had been neutralized—as the first hypothesis proposed—this should work "to refine and enlarge the public views, by passing them through the medium of a chosen body of citizens," so that "the public voice, pronounced by the representatives of the people, will be more consonant to the public good than if pronounced by the people themselves, convened for the purpose." This was the great republican hope that *Federalist* 10 proposed: to improve the quality of deliberation and decision beyond what "the people themselves" could achieve, to improve on unrefined public opinion through deliberation among a superior class of lawmakers.

These arguments are essentially hypotheses—predictions of the benefits that the creation of a diverse extended republic might bring. When Madison turned to the subject of the separation of powers, he drew more directly on his experience in Virginia and his observations of the other states. Here his direct target was again Montesquieu, "the oracle who is always consulted and cited on this subject."[58] But refuting Montesquieu on this issue was a more complicated task than dealing with the idea that stable republics had to be small and homogenous. One first had to determine what Montesquieu and his American acolytes actually meant by the separation of powers. This was the subject of *Federalist* 47, which used both the evidence of the British constitution on which Montesquieu had relied and the way in which the American constitution makers had applied his axioms to demonstrate that his theory did *not* demand a wholly rigid separation of the three domestic departments. Any empirical effort to describe what separation meant in operation confirmed the pointed observation of *Federalist* 37: "Questions daily occur in the course of practice, which prove the obscurity which reigns in these subjects, and which puzzle the greatest adepts in political science."[59] The true problem was not to bring theoretical rigor to an inherently murky topic. It was rather to identify the specific challenges that republican constitutions were most likely to generate, and then to propose some workable cures.

That was the problem Madison took up in *Federalist* 48, where he restated the problem of separation in fresh terms. The dominant fact was that "the legislative department is everywhere extending the sphere of its activity, and drawing all power into its impetuous vortex." The constitution makers of 1776 had not foreseen this danger. With their eyes fixed on their own history, where the "all-grasping prerogative of an hereditary magistrate" was the source of their grievances, "they seem never to have recollected the danger from legislative usurpations." The swirling force of this new vortex depended on two other factors. One was the political superiority that the legislature would draw from its "supposed influence over the people." The other was the advantage it gained from its rule-making authority, allowing it to "mask, under complicated and indirect measures, the encroachments it makes on coördinate departments."[60]

On this subject, Madison's analysis in 1787–88 lay closer to his experience, and thus closer to the thinking that had shaped his

agenda of constitutional reform. By contrast, the argument about
the merits of an extended republic, though it has figured more
prominently (or even predominantly) in the scholarly literature,
was initially driven more by the rhetorical need to counteract
received wisdom. That does not lessen its theoretical significance,
which Madison continued to ponder.[61] Madison understood that
this conventional wisdom about the size of republics needed
correction. But his constitutional agenda was more closely tied
to his criticism of the workings of American legislatures. With
its vision of creating a better level of deliberation, *Federalist* 10
expressed a Madisonian ideal. But *Federalist* 48 identified a real
problem that had to be solved.

The leading conclusions of *Federalist* 10 and 48 thus identify
an important line of tension in Madison's thinking. *Federalist* 10
promoted a plausible way of improving the quality of legislation
by neutralizing the play of faction in society and then promoting
ways to allow a superior class of representatives to deliberate
over public matters. Whether that remedy would work, however,
remained to be tested. *Federalist* 48, by contrast, presupposed
that, even if this model of deliberation was effective, Congress
(and particularly the House of Representatives) would remain
the most dangerous institution of the government.

Even in *Federalist* 10, however, Madison also offered a realistic
assessment of other commitments that would work to compromise legislators' independence. He identified these difficulties
in the paragraph that follows the famous account of the multiple
sources of faction. That account concludes with the observation
cited at the opening of this chapter: "The regulation of these various and interfering interests forms the principal task of modern
Legislation, and involves the spirit of party and faction in the
necessary and ordinary operations of Government."[62] But the
development of this thought in the next paragraph illustrates
how this seemingly obvious remark subsumed a more probing
analysis of the problem of collective deliberation.

Madison began with the commonplace maxim that no one
should "be a judge in his own cause." What is true of individuals
also holds for collective bodies. Here Madison again posed a
question that was far more analytical than rhetorical: "Yet what
are many of the most important acts of legislation, but so many

judicial determinations, not indeed concerning the rights of single persons, but concerning the rights of large bodies of citizens? And what are the different classes of legislators but advocates and parties to the causes they determine?"

Madison then provided three examples of economic legislation in which questions of public policy and justice inevitably intertwined: laws relating to debtors and creditors, to the protection of domestic manufactures, and to the "apportionment of taxes." In each case, the government had to act, one way or another. Each example involved the possession of property, where the *rights*, and not merely the *interests*, of individuals and social classes were inherently at stake. Each therefore implicated a matter of justice, because the decisions taken would invariably benefit and disadvantage some groups more than others. And each would affect the actions of lawmakers, not merely out of self-interest but also because representatives would need to respond to the dominant interests of their constituents.

Anyone who had been involved in American legislative deliberations in the mid-1780s would be aware of these issues. But Madison's analysis altered and, in a sense, elevated the stakes. His characterization of legislative acts as equivalent to "so many judicial determinations" is especially interesting. Like his rationale for the council of revision, it illustrates his impatience with the familiar categories of the separation of powers. It was one thing to protect the formal independence of each department of government. But in Madison's thinking that goal was secondary to a greater good, which was to improve the quality of legislative deliberation, not by making lawmakers more like judges but by making their decisions more judicious.

One can read this aspiration in either of two ways. Commenting on this same passage, Gordon Wood argues that Madison's "use of judicial imagery to describe the factional and interest group politics in the state legislatures" was actually a traditional, even utopian, and hardly modern conception at all. In many ways his ideas "point back toward the colonial world, not toward our world at all." Rather than providing a model of "hardheaded realism," as so many commentators on Madison's political science have observed, this notion was just as idealistic, Wood suggests, as the vision of republican virtue that the revolutionaries originally shared in 1776. What Madison longed for was to constitute representative assemblies composed of men like himself—elites who could "transcend the interest-mongering of the many in the society and be able to act as neutral judges or referees in the new national Congress."[63]

Just as Wood has elsewhere characterized the Federalists of the late 1780s in almost elegiac terms, so this insight into Madison catches the retrospective, conservative facets of his thought. Yet Wood also fails to capture, I believe, other crucial aspects of Madison's thinking that were indeed modern. Had Madison really envisioned Congress (or the state legislatures) acting like their colonial ancestors, his concern with the process of legislation would not have been so pronounced. Colonial legislatures indeed often acted as adjudicative bodies, receiving petitions from communities asking them to resolve and mediate local conflicts. The enactment of ordinary legislation, or of acts of the kind Madison described in *Federalist* 10, were rare occurrences before 1776. The tax burden of colonial governments was low; acts regulating commerce came from Parliament; and debtor-creditor issues raised few legislative tensions as individuals carried their obligations over protracted periods. Moreover, however weak the British empire may have appeared in allowing the colonial assemblies to acquire so much autonomy, governors and the privy council still intervened to supervise legislative acts that had serious policy implications. But the revolution altered these practices significantly, forcing legislatures to act—to make law, in the positive sense of the term—to a degree wholly unprecedented in the colonial past. The consequences of that legislation carried over into the "critical years" of the post-revolutionary era to form the basis of the experience on which Madison was generalizing. Nor was it unrealistic for Madison to imagine that the development of an expanding society would bring demands for improvement that would encourage private interests to attempt to capture public support. The legislature would be the branch of government that these interests would address. To worry whether Congress would become the mere vehicle for their expression, or whether its members would simply act as "advocates and parties to the causes which they determine," was not a nostalgic sigh to restore the standards of an earlier day. It assumed instead that the making of positive law would be the principal function of Congress, and that this duty would best be met if the conditions of deliberation were somehow improved.

If representatives carried these commitments with them, it became important to explain how they might be prompted to act more judiciously. Percolating through Madison's later essays on Congress (*Federalist* 52–58 and 62–63) is a concern with the knowledge and information on which they would deliberate, and a latent assumption—which proved correct for the better part of a century—that both houses of Congress would be largely stocked with members who would serve only a term or two. Representatives would come from the far corners of the union, carrying parochial loyalties that would need to be modified. To be "a competent legislator," Madison observed in *Federalist* 52, one would need to "add to an upright intention and a sound judgment a certain degree of knowledge of the subjects on which he is to legislate." Some of that knowledge might come from one's "private station," but "another part of it can only be attained, or at least thoroughly attained, by actual experience in the station which requires the use of it." The length of the term a national legislator needed to serve should be a function of how much he would need to learn. In this sense, there is nothing unreasonable about the two-year term, notwithstanding the "current observation" holding that "where annual elections end, tyranny begins." Unlike the "small compass" and "not very diversified" realm of the states, "the great theatre of the United States" would require lawmakers to learn about the variety of laws and conditions prevailing throughout the country. Lawmakers would "bring with them a due knowledge of their own State," but they "will have much information to acquire concerning all the other States." They would have to serve as both rapporteurs and students, conveying information and absorbing it in turn.[64]

The quality of those deliberations, Madison deeply believed, would also be affected by the size of the representative body. At the same time, he confessed, "no political problem is less suscep-tible of a precise solution," as the enormous variance in the size of the state legislatures itself indicated. "Nothing can be more fallacious than to found our political calculations on arithmetical principles." Some means of moderation would have to be applied, steering between dual dangers. One needed enough members "to secure the benefits of free consultation and discussion" and to protect against a cabal for "improper purposes." But too large an assembly would produce "the confusion and intemperance of a multitude." Madison retained his horror of over-large bodies, even when they contained the wisest of men. As he famously remarked of the Athenian popular assembly, "Had every Athenian been a Socrates, every Athenian assembly would still have been a mob."[65] Legislative bodies, in Madison's sincere view, were vulnerable to a similar woe: "The more multitudinous a representative assembly may be rendered," he warned in *Federalist* 58, "the more it will partake of the infirmities incident to collective meetings of the people." Members would lose the sense of conscience required to deliberate. "Ignorance will be the dupe of cunning, and passion the slave of sophistry and declamation."[66]

A skeptic could read statements like these as evidence of Madison's own sophistry. But this concern recurs often enough to suggest his underlying conviction that serious deliberation did require capping the collective size of a legislative body. That conviction also entered into the defense of the Senate that Madison offered in *Federalist* 62 and 63, his final essays as Publius. Madison outlined his discussion with four headings, three of which he dismissed as quickly as possible: the qualification of senators; the method of their appointment by the state legislatures, a topic that rated all of three sentences; and the equal state vote, which got three paragraphs but pivoted on the idea that it was, in the end, simply a compromise. Madison ended this part of the discussion on a final barbed note. The "peculiar defence which it involves in favor of the smaller States, would be more *rational* [emphasis added], if any interests common to them, and distinct from those of the other States, would otherwise be exposed to peculiar danger."[67] Readers could readily infer that this defense was really not rational on any grounds other than compromise.

Madison thus gave the issues that had preoccupied the Convention almost nugatory treatment. Had he been writing these essays as a propagandist, a simple celebrant of the Convention and the Constitution, he could have taken a different tack. Then he could simply have deployed the reasons his opponents at Philadelphia—delegates like William Paterson and Oliver

Ellsworth, if not the tipsy former Princetonian, Luther Martin—
had offered for their position, privately distasteful as they might
have been.[68] Madison's serious discussion of the Senate in *The
Federalist* began only with his fourth main category, "the number
of senators, and the duration of their appointment." This heading,
too, sounds innocuous, but Madison translated it to cover both
the basic purposes the Senate was conceived to serve "and the
inconveniences which a republic must suffer from the want of
such an institution."

Madison began his case with two cautionary points that he
stated quickly. The Senate would provide a security, first, against
"schemes of corruption or perfidy," and also against a single
assembly "yield[ing] to the impulse of sudden and violent passions" or being "seduced by factious leaders into intemperate and
pernicious resolutions." These were hoary maxims that any rhetorical novice could adduce. But then Madison explicitly returned
to the themes of his pre-Convention memorandum on the vices
of the political system to describe the true advantages of a senate.
Legislatures were ordinarily stocked by individuals "called for
the most part from pursuits of a private nature, continued in
appointment for a short time, and led by no permanent motive
to devote the intervals of public occupation to a study of the laws,
the affairs, and the comprehensive interests of their country." This
was the consequence of having legislatures staffed with amateur
lawmakers who came and went with every passing year; their
inexperience went far toward explaining the manifest defects of
state legislation. "What indeed are all the repealing, explaining,
and amending laws, which fill and disgrace our voluminous
codes," Madison asked, echoing items 9 and 10 of "the Vices,"
"but so many monuments of deficient wisdom?"[69]

In *Federalist* 62–63, Madison took the time he had not expended
in that earlier document to enumerate the consequences of this
"mutability in the public councils." Had he wished to do so, he
noted, "he could fill a volume" with its "mischievous effects."
For now, a few would have to do. Internationally, the mutability
of legislation had brought Americans into disrespect, depriving
them of "all the advantages connected with national character."
But the domestic consequences were "still more calamitous."
What good would it do ordinary Americans "if the laws be so

voluminous that they cannot be read, or so incoherent that they cannot be understood; if they be repealed or revised before they are promulgated, or undergo such incessant changes that no man, who knows what the law is to-day, can guess what it will be tomorrow." Under these conditions, the only beneficiaries of legislation would be the "enterprising, and the moneyed few" who expended the time and energy to track the law in its fluidity."[70] Conversely, instability in law would discourage the systemic rational planning that prudent citizens would otherwise do.

Madison's public defense of the Senate in his final essays as Publius fully echoed the opinions he had expressed in his 1785 letter to Caleb Wallace. The role of the Senate was to provide the wisdom and stability that republican legislatures might otherwise lack or carelessly abandon. That concern rested upon the conviction that legislatures would be the active source of law, that representatives would too often serve the narrow interests and opinions of their constituents, and that many of them would lack the knowledge and experience to perform their work competently. The ideal of senatorial deliberation, conducted by lawmakers given six years to learn their task and the advantages of discussion in a compact body, thus remained part of the Madisonian constitution.[71]

Yet for all the advantages the Senate might possess, and despite the fact that its powers exceeded those of the House, it was also "the weaker branch of the stronger department." As Madison argued in the concluding paragraphs of *Federalist* 63, history provided ample evidence that the great Anti-Federalist fear that the Senate would dominate the government, abusing its joint legislative-executive-judicial powers, was wildly misplaced. Rather than seek a seat in the upper house, Madison intended all along to serve in the House of Representatives (although he grudgingly accepted his nomination for senator by Virginia Federalists, who were a minority in the state assembly, and was content to finish third in the voting, behind the Anti-Federalist victors Richard Henry Lee and William Grayson). The logic of this position rested on the belief that controlled Madison's political thinking in the late 1780s, that the institution most directly representative of the people would be the dominant force in republican politics. As he observed in his last sentence as Publius, "Against the force of the immediate representatives of the people, nothing will be able to maintain even the constitutional authority of the people, but such a display of enlightened policy, and attachment to the public good, as will divide with that branch of the legislature the affections and support of the entire body of the people themselves."[72] The Senate would succeed, not by force of political influence but only by being the best legislative body it could possibly become—by acting senatorially.

CHAPTER 3

"WHEREVER THE REAL POWER LIES"

Public Opinion and the Protection of Rights

On January 10, 1788, Madison wrote a remarkably revealing letter to his "dear friend" Governor Edmund Randolph. At Philadelphia, Randolph had joined Elbridge Gerry and George Mason in refusing to sign the Constitution. Yet Randolph had his mercurial moments—he could be a "trimmer," in the political vernacular—and the report the governor prepared for the Virginia legislature gave more support to the Constitution than to the changes that its Anti-Federalist critics desired. In late December, Randolph sent this report to Madison. Anxious to woo Randolph back to the Federalist side, Madison noted that "the spirit of it does as much honor to your candour, as the general reasoning does to your abilities." But on one issue Madison wrote with equal candor himself. Randolph still wanted the state ratification conventions to recommend their proposed amendments to a second general convention, which could then revise the Constitution in response to these public sentiments. Madison thought this was a formula for political disaster, and he minced no words in explaining why this scheme was wholly misguided. Not only was Randolph naive in gauging the capacity of the critics of the Constitution to agree on the changes they sought, but he was also badly misjudging the political animus behind their objections. Should a second convention meet, opponents of the Constitution would find their way into the state delegations. The chances that such a body could attain the consensus that the Convention of 1787 had achieved were minimal.[1]

Madison's alarm on this issue rested on both theoretical principles and pragmatic calculations. Finding a way to ground the authority of the Constitution in a clear and wholly unambiguous expression of popular sovereignty was a supreme achievement of the Federalist movement that he was captaining. Today we take the Constitution's legal supremacy so much for granted that we overlook how remarkable a project its ratification really was. Madison grasped the significance of ratification from the start. It was the first substantive point he discussed when he sent Jefferson his initial agenda in March 1787: "It will be expedient in the first place to lay the foundation of the new system in such a ratification by the people themselves of the several States as will render it clearly paramount to their Legislative authorities." The same subject reappeared as item 8 of "The Vices of the Political System of the United States."[2] Under a constitution approved only by the state legislatures, the doctrine of *leges posteriores priores contrarias abrogant* (later laws contradicting earlier ones abrogate them) would give any subsequent legislative act that violated a constitution superiority over the prior act of ratification. Because that was the basis on which the Articles of Confederation had been approved, acts of the state legislatures infringing its authority were seemingly permissible. Drawing on precedents set in Massachusetts between 1776 and 1780, Madison concluded that the model of having a specially appointed convention frame the constitution, and then having that text ratified by the people through specially elected conventions, would elevate its authority above the laws and the constitutions of the states.[3]

Creating a separate form of popular representation through ratification conventions, rather than relying on the existing legislatures, could be characterized as a clever legal fiction. Even so, this expedient marked an essential step in distinguishing a constitution from ordinary legislation. The former would embody supreme law, as Article VI of the Constitution provided; the latter would be subject to constitutional review. Equally important, Madison and his Federalist allies imposed constraints on how the people could utter their sovereign voice. That voice would speak loudly and deeply, but when it spoke, it could decisively utter only one of two words: yes or no. The proposed constitution, Federalists insisted, must be approved or rejected in its entirety. It could not be ratified conditionally or in piecemeal fashion—one article up, another down, a third awaiting amendment. The state

conventions were free to *propose* amendments but not to make
ratification contingent on their prior approval. Federalists worked
hard to implement this rule, guaranteeing that the decisions of
their states were clear and unambiguous.

When Madison wrote Randolph in early January 1788, however, the outcome of this struggle was uncertain. The Federalists
adopted a brilliant strategy for ratification, but their political
calculations, predicated on gaining decisive victories in easy
states, provoked some sharp reactions. In Pennsylvania, as Pauline
Maier has demonstrated, the Federalist refusal to publicize the
dissent of the minority Anti-Federalists became a political embarrassment that supporters of the Constitution elsewhere struggled
to overcome. Whether the ratification conventions should recommend *subsequent* amendments became an issue that Federalists
faced only after the Massachusetts convention assembled a few
days later.[4] Madison thus had good reason to worry whether
each state's decision on the Constitution could be limited to a
single unequivocal vote. Popular sovereignty was a powerful
weapon to wield but a dangerously awkward one to aim. Losing
control of the process of ratification, in the way that Randolph
was suggesting, could open up new obstacles far more difficult
to surmount than those that had confronted the Convention.[5]

Constitutional theory and expedient practice thus merged decisively in Madison's mind. But his letter to Randolph is remarkable
in one other respect. The challenge of ratification was not limited
to controlling the rules of deliberation and decision within the
state conventions. It also depended on the sway of public opinion.
On this issue, Madison added one of those typically concise comments that exposes concerns he did not dare to voice in public.
Suppose a second convention did meet, "and the Constitution
re-edited with amendments," he wrote,

> the event would still be infinitely precarious. Whatever respect
> may be due to the rights of private judgment, and no man feels
> more of it than I do, there can be no doubt that there are subjects
> to which the capacities of mankind are unequal, and on which
> they must and will be governed by those with whom they happen
> to have acquaintance and confidence. The proposed Constitution
> is of this description. The great body of those who are both for
> & against it, must follow the judgment of others not their own.

Here a mask drops away, and Madison reveals a deep personal skepticism about the capacity of public opinion. On complicated questions, on which citizens are not well informed or cannot develop a proper mode of judgment, they depend on the guidance of others. In the gentry world of eighteenth-century Virginia—the world in which Madison was reared, and of which he remained inextricably a part—that still meant the leadership of a politically active planter elite. Had Randolph, Mason, R. H. Lee, and (perhaps worst of all) Patrick Henry not stirred up so much trouble, Madison almost grumbled, "I have no doubt that Virginia would have been as zealous & unanimous as she is now divided on the subject."[6]

The greater problem with Randolph's idea, then, was not only that it would complicate the procedure Madison had carefully developed; it also risked destroying the general confidence of the people in those who had recommended it: "The very attempt at a second Convention strikes at the confidence in the first; and the existence of a second by opposing influence to influence, would in a manner destroy an effectual confidence in either, and give a loose to human opinions; which must be as various and irreconcilable concerning theories of Government, as doctrines of Religion; and give opportunities to designing men which it might be impossible to counteract." Nothing better conveys Madison's anxiety about the entire process of constitutional formation than this strikingly pessimistic assessment of the very basis on which public opinion would form. Here was a problem not of constitutional governance per se but of the political basis on which a republican society must operate.

The day after Madison wrote Randolph, *Federalist 37* appeared in the New York *Independent Journal*. This was only his sixth essay as Publius, but it marked the point where he took over the principal writing burden from Hamilton. Its general objective (to be discussed at greater length in the next chapter) was to explain all the difficulties that the work of constitution making entailed. But Madison opened his essay by echoing points Hamilton had raised in *Federalist 1*, which emphasized the considerations that conscientious citizens must keep in mind when they engage in a debate as momentous as the one now occurring. Madison's opening plea, like Hamilton's, was for citizens to attain a spirit of "moderation" as they joined the public debate over the Constitution.

That term had a meaning different from the one we now give it. Today moderation often means holding a midpoint in a debate, or seeking to balance the competing claims of both sides of an argument. For Publius, however, moderation was more an attitude than a position. It was the reasonable (or reasoning) frame of mind that a thoughtful person should adopt when considering a complicated question. Such an attitude would not prevent the citizen from coming down decisively on one side of a debate and rejecting the other. Moderation was not about finding midpoints or compromises; it was instead about the nature of reasoning analytically. To act with moderation in 1787–88 involved adopting a critical posture toward the active participants in a debate. But it also required thinking carefully, even empathetically, about the problems the constitution makers had set out to solve.

The Madison who worried about these problems in 1788 was manifestly not a wild enthusiast for the vigorous, unchecked expression of public opinion. His January letter to Randolph marked only one expression of his reservations about the deliberative capacity of ordinary citizens. The famous analysis of *Federalist* 10, resting on the conclusions first sketched in item 11 of "the Vices," presupposed that self-interest, opinion, and passion would dominate the political commitments of ordinary citizens. One of the main purposes—indeed, arguably the most important—of constitutional government was to create a space within which the people's elected officials could deliberate with each other. When they did, they should learn to transcend both the ordinary vices of popular government and the parochial perspectives they would carry into office. That was the principal aim of a republican system of representation, Madison observed in a key passage of *Federalist* 10: "to refine and enlarge the public views, by passing them through the medium of a chosen body of citizens," in the hope that "the public voice pronounced by the representatives of the people, will be more consonant to the public good, than if pronounced by the people themselves convened for the purpose."[7]

This tension between the possibility of reasoned deliberation and the impassioned flow of public opinion identifies the decisive fault line separating the domain of Madison's constitutional theory from the surrounding environment of his political thinking.[8] As a *constitutionalist*, Madison was concerned with the workings of institutions; as a *political theorist*, with the play of interests, opinions, and passions both among the citizenry and upon the institutions of government. The challenge framing his analysis of the American political system pivoted on the connections and tensions between these adjoining realms of action. In critical passages in his political thinking, Madison played these two areas of political behavior against each other. In item 11 of "the Vices," for example, he juxtaposed the potential sources of legislative injustice emanating from the improper motives of lawmakers with "the still more fatal if not more frequent cause [that] lies among the people themselves." In *Federalist* 45–46, he compared the relative powers of the national and state governments with the greater sources of political affection the states would enjoy through their ordinary operations and familiarity with their citizens. Three essays later, in *Federalist* 49, Madison again implied that Jefferson's idea of using popularly elected conventions to monitor constitutional encroachments by one institution or another would prove ineffective because citizens were most likely to favor the legislature. And, perhaps most famously, Madison closed his discussion of the separation of powers in *Federalist* 51 not by explaining in full detail exactly how "ambition must be made to counteract ambition" among the departments, but rather by restating the argument of *Federalist* 10, thus suggesting that the strongest support for preserving the independence of the departments might actually be found in the operation of factious politics "out-of-doors."

The point of this argument, Madison reminded his readers, was "not only to guard the society against the oppression of its rulers; but to guard one part of the society against the injustice of the other part."[9] In both cases, the objective was to preserve the liberty and rights of subjects. Republican institutions had to be designed with this goal in mind. But the defenders of republicanism also had to understand that the play of interest, opinion, and even passion within society could be exploited to the same end. That exploitation, however, was passive. It depended on allowing interests to multiply and opinions to be expressed. In a society as diverse and extensive as the United States, the materials were already present that would provide the greatest security to the rights and liberties of individuals.

There was thus a bleakly conservative tone to Madison's view of the political intelligence of ordinary citizens, a nagging belief that the source of republican injustice lay in their desires and ambitions. Yet his view of the capacity of public opinion was not static. It evolved significantly between the late 1780s and the mid-1790s, pushing Madison's thinking about republican politics along lines he had not anticipated. Equally important, his skeptical view of collective public opinion must be reconciled with his absolute commitment to the rights of individual judgment that he ascribed to the realm of religious belief. When Madison reminded Randolph that "no man feels more [respect] due to the rights of private judgment . . . than I do," this was the sovereign source of individual autonomy that he initially had in mind. Madison's approach to the religion problem proved fundamental to his thinking in the late 1780s. That commitment was deepened by the intense struggle he waged in Virginia in 1784–86 to defeat the general assessment bill and then to enact Jefferson's landmark Bill for Religious Freedom. As Lance Banning, one of Madison's keenest scholars, has observed, "The lessons that he learned from the Virginia struggle over church and state were probably the most important catalyst for the conclusions that became his most distinctive contribution to the Founding."[10] Those conclusions pivoted in critical ways on Madison's understanding of the nature of opinion, both individual and collective, and the roles it should play in the politics of a constitutional republic.

It is altogether fitting and proper that Madison's first public act, at age twenty-five, was to secure a noteworthy amendment to the religion article of the Virginia Declaration of Rights. As it came from the constitution-drafting committee, the article stated, in full,

> That religion, or the duty which we owe to our CREATOR, and the manner of discharging it, can be directed only by reason and conviction, not by force or violence; and therefore, that all men should enjoy the fullest toleration in the exercise of religion, according to the dictates of conscience, unpunished and unrestrained by the Magistrate, unless, under colour of religion, any man disturb the peace, the happiness, or safety of society. And that it is the mutual duty of all to practice Christian forbearance, love, and charity, towards each other.[11]

To a modern reader, the language of Article XVI seems at once appealing and puzzling. The article rests upon a broad statement of the moral autonomy of individuals, implicitly defining religious liberty as a matter of interior conviction. Yet the draft also recognizes a significant measure of public authority over some forms of religious behavior. Toleration operates as a legal privilege the state is extending, not a right inherent in the individual. Moreover, the state retains authority to judge when religious enthusiasm jeopardizes the public weal and thus to regulate its conduct.[12] Then, too, modern "rights talk" might find it a challenge to know how to incorporate the moral principles expressed in the final sentence of the article into its legal vocabulary. What kind of a legal right is "Christian forbearance, love, and charity"? To our way of thinking, are these not moral duties rather than legal claims?

The points that Madison proposed to the Fifth Provincial Convention helped to secure two changes in this article. One deleted the reference to toleration and replaced it with language that affirmed that "all men are equally entitled to the free exercise of religion." The other eliminated the reference to the authority of the magistrate. Madison originally drafted language holding that civil authorities could act only when "the preservation of equal liberty and the existence of the State are manifestly endangered," standards of scrutiny higher than the original concern with "the peace, the happiness, or safety of society." In the end the convention dropped these behavioral cautions entirely.[13]

Madison was not solely responsible for the revision of the religion article. In pursuing his amendment, he gained important support from older, influential members like Patrick Henry and Edmund Pendleton. Yet Madison brought to this struggle a youthful passion of his own, nurtured in his studies at Princeton. There were moments in the early 1770s when the young graduate felt he was dealing with a cadre of backwoods primitives in his native province. In an oft-cited letter written to his college friend William Bradford, Madison raged against the "persecution" in a nearby county of half a dozen Baptist dissenters "for publishing their religious sentiments," which Madison judged "very orthodox." He had lost his "common patience" over this matter, Madison railed, "for I have squabbled and scolded abused and ridiculed so long about it" to no effect.[14]

Madison's disparaging judgment may have missed how much progress colonial society was already making on the religion question. By the 1770s the idea that toleration was an adequate solution to the existence of religious diversity in American society was already a paling belief. In the late colonial era, in the ample realm of public religious discourse, claims for equality among all denominations were already supplanting the traditional plea for toleration that would only give religious dissenters some legal protection against a dominant established church. It was an irony of the colonial situation that even the advocates of the creation of an American bishopric for the established Anglican Church had to invoke the language of toleration to support their request. If Anglicans were not allowed to exercise a right deemed essential to their ecclesiology, their advocates contended, their church would be denied the equality of religious organization that other denominations enjoyed.[15]

The adoption of the Declaration of Rights in 1776 did not unilaterally end the legal establishment of the Anglican Church within the commonwealth of Virginia. The Declaration was not, by itself, either a constitutional text or a legal command. It is better understood as a statement of principles designed to guide the behavior of all Virginians, not by imposing binding legal or constitutional rules but rather by inculcating republican values akin to the statement on Christian forbearance.[16] But the adoption of Article XVI, the religion clause, did help to create a new politics of religious contestation within the state. Inspired by its wording, religious dissenters began flooding the state's reconstituted legislature with petitions demanding disestablishment. Those petitions were delegated to the religion committee, where Madison first met Thomas Jefferson in October 1776. Fittingly, their first common cause involved thinking about ways to advance the cause of religious disestablishment that each favored.

For three reasons, this commitment mattered deeply to both men, and its influence especially on Madison's political thinking was profound. First, the pursuit of disestablishment and free exercise represented a true mark of the historical opportunity that both men believed the revolution had created—the prospect of liberating human reason from the intellectual tyranny that the demand for religious uniformity had enforced over the centuries.

As Madison proudly wrote Jefferson in January 1786, the passage of the Statute for Religious Freedom had "in this Country extinguished for ever the ambitious hope of making laws for the human mind."[17] The promotion of religious freedom in Virginia was a beachhead for the greater Enlightenment project.

Second, and more important, the clamor for disestablishment and free exercise that Virginians now expressed marked a key transition in republican politics. The dynamic element in this story lay in the petitions that religious dissenters began submitting to the legislature in the early 1770s. In both England and America, the use of petitions was a common mechanism for generating legislative action. But such petitions generally came from a particular community, or even a cluster of individuals, addressing some issue of local concern. The claims that religious dissenters were now voicing were a different phenomenon. This pressure cut across county lines, identifying an issue that could mobilize public opinion around the state. Popular agitation of the religion question gave Madison a new framework both for thinking about the role of public opinion in politics and for asking whether the people themselves were the best protectors of their own liberties. Because recognition of the claims of the religious dissenters involved a conflict between the respective rights of majorities and minorities, this issue encouraged Madison to rethink larger questions about the nature of constitutional rights—to ask, that is, whether the problem of rights under a republican government was to protect the people as a whole against their rulers or, instead, one segment of the community against another.

Beyond the question of the rights of majorities and minorities, the free exercise of religion was also ultimately about individuals. In the final analysis, the problem of religious liberty was not merely to enable small groups of like-minded believers to worship together, free from the control of an established church and its supporting government. It was, more fundamentally, about the right of individuals to decide, and redecide, which church they voluntarily wished to join (or exit). That decision ultimately rested not on birth or descent but on opinions and convictions to which each person, male and female, must come voluntarily. Following arguments that John Locke had laid down in his *Letter concerning Toleration*, Madison treated religiosity as a matter of interior conviction. In a culture imbued with a strong Protestant commitment to the choices of morally autonomous individuals, one could worship only according to the dictates of conscience, not in conformity to the rules of the magistrate or the common sense of the community. Skeptical as Madison was of the *political* wisdom and opinions of ordinary individuals, he was profoundly committed to their "rights of private judgment." And religion was the realm in which, he originally believed, these opinions mattered most.

These three concerns—with the moral appeal of free exercise, the impact of religious diversity on republican politics, and the subjective rights of autonomous individuals—were thus formative elements of Madison's political thinking from his entrance into public life in 1776. But his capacity to act upon these concerns was originally inhibited by the course of the revolution. The religion question did not entirely disappear after 1776, but it was hardly at the forefront of Virginia politics. Nor was the impact of public opinion on politics a subject that concerned Madison during the war years. Like other revolutionary leaders, he was doubtless aware of the problem of "disaffection," the catchall term that described the decline of popular enthusiasm from the sunshine patriotism of 1774–76. But that problem was less about the impact of public opinion on politics than about the very different question of maintaining an adequate level of popular support for the war. Until Madison left Congress in October 1783, his major political concerns had been with the problem of coordinating governance within the federal system—with federalism rather than republicanism. Institutional issues predominated. Only after he returned to the realm of Virginia legislative politics in 1784 did he begin to think actively about the central vice of republican politics—the sources of legislative misrule within the states. Here, too, his initial concern lay more with the characteristics of his lawmaking colleagues than with the character of their constituents. But at some point Madison began looking for a deeper explanation of the problem.

The shift or evolution in Madison's thinking can be roughly dated to mid-1785. There was no exact point of origin, no sudden aperçu that pushed Madison in a new direction. And, in any case, the conclusions he drew in the months preceding the Federal Convention mattered far more than his initial questions. Nor do scholars and biographers entirely agree how to portray his temperament on this journey. Visitors to his well-restored home at Montpelier now often hear how Madison sat in his second-floor study, gazing off at the Blue Ridge, patiently working his way through the "literary cargo" Jefferson sent him as he reviewed the first principles of republican and constitutional government. In Douglass Adair's most influential essay—the source of much scholarly controversy—Madison had a sudden decisive burst of inspiration derived from reading (or rereading) several of David Hume's political essays. The most vivid account of Madison's intellectual voyage may come from Lance Banning, whose study *The Sacred Fire of Liberty* remains the best analysis of Madison's ideas and goals in the 1780s and 1790s. For Banning, the culmination of these developments in the period just before the Convention amounted to a virtual "crisis" for Madison. He found himself "entrapped in a profoundly agonizing reexamination of his early revolutionary suppositions," Banning observes, "still imprisoned in a mental trap from which he found no obvious escape."[18]

However one characterizes this movement, there is no question that the period 1785–87 proved absolutely formative for Madison's constitutional and political thinking. The debate over the general assessment bill is the best place to begin this story. The basic question of public policy that the bill raised was not one that Madison had to rethink. Even though the assessment would operate on nonpreferential lines, providing support for all denominations, it still violated Madison's conception of the relation between church and state. The real puzzle implicated a basic value of Anglo-American constitutionalism. In conventional Whig thinking, legislative assemblies and juries were the two institutions that were designed to protect the rights of the people against the arbitrary exercise of power, principally by the executive. What would happen, however, if the violation came not from the executive but from the people's elected lawmakers? Madison wrestled with this problem in several items of his *Memorial and Remonstrance against Religious Assessments*. One critical observation closed the first item: "True it is, that no other rule exists, by which any question which may divide a Society, can be ultimately determined, but the will of the majority," he conceded; "but it is also true that the majority may trespass on the rights of the minority." This observation, seemingly so obvious to us, was not a commonplace of the time. The idea that a popular majority would be inclined to violate rights rather than preserve them was counterintuitive, especially in a republican society. Perhaps in epochs of disorder and anarchy that might prove true. But in a republic whose citizens should be morally committed to the protection of civil rights this was an improbable case. Should they submit to a law that would "overleap the great Barrier which defends the rights of the people," such a people would be "governed by laws made neither by themselves nor by an authority derived from them."[19]

In fact, the strategy that Madison and his allies used to defeat the assessment seemed to vindicate his notion of how republican politics should operate. A combination of legislative delay and an appeal to the same public opinion that had proved so vocal on the religion question in the 1770s worked. Although the state did not conduct a referendum on the general assessment bill, the petitions opposing it constituted a strong expression of public opinion that effectively doomed the measure. Once the assessment was rejected, Madison secured, at last, the enactment of the Bill for Religious Freedom. The reasonable inference to draw from this episode could thus have been that the people, once mobilized, were indeed capable of defending their rights against legislative abuse. Republican liberty was secure, and the people were its best guardians. Yet in fact that was precisely *not* the lesson that Madison was inclined to draw in the future. His thinking about the problem of the protection of rights in a constitutional republic moved in the opposite direction. It did so not because the debate over religious policy had ended badly—it had not—but rather because a different set of issues increasingly preoccupied his thinking.

That new concern lay with the security of rights of property (see chapter 2). Again, this was not an issue that had directly troubled Madison during the war. The greater concern then had been with the respective capacity and willingness of the states to comply with their obligations to the union. But as the states individually wrestled with issues of postwar economic recovery and the payment of the public debt, Madison became increasingly concerned with the justice of their policies. "With many others," Banning observed, Madison "had come to be increasingly concerned with legislation that infringed the rights of contract or prevented governments from meeting contracts of their own: paper money, stay laws, moratoriums on taxes, and the rest."[20] An early indication of his concern appeared in his August 1785 letter to Caleb Wallace, in particular his response to Wallace's first specific query, which asked whether representation should rest on population, or the possession of property, or territory. Madison responded by warning about the offsetting dangers of relying too much on either property or numbers in regulating the suffrage. Restricting it solely "to the landholders will in time exclude too great a proportion of citizens," and distributing it "without regard to property, or even to all who possess a pittance," risked vesting political power either in those who will "abuse it themselves or sell it to the rich who will abuse it." Perhaps this disparity could be resolved, he mused, if a constitution would "narrow this right" in the election of the upper house and "enlarge it" in "the more popular branch."[21]

Here Madison confronted a central problem of American constitutional thinking after 1776. In the bicameral systems that the states (except Pennsylvania) adopted in their new constitutions, there was no question that the lower house represented the citizenry as a whole. The right of suffrage would vest in property holders, to be sure, but with the recognition that ownership of property was widely distributed. But what would the upper house represent? There was no obvious answer to this question. One potential answer was to conceive that property itself could become not merely a minimal criterion for citizenship but also, when concentrated in the hands of the wealthier members of society, an interest deserving additional protection against the desires of the less fortunate. From being a fundamental right unifying the body politic, as republican theory traditionally conceived it, the possession of property could become a basis for identifying an array of social interests potentially in competition with one another. "In a general vein," Madison wrote Wallace, "I see no reason why the rights of property which chiefly bears the burden

of Government & is so much an object of Legislation should not
be respected as well as personal rights in the choice of Rulers."
    A latent premise of profound significance was embedded in
this observation. Republican political theory rested on the sup-
position that there was a true public good that the polity should
strive to pursue, and that the primary obligation of citizens was
to subordinate private interest to that public good. Within this
polity, citizens could be perceived as a homogeneous entity—the
people themselves. Madison's idea of dividing them into two
classes—one identified by their possession of common civil
rights, the other by a set of material interests distinguishing
larger property holders from their countrymen—thus exposed an
emerging tension within American republicanism. That tension
became far more pronounced after 1776 because of the burdens
that the war imposed upon the states, for the legislatures now had
to take unprecedented actions to mobilize the American population for a long, expensive, and exhausting war. Mobilization led
to the spiraling use of paper currency, its rapid depreciation,
competition among the armies for the purchase of food and other
supplies, price inflation—in short, an array of economic changes
that forced each household to calculate how its interests were
being affected by decisions it could not control. The hallowed
conception of republican virtue became unsustainable in wartime
and impossible to recover in peace. Once that war was won, the
states had to deal with its economic aftermath, including the flood
of British imports into America and the exclusion of American
ships (but not American produce) from imperial markets. Equally
important, the state legislatures had to determine what to do
about their public debt. If they tried to liquidate that debt through
effective programs of taxation, they risked provoking the sort of
protests that culminated in Shays's Rebellion in Massachusetts
in 1786–87. If, on the other hand, they continued to issue paper
money and made that depreciating currency legal tender for the
payment of private debts, their public policy would favor the
interests of debtors over the asserted rights of their creditors.
    In this debate, there was no question that Madison's sympathies
and preferences lay with the interests of his own class or, more
generally, with the rights of those possessing property over those
clamoring to acquire it through unjust means. The constitutional

implications of that commitment continued to evolve in his mind. At the Federal Convention, Madison argued for limiting the right of suffrage for the House of Representatives to holders of landed property. This class would share with their countrymen a common concern in protecting the essential civil rights of all citizens. But their additional interest in securing the rights of property—"the object deemed least secure in popular Governments"—justified giving them "the right of suffrage for one of the two Legislative branches." What made some constitutional effort to protect the rights of property even more essential was the proto-Malthusian view of society that shaped Madison's thinking in the 1780s. "In future times a great majority of the people will not only be without landed, but any other sort of property," he predicted.[22] It was, therefore, not only the costs of the revolution that placed the protection of property at risk. Over time, economic and demographic changes would have an even more profound effect.

Madison's concern with the rights of property thus rested on two conceptions of historical time. One was tied to the immediate legacy of the revolution and the policy debates of the 1780s, with their noticeable impact on the workings of the state legislatures. The other represented his assessment of the future course of economic development, a process that he imagined hardening rather than relaxing the relation between class structure and politics. Unlike Jefferson, who was a great optimist in conceiving how the nation's landed resources would work to support its republican politics—an opinion reinforced by his stay in France—Madison acted on more sober, even gloomy, expectations.

This perception profoundly shaped the political and constitutional dimensions of Madison's thinking in 1787. Although the task of constitutional design was primarily a matter of institutions, Madison discovered a new concern in the influence of factors working "out-of-doors," not within the legislative chambers where decisions were taken but instead within the larger society. That is the discovery that emerges from the crucial item 11 of "the Vices," the analysis devoted to the "Injustice of the laws of States."[23] Here Madison quickly summarized the shortcomings of state legislators in order to move on to the issue that now engaged him more acutely, the "causes" of injustice that came from "the people themselves." Legislative "injustice" did not arise primarily from the misbehavior of lawmakers—though some account did indeed have to be taken of that. It derived instead from the fidelity with which the people's representatives were acting as agents of the dominant interests of their constituents. The primary sources of misrule were thus exogenous to institutions. They inhered in society itself, in the play of interests and opinions within the communities where citizens resided, and in the likelihood that representatives would know all too well which partial interests their constituents preferred.

Thus, although Madison remained concerned with the injustice of state legislation, the political majorities that alarmed him were composed not of ambitious representatives but of ordinary citizens, with all their interests, passions, and opinions. Political loyalties per se constituted only one of the factors that explained the formation of "different interests and factions" within a state. The longer list included the familiar categories that defined diversity within modern "civilized societies" as their citizens and subjects "happen to be creditors or debtors—Rich or poor—husbandmen, merchants or manufacturers—members of different religious sects—followers of different political leaders—inhabitants of different districts—owners of different kinds of property &c &c." It was the formation of popular majorities among these different groupings that would form the political foundation for the unjust laws their elected leaders would pursue. "Whenever therefore an apparent interest or common passion unites a majority," Madison asked in the second part of item 11, "what is to restrain them from unjust violations of the rights and interest of the minority, or of individuals?" As is often the case in Madison's private writings, the posing of a question was an analytical exercise, not a rhetorical move. It identified a problem that he felt he first had to solve rather than articulating an argument meant to persuade others.[24]

"Three motives" might offer effective restraints on the behavior of self-interested individuals or majorities, Madison mused: "a prudent regard to their own good as involved in the general and permanent good of the Community," "respect for character," and "Religion." The first was essentially synonymous with the principles of republicanism and had already been "found by experience" to be wanting. The second, in Madison's treatment, was effectively psychological; its effect was diminished as individuals found their unjust inclinations confirmed by the common opinion of the majority. Similar conditions operated with religion. Considered "in an aggregate view," Madison observed, "individuals join without remorse in acts, against which their consciences would revolt if proposed to them under the like sanction, separately in their closets." When religion turned enthusiastic—a term that then connoted fanaticism—its presence would "hardly be seen with pleasure at the helm of Government." On other occasions, when it operated "in its coolest state," it would prove as much "a motive to oppression" as "a restraint from injustice." Religion, in other words, was simply another interest capable of acting unjustly.

The dominant problem, then, was the formation *within society* of majority factions, and the insecurity that individuals or minorities would feel about their rights. Any restraints that depended on the moral qualities of citizens, or on their collective civic virtue, would prove inadequate. Moreover, the injustice to which these conditions would lead appeared most evident in "the notorious factions & oppressions which take place in corporate towns limited as the opportunities are, and in little republics when uncontrouled by apprehensions of external danger." The crucial hypothesis followed:

> If an enlargement of the sphere is found to lessen the insecurity of private rights, it is not because the impulse of a common interest or passion is less predominant in this case with the majority; but because a common interest or passion is less apt to be felt and the requisite combinations less easy to be formed by a great than by a small number. The Society becomes broken into a greater variety of interests, of pursuits, of passions, which check each other, whilst those who may feel a common sentiment have less opportunity of communication and concert. It may be inferred that the inconveniences of popular States contrary to the prevailing Theory, are in proportion not to the extent, but to the narrowness of their limits.

The "prevailing Theory," of course, was the idea most frequently associated with Montesquieu—but with a distinguished pedigree beyond him—that self-sustaining republics should be small in extent and relatively homogeneous in their interests, the better to foster the self-denying civic virtue that republican citizens should possess. Madison stood this conventional wisdom on its head. He assumed, first, that self-interested, opinionated, and sometimes impassioned human nature had to be taken as a given, even for a republican people like the Americans. Second, he proposed that the checks created by size and diversity would work effectively to reduce the likelihood of the formation of factious popular majorities in the larger society. Those passions would still exist, but their capacity to coalesce would be sharply reduced.

Throughout this discussion, Madison conceived that "public opinion" would not effectively restrain the unjust desire of individuals. In this formative era of his political thinking, he regarded public opinion as far more of a problem than a solution. Whenever public opinion coalesced, its perceived existence would work not to correct but to confirm the self-interested and opinionated behavior of individuals. The larger or more coherent a popular majority, the less concern any individual would feel for his complicity in its improper actions. The "respect for character" that might brake an individual's support for unjust political acts would not work, because "as it has reference to public opinion, which within a particular Society, is the opinion of the majority, the standard is fixed by those whose conduct is to be measured by it." There was nothing elevated in this conception of public opinion. If anything, it anticipated Alexis de Tocqueville's discussion of the soft despotism of public opinion in *Democracy in America*. Tocqueville's account of the psychology of personal opinion is more subtle and extended, but the essential insight remains close to Madison's concise expression of 1787.[25]

Revealing as this similarity is, for the historian it matters less than the interest in the concept of public opinion that Madison may already have derived from reading contemporary French writers who were interested in the same subject. As Colleen Sheehan has demonstrated, the discussion of this subject was an important theme in the numerous books that Jefferson sent Madison from Paris after 1784.[26] There is no question that Madison's thinking on the role of public opinion was dynamic and that, by the early 1790s, he was conceiving appeals to a responsibly informed citizenry as an important safeguard of the Constitution.

What is more complicated, perhaps controversial, is identifying exactly when this transition in his thinking took place. In my view, Madison's conception of public opinion did shift significantly after 1788—away from the pessimism he expressed in his January 1788 letter to Edmund Randolph, and toward the idea of using the emerging "party press" of the 1790s as a vehicle for mobilizing political support. But the Madison who helped to draft the Constitution in 1787 and grudgingly accepted the need for its amendment in 1788 was not wholly enamored of the beneficial impact of popular opinion on republican politics. Indeed, in this period Madison's conception of the subject arguably lay closer to the disparaging view of *popular* opinion as a fluctuating and self-interested aggregation of partial preferences than to the enlightened ideal of *public* opinion as something that political leaders or the state itself might strive to improve. It was more a problem to be solved than a resource to be improved or directed to beneficial uses.

From this analysis of the multiple sources of faction, Madison closed "the Vices" by proposing two constitutional solutions. The first took the form of a broadly abstract statement that compared the advantages of "an extensive Republic," embracing a multiplicity of interests, to the corresponding weaknesses either of monarchy or of small republics. This passage merits quotation in full:

> The great desideratum in Government is such a modification of the Sovereignty as will render it sufficiently neutral between the different interests and factions, to controul one part of the Society from invading the rights of another, and at the same time sufficiently controuled itself, from setting up an interest adverse to that of the whole Society. In absolute Monarchies, the prince is sufficiently, neutral towards his subjects, but frequently sacrifices their happiness to his ambition or his avarice. In small Republics, the sovereign will is sufficiently controuled from such a Sacrifice of the entire Society, but is not sufficiently neutral towards the parts composing it. As a limited Monarchy tempers the evils of an absolute one; so an extensive Republic meliorates the administration of a small Republic.

In "the Vices," Madison did not exactly describe what this "modification of the Sovereignty" was, or how it would work, which is why some commentators treat this statement more as a general defense of the idea of an extended republic than as a specific proposal in his program of constitutional reform. In fact, its precise meaning is easy to ascertain. First, the statement remains part of Madison's discussion of the "injustice of state laws," and the "modification" referred to clearly pertains to the internal legislative authority of the states.[27] Second, and far more explicitly, Madison restated this problem at greater length in his letter to Washington of April 16, 1787: "The great desideratum which has not yet been found for Republican Governments" involves creating "some disinterested & dispassionate umpire in disputes between different passions & interests in the State." But here "the State" meant the individual states, for the specific proposal Madison was defending was to arm the new national legislature with "a negative *in all cases whatsoever* on the legislative acts of the States, as heretofore exercised by the Kingly prerogative." Should the national government possess this authority, the sovereignty of the states would be not so much *modified* as *negated* or *abolished*. A government that could not finally enact its own legislation would hardly be sovereign in any meaningful sense.[28]

There was, Madison continued, "an auxiliary desideratum for the melioration of the Republican form" of government. That would lie in a scheme of elections that would operate to "extract from the mass of the Society the purest and noblest characters which it contains." Neither in "the Vices" nor in his private letters did Madison say anything more about how these elections would be structured. Indeed, prior to the Convention he was initially uncertain whether the lower house should be elected by the people or by the state legislatures. This prediction was thus more a hypothesis that remained to be tested than a reliable or empirical account of how elections worked. Madison's hypothesis, as he later elaborated it in *Federalist* 10, was that "it will be more difficult for unworthy candidates to practice with success the vicious arts, by which elections are too often carried," and voters in turn would be more likely to prefer "men who possess the most attractive merit."[29]

As an "auxiliary desideratum," this claim was thus secondary in importance to Madison's larger argument about the political benefits of multiplicity and diversity within society. "The people themselves," in Madison's theory, were the source both of the factiousness of republican politics and of its potential solution (or at least a condition for its solution). In the diversity of their interests the people would generate the claims upon which government would have to act. But those claims would be so great and diverse in their extent as to require orderly deliberation by their elected lawmakers. The difficulty of securing lasting political consensus within society would thus clear the deliberative space within which lawmakers would have to act. The existence of multiple factions "out-of-doors," within society, would work either to prevent or at least to limit their formation within the institutions of government.

Was this argument for the effects of popular factions just as hypothetical as Madison's prediction about the benefits of large electoral districts? An extended national republic of the type Madison was imagining had, after all, never existed. Its character remained to be determined. Even so, Madison's conception of the inadvertent benefits of faction had an empirical plausibility that his thesis about elections necessarily lacked. First, there was nothing wildly speculative or merely academic in his portrayal of the diverse economic interests into which all modern societies were divided. Compared to the traditional (or classical) image of a society divided into the one, the few, and the many—monarchy, aristocracy, and demos—this was clearly a substantial advance in political sociology. Second, there was a paradigmatic case that already revealed the benefits that the existence of diversity could create. This lay in the realm of religion, where Madison correctly understood that in eighteenth-century America the existence of multiple denominations—from liturgical Anglicans to quietist Quakers and enthusiastic Baptists—was working to secure the blessings of religious liberty for all. This achievement had not occurred merely because American Protestants were all votaries of the free exercise of conscience, though support for that principle was increasingly widespread across the population. Rather, it had happened because the inherent divisiveness of Protestant culture, at play in a society where religious establishment was too weak to maintain confessional uniformity, had dispersed Americans across a richly sectarian map.

Madison's theory of faction rested on the social characteristics of individuals and their communities. It did not assume that the individual states, as such, had coherent interests that simply subsumed or defined the concerns of their citizens. It was the aggregated interests of citizens and local communities that defined the collective good of the individual states, not the other way around. Madison's theory did not presuppose that the central problem of forming a satisfactory national government was to provide institutional mechanisms whereby the states, as autonomous political communities, would negotiate their differences. It assumed instead that congeries of interests within and across states would permit national decisions to be made on the basis of collective deliberations.

Nevertheless, there was one critical sense in which the underlying structure of federalism still channeled Madison's concerns. At the national level of politics, factious majorities would find it difficult to form and persist. But for simple arithmetical reasons these factions might still exist far more readily and palpably in the states. The smaller the political entity, the easier it would be for the wrong kinds of majorities to form. Equally important, the states would retain significant legislative authority. Much of the ordinary legislation relating to the possession and use of property would still fall within their domain. So, too, would the regulation of religion—at least until other states followed the example of Pennsylvania and (now) Virginia and moved toward disestablishment. This was why the negative on state laws remained so essential a part of Madison's agenda for the Convention. Much of the terrain of American governance would fall (as Madison explained in *Federalist* 45) under the jurisdiction of the states. And this jurisdiction would still cover the most essential rights of the ownership of property.

It was this conviction that best explains why Madison regarded the negative on state laws as the optimal solution to the protection of individual and minority rights *within the states*. At the national level, the complexity and diversity of interests across the states would discourage the formation of the wrong kinds of majorities. That factor would be less effective within individual states, as the example of Rhode Island, with its anti-federal, paper-money politics, proved. But equally important, in a substantive sense the protection of property within the states did differ critically from the protection of religious rights. In the case of religion, it really was possible to constitutionally entrench the free exercise of religion and to conceive how it would be constitutionally feasible to prohibit public support of churches. Denying the state the authority to act in the realm of religion might depart radically from historical practice, but it remained a simple end to accomplish constitutionally. In the realm of property, however, such simple protections or restrictions were impossible. "The regulation of these various and interfering interests," Madison noted in *Federalist* 10, "forms the principal task of modern legislation."

There was every reason to think that the development of the American economy would become more, not less, important in the decades ahead, encouraging and even requiring the states to use their legislative authority to shape public policy.[30] There were specific ways in which one might build constitutional protections for property; several clauses of the Constitution and the Just Compensation Clause of the Fifth Amendment (authored by Madison) did just that.[31] Yet there were countless ways in which government would still have to act on property, with unequal effects on different interests. To take the examples cited by Madison in *Federalist* 10, any scheme of taxation, any regulation of the rights of debtors and creditors, any scheme for levying duties or protecting manufacturers, would produce different impacts on different classes of citizens or communities. The same would be true for acts authorizing the construction of a bridge or a highway or a turnpike, placing these works of improvement in one place but not another. Not everyone could benefit equally from such decisions. In effect, the basic rights of property—the value of one's estate—would always be affected by legislative decisions. If one was fearful, as Madison was, of the character of the popular majorities that would rule in the states, there was room aplenty to worry whether fundamental rights of property, as he conceived them, would be free from the populist sentiments that would swirl through the body politic.

Madison's thinking about the role of public opinion and the security of rights in 1787–88 thus pivoted on these propositions: First, public opinion remained a potentially disruptive force within republican politics. It was something that had to be managed or at least taken advantage of, primarily by recognizing that the diverse interests present in an extended republic would discourage the formation of lasting factious majorities at the *national* level of governance. Second, it followed conversely from this argument that popular opinion would remain a more dangerous factor within the states, where factious majorities could more readily form, capable of controlling the making of public policy in ways that would adversely affect the security of rights of property. The term Madison sometimes used to describe his own (and others') view of popular misrule at the state level was "disgust."[32] Third, the favored solution to this problem was to empower the national government to monitor the legislative injustices of the states, through a negative that its legislature could wield with relative impartiality. By contrast, the idea of using a bill of rights to secure that end was *not* an idea that Madison entertained. Such declarations, as he observed in *Federalist* 48, were so many "parchment barriers," nice to read as statements of fundamental principles but "greatly over-rated" and of little value in practice.[33]

The clearest statements of this concern came in the remarkable letters that Madison and Jefferson exchanged between the autumn of 1787 and the spring of 1789. In the annals of American history—and indeed in the realm of global constitutional history—few if any exchanges have ever attained a comparable level of political importance and analytical sophistication. The exchange became part of Madison's decision to make the adoption of rights-protecting amendments a critical element in his agenda for the First Federal Congress of 1789. But, equally important, the reasons both for Jefferson's early support for amendments and for Madison's reservations and grudging acceptance illuminate significant shifts and differences in the ways in which the two friends conceived the nature and function of bills of rights.

The correspondence began in early September 1787, when Madison offered Jefferson a very brief account of the Convention's movement toward adjournment. It effectively closed in mid-March 1789, when Jefferson commented on the reasons Madison had adduced, with mixed enthusiasm, for adding a declaration of rights to the Constitution. Of particular interest in this concluding letter was Jefferson's opening observation that Madison had neglected to mention one argument "which has great weight with me, the legal check which [a declaration of rights] puts into

the hands of the judiciary."[34] Between these opening and clos-
ing texts, the letters that matter most are the two that Madison
wrote, a year apart, on October 24, 1787, and October 17, 1788. The
first represents his culminating defense of the negative on state
laws, elaborating points he had developed in his pre-Convention
papers, in several speeches at Philadelphia, and in *Federalist* 10.
This defense, which he apologetically called an "immoderate
digression," consumed roughly half of a seventeen-page manuscript and indicates how attached he remained to the proposal
that he originally viewed as "the least possible encroachment"
that should be made "on the State jurisdictions." The second
letter, though also detailed, is more typically Madisonian in the
economy of its leading statements—another of those texts about
which one wishes that Madison had given his quill a bit more ink.

The experience of debate at Philadelphia, Banning argues, did
shift Madison's convictions in significant ways, moving him away
from the strongly nationalist positions of figures like Hamilton
and Gouverneur Morris and closer to the claims made by his
small-state opponents like John Dickinson and Roger Sherman.
Perhaps in many instances that did prove the case, as Banning
urges us to think.[35] Yet on the critical point of the negative on
state laws Madison's private opinion remained unchanged. He
would not have defended this idea at so great a length merely to
satisfy Jefferson's intellectual curiosity about an idea that Madison
knew his correspondent was likely to reject.

In a letter written on September 6, 1787, eleven days before the
Convention adjourned, Madison signaled Jefferson that he would
later explain his lingering fear that the Constitution "should it
be adopted will neither effectually answer its national object nor
prevent the local mischiefs which every where excite disgusts
agst. the state governments."[36] Those two counts—"national
object" and "local mischiefs"—correspond to the two headings
under which Madison addressed the negative seven weeks later.
"Without such a check in the whole over the parts," he observed,
"our system involves the evil of imperium in imperio"—a state
within a state, or two sovereign jurisdictions within one realm,
which a familiar maxim described as a "monster" or a "solecism in
politics." Madison expected the states to retain individual incentives to disagree with national decisions, not only on particular

policies but also because their jurisdictions must overlap. Here Madison invoked his long-standing concern with the very nature of legislative power—"the impossibility of dividing the powers of legislation, in such a manner, as to be free from different constructions by different interests, or even from ambiguity in the judgment of the impartial." If such conflicts were inevitable, a decisive power had to be lodged somewhere to resolve them. Such a power, in theory, could be vested in the judiciary. But depending on that institution would involve overlooking crippling, even fatal flaws by relying on legal cases and controversies to ascertain the meaning of the Constitution. "It is more convenient to prevent the passage of a law, than to declare it void after it is passed," Madison noted. Moreover, a state that would be willing to defy the legislative powers of the union "would not be very ready to obey a Judicial decree in support of them." Analytically, Madison believed that the states had to be denied their claim to legislative sovereignty.[37]

Madison pursued the theme of legislative ambiguity in the second heading of his rationale for the negative, as a device "equally necessary to secure individuals agst. encroachments on their rights." Here he again declared his opinion that "the evils issuing" from the "mutability" and the "injustice" of state legislation had "contributed more to that uneasiness which produced the Convention" than the obvious failings of the Confederation. The proposed constitution dealt with these problems through the restrictions on "paper emissions, and violations of contracts" in Article I, Section 10. But these "restraints . . . are not sufficient," Madison held. "Injustice may be effected by such an infinitude of legislative expedients, that where the disposition exists it can only be controuled by some provision which reaches all cases whatsoever." This remark provided the transition to the lengthy restatement of Madison's general concept of the beneficial effects of faction, which would "unfold the true principles of Republican Government, and prove in contradiction to the concurrent opinions of theoretical writers" that republics "must operate not within a small but an extensive sphere."[38]

Four weeks after Madison wrote this letter, *Federalist* 10 appeared in the New York *Independent Journal.* Although a century and a quarter passed before scholars came to recognize its authority, there is no question that this essay represents a major contribution to political theory. Madison had developed and expressed its main ideas both before and during the Convention, and he understood perfectly well the importance of rebutting and refuting the reigning paradigm of republican *thought*. A space had to be cleared within which Americans could compare the relative advantages of small and large republics. But this exercise, this response to the doctrines of "theoretical writers," marked only a partial expression of Madison's political *thinking*. *Federalist* 10, for example, ignores his concern with the difficulty of classifying and thus constraining the uses of legislative power. More important, because the negative on state laws was not part of the Constitution, Madison had no reason to discuss its absence. *Federalist* 10 could demonstrate why minority rights would be less vulnerable to factious attack at the national level of government without having to discuss why their security would remain so problematic within the states.

When Jefferson answered Madison's letter, he did not address the idea of the negative or its rationale.[39] Still, Madison could not have been overly thrilled by his friend's response. After briefly noting the decisions of the Convention that he admired, Jefferson spelled out at greater length "what I do not like." Atop this list was the omission of a bill of rights, which he deemed a constitutional necessity, something that "the people"—or all peoples—"are entitled to against every government on earth, general or particular, & what no just government should refuse or rest on inference." After next discussing "the abandonment in every instance of the necessity of rotation in office," especially "in the case of the President," Jefferson closed his reflections in a somewhat bemused and philosophical tone. Jefferson confessed he was uncertain how the ratification process should end. Perhaps the Constitution should take effect, with a later consideration of amendments. Or perhaps the people should be allowed to register their thoughts, pro and con, and send their deputies to a second convention to adjust the differences.[40]

This was exactly the idea that Madison strongly opposed, as the letter to Randolph cited in opening this chapter makes ever so clear. But Madison must have chafed even more at the final confession of Jefferson's letter, which was, in its own way, a subtle rebuke of the idea of a negative on state laws. "I own I am not a friend to a very energetic government," Jefferson admitted. "It is always oppressive." His countrymen at home seemed over-wrought about their governments; they had shown too much "alarm" over "the late Rebellion in Massachusetts." For Madison, Shays's Rebellion helped inspire the Republican Guarantee Clause of Article IV; for Jefferson it was simply a point of comparison that should enable Americans to realize that their governments were far less tyrannical than any to be found in the Old World. Perhaps sensing he had gone too far for Madison's tastes, Jefferson closed his letter with a curious postscript which noted "that the instability of our laws is really an immense evil." But Jefferson's preferred answer to this concern was to require a year to pass "between the ingrossing a bill & passing it," and then to prevent any alteration in its language![41]

That formula for delay was hardly Madison's model of how to improve legislative deliberation. Nor was he yet amenable to Jefferson's fondness for a bill of rights as a universal necessity. At the time Jefferson wrote this letter, Madison was worrying that any concession on this point would allow Anti-Federalists to pursue structural changes to the Constitution. He did not welcome the later publication in the United States of another letter Jefferson had written in February 1788, which expressed the hope that nine states would ratify the Constitution while the remaining four "may refuse to accede to it till a declaration of rights be annexed."[42] But Jefferson's initial letter of December 20 reached Madison only after he returned to Virginia in early March. He mentioned its arrival to Jefferson only after he returned to New York City in July and did not really respond to it until mid-October.

By then Madison had a full year of public debate to absorb and consider, as well as the satisfaction of seeing the Constitution ratified by eleven states. He still opposed any measure that might permit a second convention or lead to substantive changes to the Constitution. The passage of "a few years," he wrote Jefferson in August, would identify "the faults which really call for amend-ment." More important, "at present the public mind is neither sufficiently cool nor sufficiently informed for so delicate an opera-tion." Here was another powerful reservation about the capacity of public opinion to deal, with moderation, with so complicated a question as the formation of a constitution.[43] He restated his concern two weeks later: "A trial for one year will probably suggest more real amendments than all the antecedent speculations of our most sagacious politicians."[44] Better to wait until "time shall have somewhat corrected the feverish state of the public mind, and trial have pointed its attention to the true defects of the system."[45]

Given the choice between abstract speculation and concrete experience, then, Madison clearly preferred to make lessons learned from practice the foundation of his own contributions to political and constitutional theory. That attitude shaped his complex response to the specific question of adding amendments protecting constitutional rights. At the Virginia ratification convention in June 1788, Madison resisted adding any amendments to the Constitution until the narrow margin of votes separating the two sides indicated that such a concession had to be made. He generally supported the arguments that James Wilson had initially laid down in his widely reprinted public speech of October 6, 1787. Adding a declaration of rights would be both "unnecessary" and "dangerous," he told the Convention on June 24, because it might imply that the national government had been given more power than had actually been delegated, and because an enumeration of specific rights "which is not complete, is not safe," because rights left unmentioned would be relegated to an inferior status.[46] Once it became evident that acceptance of some amendments was the price to be paid for ratification, Madison insisted that the Convention's two sets of articles—one relating to rights, the other to structural aspects of the Constitution—had to be approved as recommendations to the new Congress, not prior conditions of the state's ratification.[47]

Not until October 17 did Madison address Jefferson's commitment to adding a bill of rights. The stimulus was the arrival two days earlier of another letter from Paris (dated July 31), which itemized the particular subjects Jefferson believed a bill of rights should cover: "Juries, Habeas Corpus, Standing armies, Printing, Religion and Monopolies." Jefferson argued that it would be better to have blanket prohibitions on the authority of government than to allow exceptions that could be exploited over time. Thus he would rather eliminate the clause of Article I, Section 9, that allowed Congress to suspend habeas corpus in times of insurrection or rebellion than allow it to survive as a basis for habituating the public mind to the possibility of suspension.[48]

Jefferson's mode of political thinking was much on Madison's mind in the early autumn of 1788. In response to a request from a Kentucky correspondent, he had just drafted the critical "Observations on the 'Draught of a Constitution for Virginia,'" a draft Jefferson had written in 1783 and appended to his *Notes on the State of Virginia.*[49] And, of course, in his discussion of the separation of powers in *Federalist* 49–50, Madison went out of his way to criticize (though quite respectfully) Jefferson's proposal to submit constitutional disputes among the departments to popularly elected conventions. However much these two epistolary friends agreed on political positions, on constitutional issues there were still significant differences between them. Indeed it is one tribute to their remarkable friendship, lasting half a century, that two men who agreed on so many things could nonetheless find room to argue about fundamental questions, or to apply their distinct intellectual temperaments to discuss positions they shared. In the five years after Jefferson sailed to France, their individual political experiences sharpened the differences in their perspectives even as their correspondence deepened their personal friendship.

When Madison promptly answered Jefferson's letter of July 31, he wrote with the concision and directness that often marked his thinking. His acceptance of the idea of adding a statement of rights to the Constitution hardly brimmed with enthusiasm. While claiming, perhaps a shade disingenuously, that he had "always been in favor of one," he immediately indicated that he had never been troubled by its omission "nor been anxious to supply it even by *subsequent* amendment," except that "it is anxiously desired by others." There were four reasons why he had "not viewed it in an important light." The first accorded, at least partially, with James Wilson, who had argued that the delegation of particular legislative powers obviated the need to protect rights. If, for example, the Constitution gave Congress no authority over religion, a clause protecting its free exercise might prove both superfluous and dangerous, because its inclusion might imply that a regulatory power actually did exist. Second, the effort to convert a right to a textual formula could run its own political risks: "There is great reason to fear that a positive declaration of some of the most essential rights could not be obtained in the requisite latitude." That might well prove the case in the realm of "the rights of Conscience," a subject that concerned Madison deeply. Third, developing a point he had argued in *Federalist* 51, "the jealousy of the subordinate Governments" of the states would also work as a check on federal power.[50]

It was, however, the fourth point that revealed the decisive argument, much as item 11 of "the Vices" had created the forum for Madison's initial critique of the sources of faction. Nor is this parallel merely coincidental, for his explanation of the inadequacy of bills of rights derived from the same concerns that previously justified his devotion to the negative on state laws. The fourth point rested on recent lessons of history: "Because experience proves the inefficacy of a bill of rights on those occasions when its control is most needed. Repeated violations of these parchment barriers have been committed by overbearing majorities in every State." In their own state, continued Madison, "I have seen the bill of rights violated in every instance where it has been opposed to a popular majority." Even in the realm of religion, the one area where he and Jefferson might have taken the greatest pride, Madison believed that the legislative majority would have ignored the strictures laid down in the state's declaration of rights and adopted the general assessment bill had they discovered that public opinion was on their side. In other words, even from an issue that Madison had effectively won, skeptical conclusions were to be drawn.

The dominant conclusion and lesson immediately followed:

> Wherever the real power in a Government lies, there is the danger of oppression. In our Governments the real power lies in the majority of the Community, and the invasion of private rights is *ch[ie]fly* to be apprehended, not from acts of Government contrary to the sense of its constituents, but from acts in which the Government is the mere instrument of the major number of the constituents. This is a truth of great importance, but not yet sufficiently attended to: and is probably more strongly impressed on my mind by facts, and reflections suggested by them, than on yours which has contemplated abuses of power issuing from a very different quarter.

Embedded in this statement are three propositions or assumptions that defined Madison's active thinking about rights. First, how one thought about the protection of rights had to be a function not of abstract speculation but of a concrete analysis of the actual dynamics of power. Second, the problem of rights in a republic was therefore not identical to the problem of rights in a monarchy. The dominant power in a republican government lay in the people themselves, and institutions were merely the vehicles of their desires. Third, Jefferson could not yet empirically grasp this point because his own experience the past four years had diverged from Madison's. Observing the dying ancien régime of France, Jefferson could adhere to the traditional idea that the concentrated power of arbitrary government posed the great danger to the rights of the people, viewed as a collective entity outside of government. Madison had a different model of government in front of him, one that would act on the basis of the political preference of popular majorities, but potentially adversely to the rights of individuals and minorities. Here, as in his case for an extended republic, Madison was challenging a dominant theory that construed the problem of rights primarily as a conflict between the power of government and the collective rights of the people as a whole.

Having laid down these propositions, Madison then asked what role a bill of rights would play if it were to become something more than a parchment barrier. His conception of its value remained political, not legal. In a monarchy, where "the latent force of the nation is superior to that of the sovereign," such "a solemn charter of popular rights" could still serve a vital function, "as a signal for rousing & uniting the superior force of the community." That function would not work in a republic, where "the physical and political power" resided "in the same hands, that is a majority of the people." If the majority were disposed to violate a minority's essential rights, they would not be dissuaded by the existence of a statement of principles.

Madison then posed another of those reflective questions that illustrate his engagement with the subject at hand: "What use then it may be asked can a bill of rights serve in popular Governments?" He offered two answers that justified its adoption, even if it still seemed "less essential than in other Governments." The first, and more intriguing, came in one of those single-sentence observations that the scholar wishes he had expanded: "The political truths declared in that solemn manner acquire by degrees the character of fundamental maxims of free Government, and as they become incorporated with the national sentiment, counteract the impulses of interest and passion." For Madison, a bill of rights thus remained not a set of legal commands and prohibitions but an essentially *political* text. It would operate not by creating a legal rule or standard that courts could enforce but by modifying the behavior of self-interested or impassioned citizens. Its purpose would be primarily educative, a way of developing over time the civic virtue that Madison believed ordinary citizens lacked.

The second reason reverted to the traditional argument for bills of rights. Even if "the danger of oppression lies in the interested majorities of the people rather than in usurped acts of the Government," the latter danger also has to be weighed. In such cases, the existence of "a bill of rights will be a good ground for an appeal to the sense of the community." This, too, was a political argument, not a legal one. It was, in fact, quite similar to the writings of the Federal Farmer (the moderate New York Anti-Federalist Melancton Smith) in his *Letters* against the Constitution. How would the people know when to resist the arbitrary acts of government, the Federal Farmer asked, if they lacked a bill of rights to educate them on its proper authority?[51] Yet having conceded this point, Madison indicated that he did not regard the theory—so central to radical Whig beliefs—of government continuously augmenting its "power at the expence of liberty" to be "well founded." In the American situation, he was more worried that "the abuses of liberty" in a government that was too weak would "beget a sudden transition to an undue degree of power." This was the classic theory of anarchy leading to tyranny.

Nothing in this letter indicates that Madison had revised the central tenets of his political thinking. There were expedient reasons to adopt a bill of rights, arising from the ratification debates, and these calculations became even more compelling—at least for Madison—in the forthcoming elections for the First Federal Congress. But writing to his closest political correspondent, Madison both elaborated his views and demonstrated how little had changed. The principal danger to rights would still arise from the people at large, as their interests and passions determined public opinion and turned government into its "mere instrument." That instrument would be the branch or level of government most responsive to the public—the lower house of the legislature in both the state and national governments, but also the individual states far more than the federal union. Against the dominant force of public opinion, neither bills of rights nor an independent judiciary could be relied upon to be efficacious.

That consideration also shaped Madison's initial evaluation of the specific rights Jefferson wanted to protect. Unlike Jefferson, who was willing to accept absolute prohibitions, Madison wanted to avoid "*absolute* restrictions in cases that are doubtful, or where emergencies may overrule them." The decisive consideration was, again, his fear of the force of public opinion triumphing over parchment barriers. "The restrictions however strongly marked on paper," he wrote, "will never be regarded when opposed to the decided sense of the public; and after repeated violations in extraordinary cases, they will lose even their ordinary efficacy." If a rebellion or insurrection justified the suspension of habeas corpus, "no written prohibitions on earth would prevent the measure." If Britain or Spain placed strong military forces in Canada or Mexico, Americans would gladly accept "a standing force for the public safety." And although Madison agreed that monopolies ranked "among the greatest nusances in Government," one could easily identify cases where they would be valuable. Moreover, the fear of monopolies supposed that the good of the many would be sacrificed to the interests of the few. That might hold in other regimes, but in the American republic "it is much more to be dreaded that the few will be unnecessarily sacrificed to the many."[52]

In considering these cases, however, Madison was turning his attention to the question of how rights could be concretely stated. This was, in effect, a problem of legislative draftsmanship, not so different from his concerns with the quality of lawmaking. Getting a right properly stated had been his concern back in 1776 when he proposed grounding the religion article of the Declaration of Rights on the principle of free exercise rather than toleration. If one worried, as Madison manifestly did, that bills of rights were prone to become parchment barriers, then how one defined or stated a right might have some effect—even if only a partial one—on its legal and moral authority. This was especially the case if one considered the character of the texts that the American constitution makers had "compiled" (to use one of his favored words) back in the 1770s. Many of the articles in these texts stated republican principles rather than legal commands. They could, for example, endorse the principle of rotation in office without imposing a legal requirement to that effect, or endorse the liberty-preserving value of the separation of powers without clearly distinguishing the three forms of power in ways that would satisfy Madison's desire for analytical precision.[53] The state declarations of rights typically used the monitory verb "ought" rather than the mandatory "shall," implying that the obligation to respect a right was moral rather than legal. To modern critics, such as the distinguished constitutional historian Leonard Levy, these texts seem partial and deficient—inadequate versions of what a proper bill of rights ought to contain. This criticism is itself anachronistic, however. It ignores the crucial fact that the constitutional and legal authority of bills of rights remained uncertain in 1776, which is hardly surprising if one recalls that the authority of written constitutions also posed a problem that Americans—Madison foremost among them—were struggling to work out.

Thus, when Madison turned his attention from the general purpose of a bill of rights to its substance, he found ample room to rethink exactly how such statements should operate. The amendments proposed by the state conventions were partly helpful. Relying on a pamphlet that he also sent Jefferson, Madison identified the subjects that Americans wanted to address, while distinguishing these affirmations of rights from the structural changes that he intended to ignore.[54] But, perhaps more important, Madison began thinking critically about the proper form that a statement of rights should take. That had not been an essential task at the Virginia convention. Then, his paramount goal was to prevent the proposed amendments from becoming a condition of the state's ratification. Madison had served on the committee that was responsible for drafting the convention's amendments.[55] The committee had only a day to do its work. One can be skeptical how far its debates went. Its twenty-five members included George Mason, the leading author of the 1776 Declaration, and they relied extensively on a draft prepared by a caucus of Anti-Federalist members (including Mason) a fortnight earlier.[56] Both that draft and the amendments the convention adopted were largely modeled on the Virginia Declaration, stating principles that ought to be followed rather than legal commands that had to be obeyed. The question of how one would textually incorporate the statement of a right into a written constitution that proclaimed itself the supreme law of the land thus opened a fresh field for inquiry.

Madison's thinking about the subject was sharpened by the course of Virginia politics, in which Anti-Federalists in general and Patrick Henry in particular dominated the new legislature. His decided preference was to serve in the House of Representatives, in part because that would be the more important half of Congress, but also because he naively hoped that "the arrangements for the popular elections" would spare him any need to engage in "a spirit of electioneering which I despise."[57] In fact, he was doubly disappointed. Federalist legislators, with a strong push from George Washington, made Madison their leading candidate for the Senate; he finished a respectable third to two Anti-Federalists, Richard Henry Lee and William Grayson (though Henry also reportedly declared that Madison's "election would terminate in producing rivulets of blood throughout the land").[58] Worse, Henry manipulated the drawing of district lines for the House, placing Madison in a potentially unfriendly district where his eventual opponent was the Anti-Federalist James Monroe, his former ally and correspondent. Yielding to personal appeals, Madison reluctantly returned to Virginia, where he had no choice but to "electioneer," an activity "which I always despised and wish to shun."[59]

The pressures on Madison to return to Virginia were an early indication that his naive expectations about the potential nature of national politics might not accord with the new conditions the Constitution was already creating.[60] Henry and other Anti-Federalists repeatedly asserted that Madison was "utterly against any kind of alteration in the Govt.," that he was "dogmatically attached to the Constitution in every clause, syllable & letter," even that he thought "that it was the nearest to Perfection of any thing that Could be obtained."[61] These allegations were widely repeated throughout the district, swaying the gullible as well as the partisans and compelling Madison to formulate a public response to the innuendoes swirling against him. Notwithstanding his distaste for "electioneering appearances," exigent circumstances required Madison to fashion his own strategy for mobilizing public opinion. This was not like the situation he faced in 1777, when his defeat for reelection to the House of Delegates foundered on his refusal to refresh the voters in the usual way. Nor was it the same kind of struggle that he had joined in writing learned essays for *The Federalist*.

Seeking election to Congress in 1789 involved political novelties that Americans had not yet experienced. Representative elections before then were held in existing political communities, either townships or counties, where candidates already enjoyed significant connections. But the new electoral districts were multicounty entities that existed for the sole purpose of electing representatives. They had no other civic function. Madison had to recruit a cluster of sympathetic correspondents in his own and neighboring counties to make an "interest" for him, to use their personal networks of influence in his behalf. These friends in turn had their own notions of how public opinion should be mobilized, which they shared freely with the candidate: "Mr. Munroe is writing myriads of Letters to the different Counties," George Lee Turbeville reported, but "Yr. Friends are not less active." At the start, Madison's correspondents simply wanted to make sure that he returned home, even though that might prove "very irksome to you," and to ensure that he appeared in populous Culpeper County, which loomed as the critical site of contestation.[62] Once he was back in Virginia, their suggestions became even more specific. In mid-January he learned that Monroe would appear at the next court day in Culpeper to answer Madison's discussion of the Constitution. "Many of your friends," he was also told, "solicit most earnestly that you will favour us with your Company on that day" to answer Monroe directly.[63]

In defiance of his intentions, then, Madison found himself engaged in an early version of an active campaign, attending court days in several counties and even debating Monroe in freezing temperatures after they jointly attended a Lutheran service. Madison's most important action, however, came in the letters that he wrote well-placed contacts. If circumstances forced one to campaign, it was still essential to remain consistent with one's record and conscience. Starting with his January 2, 1789, letter to George Eve, a prominent Baptist preacher three years his senior, Madison explained in some detail the nuances of his positions. In these letters, he carefully outlined his concerns about the entire amendment process, in terms consistent with the arguments he had already made. This included his insistence that amendments be considered only by Congress, rather than at a second constitutional convention that the Virginia legislature, in alliance with the dominant Anti-Federalists in New York, desired. Madison signaled his willingness to pursue the subject of amendments as soon as the new Congress met. He would attempt to secure "the most satisfactory provisions for all essential rights, particularly the rights of Conscience in the fullest latitude, the freedom of the press, trials by jury, security against general warrants &c."[64] (What the "&c." would be soon became an ongoing project for Madison, as he reviewed what the states had proposed.) There were several other provisions of the Constitution with which he was also willing to tinker. But on one key point that Anti-Federalists sought, Madison remained adamant. Drawing on the same analysis that he had been voicing since the early 1780s, he held that it would be a grave error to allow the states to meet their national obligations through a system of requisitions from Congress, with direct national taxes to follow only after they had failed to comply.[65]

Ten inches of snow two days earlier and subzero temperatures accompanied the voting on February 2. Madison outpolled Monroe by 336 votes across the eight counties, carrying 57 percent of the vote, with a substantial victory in hotly contested Culpeper County.[66] Conventional historical wisdom correctly holds that Madison benefited from the support of religious dissenters who knew his role in promoting the free exercise of religion in Virginia. Explicit evidence of this comes from George Eve's church, where one Anti-Federalist urged the church meeting of January 18 to unite against Madison's candidacy. In the ensuing discussion, Madison learned, Eve "took a very Spirited and decided Part in your favour," invoking the defeat of the general assessment bill and the enactment of the Statute for Religious Freedom.[67] Madison thus reaped the political rewards of his principled commitment to religious liberty. Similarly, the campaign that circumstances led him to wage proved distinctly Madisonian in its substance. Madison presented his views with the same distinctions and assessments that shaped his private thinking.

Still, politics carries its own logic, and Madison responded to this quickly. There were, of course, no precedents for the congressional elections of 1789. But in critical ways the experience of the ratification debate of 1787–88 carried lessons beyond its own remarkable result. It had demonstrated how national public opinion could be formed and brought to a decisive conclusion. Nothing like this had occurred since the crisis of independence in 1774–76. Revolutionary politics after 1776 was decidedly state-based, although on a few occasions—notably in 1779—particular episodes did focus national public attention.[68] The ratification struggle also created intra- and interstate alliances that continued to operate in the first federal elections. It defined new commitments that helped to shape the agenda of the First Congress, notably on the issue of amendments that Madison took responsibility for advancing. The publication in newspapers and pamphlets of the debates in the state ratification conventions also marked a significant step in the development of public interest in the nature and content of political deliberations. Before 1787, only a handful of state legislative debates had appeared in American newspapers. After ratification, the prevailing expectation was that debates in the House of Representatives, where the people's directly elected lawmakers would sit, should be available to the public. The New York City press quickly began reporting debates in the House, and other papers reprinted their accounts. Representatives mindful of their reputation naturally acquired the incentive to see their names in print. One New York congressman even asked a friend to "draw up some suitable speech for me, not to[o] long or to[o] short," on Madison's proposed amendments.[69]

Public opinion was very much on Madison's mind in the spring of 1789 as he insisted on pushing his rights-based amendments through Congress. He did this against the misgivings of Federalists, who controlled both houses of Congress, and the indifference of Anti-Federalists, who knew they would not get the changes they really wanted. Some Federalists thought Madison was *too* sensitive to public opinion. Robert Morris, now a senator from

Pennsylvania, scoffed that Madison had got "frightened in Virginia and 'wrote a book,'" an allusion to Madison's published letters in support of ratification.[70] But the attention to public opinion that Madison felt as he pushed the case for amendments in the spring and summer of 1789 did not depend on personal political calculations. It was tied instead to his conviction that the prompt adoption of amendments would bring the entire process of adopting the Constitution to an appropriate closure.

Again, little had changed in his assessment of the real value of a statement of rights. The most creative element of his thinking involved the form the amendments should take. Rather than publish a separate bill of rights, as the states had done, Madison wanted to insert his proposals at the specific point in the Constitution where they would take legal effect. These clauses would operate not as a statement of principles in the voice of 1776 but rather as a set of constitutional commands. Their placement in the text would indicate the mode of their enforcement, primarily as restrictions on the legislative power of Congress. In presenting his proposals in his major speech of June 8, Madison did not concede that the framers had erred in omitting a statement of rights, or that Federalists had done wrong to resist making the adoption of amendments a condition for the ratification of the Constitution. In his notes for this speech, Madison identified four "reasons urging amendts. 1. to prove fedts. [Federalists] friends to liberty 2. remove remaining inquietudes 3. bring in N. C. & R. Island 4. to improve the Constitution."[71] The fourth point, which we regard as the most important, was almost certainly fourth in importance to its author. In his actual speech, Madison went on to discuss whether bills of rights were valuable or not, and to identify shortcomings in the existing versions Americans had adopted. He made the same fundamental point to the House that he had made to Jefferson: "The prescriptions in favor of liberty, ought to be leveled against that quarter where the greatest danger lies," he noted. "But this [is] not found in either the executive or legislative departments of government, but in the body of the people, operating by the majority against the minority."[72] Madison also made a last attempt to extend the federal protection of rights against the states, by inserting a clause in Article I, Section 10, holding that "no state shall violate the equal rights of conscience, or the freedom of the press, or the trial by jury in criminal cases." In later debate, he boldly described this provision "as the most valuable amendment on the whole list."[73] That argument carried enough weight in the House to keep the clause in its proposed list of amendments, but not in the Senate, where the proposal was deleted. This was less of a blow than the rejection of the negative on state laws in the Convention, but it still stung.

Like other members of the House, Madison was aware that he was now addressing two audiences: his fellow representatives, operating in a chamber where collective debate did matter, and the public at large. Thinking about how to reach that public—indeed, how to educate and influence it—was one of the discoveries that emerged from both the ratification process and the publicity of the new Congress, which contrasted so sharply with the obscurity in which the Continental Congress had labored. Madison entered the constitutional debates of the 1780s conceiving public opinion as something that the deliberations of republican institutions had to overcome. But active participation in the debates over ratification and his reading in the sources Jefferson had sent him complicated his approach to the problem. He captured this tension in his reading notes from 1791. "In proportion as government is influenced by opinion, must it be so by whatever influences opinion," he mused. "This decides the question concerning a bill of rights, which requires ['acquires' was the intended word] efficacy as time sanctifies and incorporates it with the public sentiment."[74] Public opinion might have a valuable function to play, he was now realizing, in maintaining constitutional government—one of the great problems he wrestled with for the rest of his life.

CHAPTER 4

"THESE EXPERIMENTS ARE OF TOO TICKLISH A NATURE TO BE UNNECESSARILY MULTIPLIED"

The Problem of Thinking Like a Constitution

On January 11, 1788, the day after Madison wrote his letter on public opinion to Edmund Randolph,[1] *Federalist* 37 appeared in the New York *Independent Journal.* This was Madison's sixth contribution to the series. It marked the point when the task of writing as Publius passed from Hamilton to Madison. He wrote twenty-three of the next twenty-six essays before preparing to return to Virginia. More important, *Federalist* 37 gave *The Federalist* what was in effect its second introduction. The main purpose of the prior essays, written primarily by Hamilton, was to make the *nationalist* case for an effective federal union. But *Federalist* 37 turned attention to the structure of the Constitution—to its animating principles; to its relation to republicanism, federalism, and separation of powers; and finally to its institutions. Madison wrote most of the essays on Article I and Congress, then Hamilton took back the quill to discuss the executive and judiciary. Fittingly, when the second volume of the book-length M'Lean edition of *The Federalist* appeared in May 1788, *Federalist* 37 was its opening essay.

This essay is as remarkable a contribution to the American science of politics as *Federalist* 10 and 51. Those two essays present Madison's leading hypotheses on an extended republic and separation of powers. But *Federalist* 37 is a meditation about the nature of constitution making. Its lessons were immediately intended to apply to the current deliberations over ratification, but they also remain relevant to the continuing task of maintaining a constitution after its establishment. It laid down guidelines for constitutional analysis that Madison pursued in later essays, notably in discussing federalism in *Federalist* 39 and separated powers in *Federalist* 47–48. It is, arguably, the one place where Madison explored most self-consciously what the task of thinking like a constitution really meant.

Madison opened the essay by restating the central theme of *Federalist* 1. In the opening paragraph of that essay, Hamilton observed that Americans enjoyed the unique opportunity "to decide the important question, whether societies of men are really capable or not of establishing good government from reflection and choice, or whether they are forever destined to depend for their political constitutions on accident and force." To do this, Americans had to apply the "lesson of moderation" in forming their judgments by adopting the proper attitude to participate in a public debate.[2]

Federalist 37 began by enlarging Hamilton's point, noting that the "spirit of moderation" that was needed "is more apt to be diminished than promoted, by those occasions which require an unusual exercise of it." But then Madison shifted the emphasis away from the attitude that citizens should maintain and toward a different problem—the fact that "many allowances ought to be made for the difficulties inherent in the very nature of the undertaking referred to the convention." Citizens had to do more than acknowledge the fallibility of their own judgment. They also needed to weigh the "difficulties" the constitution makers themselves had faced, to appreciate that their efforts were an act of creative political thinking in real time, and thus to attempt to apprehend what the process of forming a new government actually entailed.[3]

Madison identified four major problems that must have affected the Convention. The first was the absence of precedent. Knowledge of the history of other confederacies, a subject that Madison had studied in 1786 and discussed in *Federalist* 18–20, could only "give warning of the course to be shunned, without pointing out that which ought to be pursued." Madison's second point developed another theme of *Federalist* 1. Constitution making involved balancing values and principles that were not wholly compatible. On the one hand, one wanted to attain "energy" and "stability" in government while avoiding the "irregular and mutable legislation" that "characterize the state administrations." These concerns

justified vesting power in relatively few hands and allowing them
to govern "for a length of time." Yet "the genius of republican
liberty" required a high measure of popular accountability and
rotation in office, criteria that threatened the norms of stability.
Balancing these two commitments "must clearly appear to have
been an arduous part" of the Convention's labors.[4]

Madison's third point began with a nearly superfluous observation that identified a central problem the Convention must have
faced—"marking the proper line of partition between the authority of the general, and that of the state governments." He might
have answered this question by delineating the essential tasks of
national and state governance. Instead he sounded a strikingly
epistemological tone by comparing the difficulties of reasoning
about political phenomena with other efforts "to contemplate and
discriminate objects, extensive and complicated in their nature."
In effect, Madison was contrasting the artificial institutions only
humans could create with aspects of the natural world, such
as the sensations and faculties of the human mind as well as
inanimate objects and animate entities. Madison concluded his
discussion by alluding to the problems the framers must have
faced in reconciling the interests each represented. The conflict
between large and small states was one obvious division. But
"other combinations, resulting from a difference of local position
and policy," also intervened. No special genius was required to
recall the sectional fault line between free and slave societies.[5]

If citizens acting with moderation surveyed these factors, they
would readily grasp that the Convention "should have been forced
into some deviations from that artificial structure and regular
symmetry which an abstract view of the subject might lead an
ingenious theorist to bestow on a Constitution planned in his
closet or in his imagination." Irregularities, imperfections, and
deviations from abstract principles were inevitable. The success
of the whole event, Madison concluded, should be seen as a "real
wonder" and a genuine source of "astonishment." Indeed, for
those "of pious reflection" it was yet more evidence that "a finger
of that Almighty Hand" that had helped save the revolution at
its "critical stages" was still moving.[6]

Nothing quite like *Federalist* 37 exists anywhere else in the vast
archive of the ratification debates. Other writers happily cited

lessons drawn from their reading. But analyzing the inherent difficulty of the constitutional project was another matter. Madison was producing an account that not only subsumed the broad problems the framers had faced but also reflected about political reasoning itself. The nature of that activity could be understood only when one compared it to other ways of knowing.

Of these four main points, the one that best illustrates Madison's *thinking* is the third, with its epistemological comparisons. This comparison may not have served every reader equally well, for it was addressed to those who were "accustomed to contemplate and discriminate objects, extensive and complicated in their nature." Madison offered two examples of how these difficulties could be compared to other fields of study. One involved "the faculties of the mind," long the object of study by "the most acute and metaphysical philosophers." The other covered "the great kingdoms of nature" and the task of "tracing with certainty, the line which separates the district of vegetable life from the neighbouring region of unorganized matter, or which marks the termination of the former and the commencement of the animal empire." Madison's use of territorial and political terms to describe natural phenomena served as a transition to his real topic. In nature one had to assume that "the delineations are perfectly accurate"—that they really existed—but "appear to be otherwise only from the imperfection of the eye which surveys them." But in viewing "the institutions of man," one had to recognize that "the obscurity arises as well from the object itself, as from the organ by which it is contemplated." Here was another reason for "moderating still farther our expectations and hopes from the efforts of human sagacity."[7]

The ostensible subject of this analysis was the difficulty of marking a clear "partition" between national and provincial jurisdictions. But to illustrate this point Madison turned naturally, perhaps almost inadvertently, to the complementary problem of the separation of powers. Here, following Montesquieu, everyone knew there were "three great provinces" of power. Abstractly, distinguishing legislative, executive, and judicial power should not be that difficult. Yet "questions daily occur in the course of practice, which prove the obscurity which reigns in these subjects, and which puzzle the greatest adepts in political science." Even more

complicated was the nature of law itself, and the "different tribunals of justice" where cases could be tried. This subject had been
most "industriously pursued" in Britain. But even there it remained
"a source of frequent and intricate discussions" often leading to
"indeterminate" results. The full meaning of a statute could not
be known at the moment of passage. Indeed, in a single sentence
that speaks volumes for the whole enterprise of constitutional
interpretation, Madison noted that "all new laws, though penned
with the greatest technical skill, and passed on the fullest and most
mature deliberation, are considered as more or less obscure and
equivocal, until their meaning be liquidated and ascertained by
a series of particular discussions and adjudications."[8] No piece of
legislation in the entire corpus of American history had received
as much deliberation as the Constitution; no other form of law has
since been exposed to more complicated interpretation.

To these difficulties Madison added a final source of "embarrassment": language. Drawing directly on John Locke's critique of
language in Book 3 of the *Essay concerning Human Understanding*,
Madison succinctly noted that "no language is so copious as to
supply words and phrases for every complex idea, or so correct
as not to include many equivocally denoting different ideas." The
more complex the object of observation was, the more likely it
was that the unavoidable ambiguity of language would introduce
further uncertainties.[9]

One might dismiss these reflections on the science of politics
as an intellectual nod to Madison's Princeton education. Not
every reader of the Constitution would be tempted to compare
the classification of political institutions to the "delicate shades
and minute gradations" among "sense, perception, judgment,
desire, volition, memory, imagination," or to benefit from a
metaphorical juxtaposition of the natural estates of animal, vegetable, and mineral with empires, kingdoms, regions, or districts.
Yet the epistemological musings of *Federalist* 37 were no mere
academic digression from the real business of constitutional
deliberation. Instead they set the foundation for the arguments
Madison deployed as he turned to the task of publicly justifying
key elements of the Constitution. Some of his most important
and instructive contributions to *The Federalist* were applications
of the rules for political study that *Federalist* 37 laid down. Nor

were these rules meant solely for the moment of ratification. In the 1820s and 1830s, the aging statesman still believed that Americans should apply moderation to their constitutional reasoning.

The Madisonian method of thinking like a constitution (to indulge that phrase) rested on two complementary propositions.[10] First, there was no alternative to describing the new system in all its messy details. One could not rely on hoary maxims that pretended to express iron rules of politics. It was not enough to say that *"imperium in imperio* [a state within a state] is a solecism in politics" in order to dismiss the division of sovereign powers under the new federal system as a recipe for a nationalist consolidation. One instead had to map the complex ways in which the federal system would operate. Nor could one merely conclude that the Constitution was defective because it violated the formulaic statements of the principle of separated powers that appeared in the state constitutions. To understand what separation of powers really meant, one had to examine how it worked in practice, and that would necessarily take some time to observe.[11]

Second, a moderate analysis of constitutional phenomena demanded greater accuracy in the use of language. Locke's lessons had to be applied. "Perspicuity therefore requires not only that ideas should be distinctly formed, but that they should be expressed by words distinctly and exclusively appropriated to them."[12] The difficulty of doing that in practice provided an incentive and rationale for linguistic clarity. One path to this clarity could be essentially definitional in nature. Madison offered two noteworthy examples of this in *Federalist* 10 when he defined the key words "faction" and "democracy." But the ideal of perspicuity needed more than definitional precision. It also required what modern scholars (in other contexts) call "thick description." One could not reduce an open-ended, multifaceted concept like federalism or sovereignty or the separation of powers or statehood to a simple verbal formula. Such concepts had to be constructed inductively, in part by parsing the complexities of the constitutional text but also by observing the actual practice that Americans followed. In key passages of *Federalist* 39 and then in *Federalist* 47–48, Madison directly applied the analytical model of *Federalist* 37 to describe the core concepts of federalism and separation of powers.

The argument of *Federalist* 39 rested on two questions: "whether the general form and aspect of the government be strictly republican"; and whether it would replace "the *federal* form, which regards the union as a *confederacy* of sovereign states," with "a national *government*, which regards the union as a *consolidation* of the states." In the first case, one could not adequately describe a national republic from the existing examples often cited, which included states as disparate as Holland, Venice, Poland, and England. All contained monarchical or hereditary elements that Americans could never accept as republican. One had to define a republic on other principles. Here Madison set up two criteria: it must be "a government which derives all its powers directly or indirectly from the great body of the people; and is administered by persons holding their offices during pleasure, for a limited period, or during good behaviour." This definition was less open-ended than the one John Adams had used in his *Thoughts on Government* (1776): "Of Republics, there is an inexhaustable variety, because the possible combinations of the powers of society, are capable of innumerable variations."[13] But Madison's criteria for a republic allowed a wide range of applications that could then be assessed on their merits.

A better demonstration of his method comes, however, in the second half of *Federalist* 39, where he rebutted the accusation that the Constitution treated "the union as a *consolidation* of the states."[14] To weigh this charge, one first had "to ascertain the real character of the government in question." The idea of "real character" is another illustration of Madison's underlying empiricism, his aversion to systems planned in the "closet" or "imagination" of an abstract theorist. In 1788 one could not yet test the character of the Constitution against the lessons of experience. But its dimensions could still be mapped by identifying the specific modes or vectors along which "federal" and "national" characteristics would operate. To those who conceived the future of American federalism as a zero-sum struggle between the union and the states, Madison's analysis would seem deeply flawed or overly complex. No fewer than five categories defined the matrix of federal relations, he argued, and that configuration was hardly elegant. As a measure of Madison's patience with distinctions, descriptions, and nuance, few of his paragraphs can surpass the conclusion of *Federalist* 39:

> The proposed Constitution therefore is in strictness neither a national nor a federal constitution; but a composition of both. In its foundation, it is federal, not national; in the sources from which the ordinary powers of the Government are drawn, it is partly federal, and partly national: in the operation of these powers, it is national, not federal: In the extent of them again, it is federal, not national: And finally, in the authoritative mode of introducing amendments, it is neither wholly federal, nor wholly national.[15]

The truths of American federalism could thus be found only in its details.

The famous analysis of the separation of powers in *Federalist* 47–51 unfolds in a similar fashion. Here, again, Madison began with the problem of definition, treating "the celebrated Montesquieu" as "the oracle who is always consulted and cited on this subject." Madison likely applied to "oracle" its dual meaning—to be at once authoritative yet also enigmatic in a pronouncement. To reconstruct both Montesquieu's meaning and its relevance to Americans, Madison continued, one had to reason from "the source from which the maxim was drawn," the British constitution that Montesquieu admired. If one discovered that existing British practice did *not* make the departments "totally separate and distinct from each other," then a vast space opened where some intermingling of the three forms of power became possible. Madison reached the same conclusion by examining how American constitutions applied the doctrine of Montesquieu in practice. Here, too, the applications proved quite varied.[16]

Once this thick description amplified the definition, one could then ask which institution posed the greatest threat to the separation of powers. The state constitutions treated these dangers as symmetrical, potentially emanating from any of the three departments. Yet that presumption hardly accorded with American experience. "But the most dangerous branch of government," Madison wrote in *Federalist* 48, was manifestly the legislature, which "is everywhere extending the sphere of its activity, and drawing all power into its impetuous vortex." Its "superiority" rested on two conditions. One was the "intrepid confidence" the legislature gained from its intimate political connections with the people. The other was the advantage it wielded because legislative power, by its very nature, was "at once more extensive, and less susceptible of precise limits," than the implementing powers exercised by the other branches.[17]

Like the discussion of federalism in *Federalist* 39, these two initial essays on the separation of powers exemplify a Madisonian mode of political analysis. That way of thinking like a constitution requires, first, a search for perspicuity in the definition of key terms; second, a willingness to derive an array of applied or potential meanings from the evidence of practice; and third, and most important, a diagnostic capacity to identify and measure the real forces that animate political action. For Madison, this last challenge involved weighing the deliberative and decision-making capacity of institutions against the life force of political life that swirled through the interests, opinions, and passions of the people themselves. That life force generated the concerns of republican politics, but for Madison the constitutionalist it operated as both a resource and a potential danger.

Nowhere is Madison's preoccupation with this challenge more evident than in *Federalist* 49–50, the surprising diversion that precedes the concluding judgments of *Federalist* 51. Here Madison went out of his way to discuss Jefferson's proposal, in his 1783 "draught" of a constitution for Virginia, to submit disputes among the departments to popularly elected conventions, which could meet occasionally or periodically either to keep the framework of government in its proper trim or to make such "alterations" (a term inherited from Locke) as now seemed necessary. There was no obvious reason in 1788 to pursue or even discuss Jefferson's idea. It was neither part of the Constitution that Madison was defending nor a remedy that Anti-Federalists were advocating. Madison's latent purpose was to show that "the people themselves" were incompetent to arbitrate constitutional disputes. Some other scheme of separated powers, embedded in institutions of government, was the default option that Americans had to accept.

Federalist 49 developed this position with three main objections to the idea of occasional conventions. The first two rested on Madison's apprehensions over the psychological dimensions of constitutional decision making. The third involved a specific political analysis of where the real danger of constitutional encroachments lay.

Madison's initial concern was with the place of *veneration* in maintaining constitutional stability. This was not an attitude that he valued blindly or with quite the same reverence that Edmund Burke soon expressed in his *Reflections on the Revolution in France*. Back in *Federalist* 14, Madison, in full rhetorical flight, had pointedly reminded his readers: "Is it not the glory of the people of America, that, whilst they have paid a decent regard to the opinions of former times and other nations, they have not suffered a blind veneration for antiquity, for custom, or for names, to overrule the suggestions of their own good sense, the knowledge of their own situation, and the lessons of their own experience?"[18] Given a choice between a failing Confederation and the promise of an extended national republic, should not Americans revive their "manly spirit" of 1776? But one could still distinguish moments when a revolutionary choice had to be made from those occurring over the long run of constitutional governance. Escaping tyranny and maintaining constitutional stability were vastly different phenomena. The first risk of Jefferson's proposal was that, if used with any frequency, it might "deprive the government of that veneration which time bestows on every thing, and without which perhaps the wisest and freest governments would not possess the requisite stability."[19] Madison's own assessment of the ambiguous nature of separation of powers implied that this would be a recurring challenge.

The problem, however, was not merely that there would be repeated appeals to popular judgment. It was also that citizens lacked the independent judgment required to assess these conflicts rationally. This observation rested on a recurring theme in Madison's assessment of the nature of *individual* opinion. Anticipating the famous analysis of democratic opinion associated with Alexis de Tocqueville, Madison assumed that the political judgment of an individual citizen would "depend much on the number which he supposes to have entertained the same opinion." If one worried that mass opinion would prove unstable, fostering a culture of veneration for the Constitution would not be "a superfluous advantage" to maintaining the stability of the republic. It would be one thing if Americans were "a nation of philosophers," capable of ruling on the basis of "enlightened reason" rather than needing to rely on the authority of precedent. But that was "as little to be expected as the philosophical race of kings wished for by Plato."[20]

Madison then turned to the conditions that would likely operate if Jefferson's proposal took effect. Thinking historically, Madison recalled the circumstances of the initial drafting of the state constitutions a decade earlier. True, conditions then had done "much honor to the virtue and intelligence of the people of America." Yet it also "must be confessed," he added, "that the experiments are of too ticklish a nature to be unnecessarily multiplied." One had "to recollect" the favorable conditions of 1776. Then,

> all the existing constitutions were formed in the midst of a danger which repressed the passions most unfriendly to order and concord; of an enthusiastic confidence of the people in their patriotic leaders, which stifled the ordinary diversity of opinions on great national questions; of a universal ardor for new and opposite forms, produced by a universal resentment and indignation against the ancient government; and whilst no spirit of party connected with the changes to be made, or the abuses to be reformed, could mingle its leaven in the operation.[21]

No such "equivalent security" of circumstances could be expected in the future.

What conditions would apply instead? If the goal of the separation of powers was "maintaining the constitutional equilibrium of the government," one had to return to the real balance of forces among the departments. The most likely source of appeals would come from the weaker branches of executive and judiciary. The legislature would enjoy all the "advantages" of numbers, proximity to "the people at large," and "connections of blood, of friendship, and of acquaintance." Historically its members were also meant to act as "the confidential guardians of the rights and liberties of the people." How could the two weaker, politically disconnected branches possibly prevail against this superiority?[22]

From a modern perspective, Madison's weighing of the respective strength of different institutions seems naive. Even in the 1780s, the examples set by two popularly elected governors—George Clinton in New York and John Hancock in Massachusetts, the dominant figures in the politics of their states—could have pointed his thinking along a different path. But Madison's driving conviction then was that the legislature was the dominant institution of popular government because of the political intimacy its members possessed with ordinary citizens. Implicit in this formulation was the recognition that the people would often prove the real source of mischief. The problem was not merely that legislators would be their political favorites but, more important, that they would also act as the instrument of their constituents' interests, opinions, and passions. When lawmakers encroached on the just powers of other departments, they would accurately reflect factious pressures coming from "the people themselves."

True, there might be occasions when the misdeeds of the legislature were "so flagrant and so sudden, as to admit of no specious coloring." At such moments, the people could readily slough their "prepossessions in favor of the legislative party." Yet, even then, their response "could never be expected to turn on the true merits of the question." It would still fall prey to improper factors—to "the spirit of preexisting parties" or new parties created by the pending controversy, the influence of prominent individuals or the participants in the disputed "measures." "The *passions*, therefore, not the *reason* of the public would sit in judgment." But it was constitutional reason that would be needed, Madison insisted, not political passion. Any controversy serious enough to warrant appealing to their authority would bring the people to a condition too impassioned and opinionated to enable them to exercise civic reason.[23]

The strange digression of *Federalist* 49 thus offers a remarkable insight into Madison's thinking. Taken to its logical conclusion, his argument implies that thereafter there would rarely if ever be a moment when the people could safely exercise their constitutional reason. Their role in constitutional decision making had to be a one-off affair. It could be exercised, with fingers crossed, only when necessity required a document to be adopted. Thereafter it had to rest, at least until an occasion for constitutional *amendment* arose. The idea of engaging the people *actively* in pending constitutional controversies risked too much. Given a choice between the veneration required for constitutional stability and the democratic propriety of allowing a sovereign people to choose for itself, Madison decisively favored the side of stability. *Federalist* 49–50 were thus entirely consistent with the reservations about public opinion that he had conveyed to Randolph only weeks earlier.

It was the great irony of the ratification struggle of 1787–88 that Federalists had to accommodate their elitist ideas to the democratic sentiments that the revolution had released. Federalists wanted the United States to be governed by a class of leaders superior to the amateurs, hacks, and demagogues who dominated state politics. In the famous phrasing of *Federalist* 10, they wanted a legislature composed "of a chosen body of citizens, whose wisdom may best discern the true interest of their country, and whose patriotism and love of justice, will be least likely to sacrifice it to temporary or partial considerations." Yet Federalists had to align this image with the popular, even populist tendencies of American politics. In Gordon Wood's influential words, "The Federalists in 1787 hastened the destruction of whatever chance there was in America for the growth of an avowedly aristocratic conception of politics and thereby contributed to the creation of that encompassing liberal tradition which has mitigated and often obscured the real social antagonisms of American politics." They had "little choice in the matter," Wood adds, because the predominance of republican ideas made it impossible to justify the Constitution on any other grounds.[24]

The dynamic nature of republican politics and the need to accommodate elite decisions to popular expectations became evident as soon as the First Congress met. Following the precedent set by the ratification conventions, the House of Representatives opened its debates to journalists. Their reports were quickly reprinted across the country. That departure immediately distinguished the new Congress from its predecessor, the Continental Congress. Though the Senate did not open its doors for another six years, a critical precedent was thus set. The people's elected representatives would adhere to new norms that made their deliberations as well as their decisions a matter of public record.

Taken together, the ratification campaign of 1787–88, the first federal elections, and the doings of Congress demonstrated the

possibility of a truly national politics. Yet an even greater departure emerged in the realization that public opinion was something
that national leaders could actively mobilize and manipulate. That
recognition grew more evident as disagreements over national
policies began to simmer and then to boil in the early 1790s.
The financial program of Secretary of the Treasury Alexander
Hamilton provided the initial basis for these disagreements.
But the impact of the French Revolution soon compounded that
domestic stimulus. After 1793 foreign policy replaced Hamilton's
program as the great source of contention in national politics.
Both sets of issues raised important questions about the relation
between Congress and the executive. With Hamilton's program,
the main issue was the dominant influence that a minister of state
seemed to hold over Congress. In the realm of foreign policy,
the primacy of the presidency in decision making challenged
standing assumptions about the principle of legislative supremacy
in a republican government.[25]

These disputes had two major consequences that transcended
the specific policies in question. One was the development of
the first political party system—the competition between pro-
administration Federalists, led by Hamilton, and the opposition
Republican party that Madison and Jefferson began forming
in 1791. That party system originated in divisions within the
national government, but it quickly escalated into partisan electoral competition at the constituency level. The climactic event
in the emergence of this system was the election of 1800–1801,
which ended in a rocky but eventually successful transition of
power from one party to another.[26]

The second major consequence involved the evolution of inno-
vative modes of constitutional interpretation as both a source
of political dispute and its continuation by other means. The
significance of this point cannot be overestimated. Constitutional
arguments had figured prominently in Anglo-American political discourse well before the revolutionary controversy. But the
adoption of a written constitution as a statement of fundamental
law added a new dimension to the rhetorical invocation of constitutional norms. The questions of how a constitution was to
be *interpreted*, of determining which methods one would use to
ascertain its proper meaning, or deciding whether an action was

constitutionally legitimate or not, were all matters for which there were as yet no definitive answers. Nor could one expect to find the answers to these questions solely within the realm of judicial discourse. Though the concept of judicial review of legislative acts was part of the original understanding of the Constitution, no one in the 1790s would have said that the courts were the only locus of interpretive authority. Congress and the president were also entitled to act on their own constitutional judgments.[27]

In formulating approaches to these questions, the members of Congress and the administration naturally had to find ways to merge their political preferences with their constitutional judgments. Constitutional uncertainties never arose in a political vacuum. They were never exercises in a purely disinterested or objective judgment. No one set out to determine what the Constitution would mean in the abstract. It was the flow of policy and events, not intellectual curiosity, which raised these questions. There was no finite or readily visible boundary between the realms of political choice and constitutional interpretation. Political disagreements readily escalated into constitutional arguments; alternative readings of the Constitution helped to generate political disputes.[28] The creation of an opposition political party could itself be seen as evidence of enmity to the Constitution, if its actions or sentiments seemed to verge toward sedition. Yet parties could also become vehicles for creative discussion, posing and sharpening the choices that citizens and their representatives had to make. Indeed, promoting the creative role that parties should play in shaping civic public opinion became another crucial innovation of the 1790s.

Madison was involved in every facet of this process, and this involvement pushed his political and constitutional thinking in new directions. When he discussed the mischiefs of faction in *Federalist* 10, he had been contemplating *not* the workings of organized political parties but rather the swirl of competing interests and opinions within society. When he observed in *Federalist* 37 that the meaning of "all new laws" must "be liquidated and ascertained by a series of particular discussions and adjudications," he was imagining a set of focused analyses of individual clauses, not the evolution of distinct theories of constitutional interpretation. When he thought about the potential role of public opinion in the mediation of constitutional disputes, he worried that the people themselves might be the real source of many controversies while doubting that citizens could exercise the collective reason required "to controul and regulate the government." The idea that political parties might appeal to the general public on constitutional questions was not yet part of his imagination.

Over the course of the 1790s, Madison's constitutional thinking evolved in new and significant ways. Numerous scholars have long fretted over what Wood calls "the James Madison problem." In its customary form, the crux of that problem lies in reconciling the "fervent nationalist" of the 1780s, the advocate of the negative on state laws, with "the strict constructionist, states' rights cofounder" of the Republican party. To put the point more simply: how did the proponent of a congressional negative on state laws in 1787 become the author of the Virginia Resolutions of 1798? Wood's answer to that problem suggests that the emphasis on this one transformation misses its true origins. The deeper source of Madison's and Jefferson's opposition politics pivoted on their accurate perception that Hamilton wanted to build an American version of the modern fiscal-military state, a nation-state that came encumbered with a potent executive, but one that could still be linked with the mechanisms of representative government.[29] As Hamilton advanced his agenda in 1791, his conception of the nature of the American republic, and more specifically of the relation between the executive and Congress, became evident, identifying constitutional questions that Madison had not previously or adequately considered.

Without challenging this interpretation, there is another way to portray Madison's evolution or transformation in the 1790s. As a political thinker, he was, above all things, deeply empirical. He had expectations for how he wanted the constitutional system to operate, and he worried actively about the means of maintaining constitutional stability. But like any engaged and contemplative leader, he also understood that the passage of time introduced new evidence and new perspectives into the political landscape. He was always mindful of the differences between the republican assumptions of 1776 and the critical opportunity that the Federal Convention could seize a decade later. When

Madison thought about the shortcomings of the republican constitutionalists of the mid-1770s, he drew on his own experience to
fashion lessons to be learned.[30] And when he considered the novel
developments that accompanied the early implementation of the
Constitution, he had fresh data to consider. As John Ferejohn
shrewdly observes, the events of the 1790s allow us to view "the
empirical and pragmatic Madison as he attempted to assimilate
new and unexpected information about how and how well the
new government worked and where it was in further need of
repair and redesign."[31]

Thus to pose the "Madison problem" as a simple matter of
explaining the ostensible inconsistency between the nationalist of
the late 1780s and the putative exponent of a states'-rights position
in 1798 overlooks a greater difficulty. When one is politically
active in the way that Madison certainly was, the continuous
challenge of public life is to adjust to the unanticipated and the
unexpected. That is exponentially more the case when public life
involves the implementation of a new constitution, the creation
of the working institutions of a modern nation-state, and the
response to the world-historical upheaval of the French Revolution. Under these conditions, there should be a better way of
explaining the changes in his thinking than fretting about an
apparent inconsistency that is itself far less significant than is
often thought. In fact, Madison had clearly anticipated the supposed heresies of the "Doctrine of 1798" a decade earlier, when
he argued, in *Federalist* 46 and again in *Federalist* 51, that the state
governments would retain some political authority to challenge
the misuse of federal authority. What he did not and perhaps
could not have anticipated then was the way in which the active
use of presidential and executive authority could reshape the
political landscape. It was in the realm of separation of powers,
far more than federalism, that the most significant departures
and developments occurred.

At the start of this period, during President Washington's first
term, Madison's constitutional concerns remained consistent with
his prior beliefs. One aspiration of 1787–88 did prove a quick
disappointment—the prediction expressed in *Federalist* 10 that
elections for the extended republic would yield a higher caliber
of representatives than the states typically produced. Scanning

the list of his future colleagues in the House, Madison grumbled that he saw only "a very scanty proportion who will share in the drudgery of business."[32] The true "genius" of the new government would still require "experimental instruction," he wrote Jefferson in late March 1789. "Were I to advance a conjecture, it would be, that the predictions of an anti-democratic operation will be confronted with at least a sufficient number of the features which have marked the State Governments."[33]

The dispute over Hamilton's proposal to secure a congressional charter for a national bank that preoccupied the third session of the First Congress in the winter of 1791 played upon Madison's fear of the unlimited exercise of legislative power. Hamilton and his supporters relied on the Necessary and Proper Clause of Article I, Section 8, to provide the requisite authority. Madison and Secretary of State Jefferson disputed that claim. Believing that the "impetuous vortex" of the legislature posed the greatest threat to constitutional stability, Madison hardly welcomed an open-ended interpretation of the Necessary and Proper Clause that left Congress free to judge the extent of its jurisdiction. The power to issue charters of incorporation was substantive and consequential in its own right. It was too important a matter to be left to constitutional inference or construction. He had acted on that assumption at Philadelphia in 1787, when he proposed giving such a power to Congress. That motion failed, not least because many framers believed that the Necessary and Proper Clause made such a power superfluous.

Yet in *Federalist* 44 he had defended that clause with a typically Madisonian set of reasons that laid out "four other possible methods" with which the Constitution might have dealt with this problem. Had it echoed Article II of the Confederation in limiting Congress to "expressly" delegated powers, it would have exposed the new government to the same embarrassments its predecessor had suffered, forcing it to rely on the "doctrine of *construction* or *implication*." Had it provided "a positive enumeration" of all the requisite powers the government might henceforth use, the Convention would have had to draft "a complete digest of laws on every subject to which the Constitution relates." Had it taken the opposite approach by listing powers the new government could not exercise, it would have pursued an equally "chimerical" path,

potentially permitting the use of every power not proscribed. Or
had it simply remained "silent on this head," it would have left
the Constitution vulnerable to all the criticisms that were being
leveled against the use of "necessary and proper." On this last
point Madison noted, "No axiom is more clearly established in
law, or in reason, than that wherever the end is required, the
means are authorized; wherever a general power to do a thing is
given, every particular power necessary for doing it is included."[34]
This was the principle and even the language that Hamilto-
nians invoked during the debates of 1791. But from Madison's
perspective in 1788 the advantage of the clause as written was
that it at least established a standard that one could dispute. One
must still search for the "true meaning" of the text. That inquiry
would begin in Congress. Should Congress err, "the success of the
usurpation will depend on the executive and judiciary departments" and then on the voice of the voters. In this controversy, the
state legislatures would stand "ready to mark the innovation, to
sound the alarm to the people, and to exert their local influence
in effecting a change of federal representatives."[35] *Federalist* 44
thus supports a reading of the Necessary and Proper Clause
that was conducive to Hamilton's claim for the constitutionality
of the bank charter; consistent with the role that Washington
played in taking constitutional counsel from Madison, Jefferson,
Attorney General Randolph, and Hamilton before signing the
act; and anticipatory of the political strategies that Madison and
Jefferson followed as their criticism of Hamiltonian policies led
them to organize the opposition Republican party.
    That opposition had both political and constitutional dimen-
sions (and personal ones as well). Hamilton and his supporters
wondered what had happened to Madison. Perhaps he had suc-
cumbed to Jefferson's dark influence, tainted with its French fla-
vors. Hamilton also recalled "an afternoon's walk" with Madison
during the Convention, when they had agreed on the utility of
uniting the national and state public debt.[36] In 1790, Madison's
opposition to the assumption of state debts led to the famous
compromise that placed the future national capital along the
mosquito-infested marshes of the Potomac. A deeper source of
division rested on a fundamental disagreement over American
policy toward Britain. Hamilton's revenue system depended on

a steady flow of British imports, but the Virginians, convinced that Britain was pursuing predatory policies against the United States, wanted to use commercial sanctions to open imperial markets to American produce.

These were, however, disputes over policy that lacked constitutional implications. The bank question was different, because a plausible interpretation of the Necessary and Proper Clause was required. Madison's departure from the ideas expressed in *Federalist* 44 was significant. Even so, his opposition to a latitudinarian reading of the Necessary and Proper Clause did remain consistent with his long-standing concern with the problem of circumscribing the scope of legislative power. Yet by 1791 Madison and Jefferson could no longer divorce this issue from the larger Hamiltonian program. As Wood observes, Hamilton's distinctive role as a state builder on the British model made it impossible for the Virginians to isolate the issue of the bank from a broader nexus of positions that they also opposed on principle.

The constitutional implications of Hamilton's agenda went well beyond his expansive reading of congressional power. Hamilton had a sophisticated understanding of his status as secretary of the treasury. No one—not even his cabinet rival, Jefferson, who had notable political skills of his own—was better prepared to realize the possibilities of his office. Hamilton had written perceptively about this in *Federalist* 36. Most nations, even those "of the more popular kind, usually commit the administration of their finances to single men or to boards composed of a few individuals," who first prepare "the plans of taxation" that "the sovereign or legislature" later adopt.[37] This was not just the role that Hamilton conceived for himself; it also conformed to the expectations that many congressmen actively expected him to fulfill.

Hamilton's conception of his ministerial role was linked to his professed fondness for the British constitution. That was well known within the political elite from his Convention speech of June 18, 1787. His Humean admiration of the virtues of political corruption, boldly pronounced at a Jefferson dinner party in August 1791, offered further evidence of his intentions. Not only did his *policies* seem contrived to enable the new government to emulate the British state, his *politics* also seemed to reflect an effort to apply a British model of ministerial influence over Congress. Madison was the single most respected member of Congress, but Hamilton was still able to develop supportive coalitions in both houses.

On the basis of these perceptions, Madison and Jefferson developed a strategy for creating an opposition political party. The initial struggle took place within the confines of the national government, where its goals were to fashion working majorities within Congress but also to appeal to the president as the ultimate decision maker. That was one of the fascinating aspects of the final phase of the bank dispute. When the framers gave the president a limited veto over legislation, they conceived it primarily as a defensive weapon against the "usurpations" and "encroachments" of Congress. Yet in *Federalist* 44 Madison did imagine the president wielding a veto for constitutional purposes. That was exactly the situation the bank bill created once it passed Congress. Washington was happy to take constitutional counsel from Madison, Jefferson, Attorney General Edmund Randolph, and Hamilton. That had been his style of command as wartime commander-in-chief, and as president he attempted to maintain it. But Hamilton was the one he asked to write last, at far greater length, and with his opponents' objections all at hand to refute.

The increasingly bitter and rancorous competition within the administration lasted well into the summer of 1792. It took the president some time to gauge the depth of this quarrel. Once he did, he made his best effort to convince his ministers to act as he had expected his generals to do during the war—to no avail. The one point that united Hamilton, Jefferson, and Madison was the conviction that Washington had to serve a second term rather than make the idiosyncratic Vice President John Adams his likely successor.[38]

Embedded within this conflict was the growing recognition that control of the government depended on command of the presidency. That perception would have been difficult to fashion in 1787, when the office's political potentiality seemed so uncertain. Moreover, Washington's presence arguably made it more, not less, difficult to assess how the office would operate with presidents who lacked his unique character. Still, his role in resolving the bank debate was a marker of the central importance of the office. That importance would only grow when questions of foreign policy came to the fore after 1793, and when the presidency became the object of direct partisan competition, as it finally did in 1796.

Before then, however, the first step that Madison and Jefferson took involved appealing to public opinion. Hamilton already had a prominent newspaper supporting his program—the *Gazette of the United States*, edited by John Fenno. Three days after Washington signed the bank act on February 25, 1791, Jefferson wrote one of Madison's classmates from Princeton, the poet Philip Freneau, to invite him to work as a translator within the State Department. He would not have that much official work, Jefferson told Freneau, should he wish to pursue "any other calling."[39] But the real calling they wanted Freneau to fill was to counter Fenno. After some dithering, Freneau accepted the invitation, and the first issue of his *National Gazette* appeared on the last day of October 1791.

Madison was an early contributor. His first essay, the lengthy "Population and Emigration," appeared in mid-November. His second paper, "Consolidation," was a better indicator of what was to come. Here Madison contrasted the dangers that any effort to consolidate the separate states into one government would produce with the advantages that would flow from whatever promoted "the mutual confidence and affection" of the states and "concord and confidence throughout the great body of the people." The more the latter existed, the better prepared Americans would be to "take the alarm at usurpation or oppression" and thus to "*consolidate* their defence of the public liberty."[40] The dozen and a half of these "party press" essays that Madison wrote in 1791–92 marked an initial though still primitive attempt to develop a party platform.[41] In length and style, these pieces contrast significantly with Madison's writings as Publius. Not only the essays themselves but their paragraphs and sentences are much shorter and more pointed. Propositions are stated clearly and directly. Readers are given relatively simple choices to make, finally culminating in a straightforward set of topics—"The Spirit of Governments"; "The union: Who are its real friends?"; "A candid State of Parties"; and "Who Are the Best Keepers of the People's Liberties?"—on which the final choices devolved into "Republican" and "Anti-republican" interests.

The underlying assumption of these essays was that "public opinion sets bounds to every government, and is the real sovereign in every free one." The first part of this sentence had become a commonplace in eighteenth-century thinking. But the second part, read either literally or liberally, supported a broader conception of the role of public opinion in republican government. Madison offered an interesting explication of this point by observing that, "in proportion as government is influenced by opinion, it must be so, by whatever influences opinion. This decides the question concerning a *Constitutional Declaration of Rights*, which requires ['acquires' was the intended word] an influence on government, by becoming a part of public opinion." This idea was consistent with Madison's thinking in 1788, when he observed that a bill of rights would "acquire by degrees the character of fundamental maxims of free Government, and as they become incorporated with the national sentiment, counteract the impulses of interest and passion."[42] But in that statement a bill of rights would operate as its values were inculcated among the citizens, acting as conscientious constraints moderating their behavior. By contrast, in 1791 Madison was imagining this incorporation of sentiment working as a restraint on government. That position was closer to the rationale that the Anti-Federalist writer Federal Farmer had laid down for a bill of rights. Without such a text to signal the limits of government power, the Farmer warned, the people would be unable to know, and thus to react, when government exceeded its just authority.[43]

From essay to essay, Madison was modeling the role that citizens should play in maintaining the constitutional structure. The success of that model depended on the diffusion of information across society, no easy matter in the extended American republic. Madison thus endorsed every mechanism that "facilitates a general intercourse of sentiments," with an emphasis on the role of newspapers and the value of having "representatives going from, and returning among every part" of the people.[44] But the broader project was to turn citizens into constitutional monitors. In a "representative republic," Madison wrote in the essay "Government," "every good citizen will be at once a centinel over the rights of the people; over the authorities of the confederal government; and over both the rights and the authorities of the intermediate [the state] governments."[45] To secure that end, Madison continued in his next essay, "Charters," Americans had to appreciate the novelty of their "revolution": "In Europe, charters of liberty have been granted by power. America has set the example, and France has followed it, of charters of power granted by liberty." Beyond the pride Americans should feel in this achievement, they also had to accept the "vigilance" that was now their duty as citizens. The "complicated" system they had created, the "compound republic" of *Federalist* 51, "requires a more than common reverence for the authority which is to preserve order thro' the whole"—that is, their own "popular charters" of government.[46]

In describing this duty, Madison was invoking a more advanced model of the role of public opinion in government. "All power has been traced up to opinion," he observed. "The stability of all governments and security of all rights may be traced to the same source." Citizens had to show "the same keenness" in marking the boundaries of "their governments as delineated in the *great charters*" that they attached to protecting their "dearest rights; until every citizen shall be an ARGUS to espy, and an Ægeon to avenge, the unhallowed deed" of a trespass on the Constitution. Opinion in this sense had a meaning quite distinct from the use of that term in *Federalist* 10, where Madison listed "a zeal for different opinions concerning religion, concerning government, and many other points, as well of speculation as of practice" first in order (though not in importance) among "the latent causes of faction." In 1787 opinion was simply another form of personal preference. Four years later, in the party press essays, public opinion was something to be constructed and then devoted to "guarantee, with a holy zeal, these political scriptures from every attempt to add to or diminish from them."[47]

Madison may well have had another project in mind when he was preparing these brief essays. As Colleen Sheehan argues in *The Mind of James Madison*, the reading notes upon which Madison drew while drafting his contributions to the *National Gazette* seem to express broader purposes. It is at least conceivable, Sheehan suggests, that Madison was planning "to produce a scholarly treatise on politics." Such a treatise would have developed a comprehensive theory of republicanism and included substantial treatment of the writings of antiquity.[48] Madison's reading notes also indicate that he wanted to develop some of the key propositions he had laid down in 1787–88. In a fascinating passage, we find Madison musing about the argument of *Federalist* 10: "The best provision for a stable and free Govt. is not a balance in the powers of the Govt. tho' that is not to be neglected, but an equilibrium in the interests & passions of the Society itself, which can not be attained in a small Society. Much has been said on the first. The last deserves a thorough investigation."[49]

Madison then left an interior note to a further reflection that appears to be a dig against John Adams and potentially Hamilton. The existence of "natural divisions in all political societies" precluded the need for creating "artificial distinctions, as kings & nobles," to form additional "checks and balances." The "existing vices—avarice and vanity—cowardice & malice—&c" would do the work without having to promote "new vices."

Madison's scholarly interest in developing his theory of republicanism was soon overtaken by the flow of events, which in turn refocused his concern with the workings of institutions. While he was writing the party press essays, Hamilton opened a new chapter in his legislative agenda with his "Report on Manufactures," which proposed federal bounties for nascent industries. Hamilton drew upon the opening clause of Article I, Section 8, which allowed Congress to use its authority over taxation to provide for the "general welfare of the United States." Taking that claim literally, Madison concluded, would destroy the basic principle of the Constitution. "If not only the *means,* but the *objects* are unlimited, the parchment had better be thrown into the fire at once."[50] This notion of general welfare "broaches a new constitutional doctrine of vast consequence," one capable of "subverting the fundamental and characteristic principle of the Constitution" by destroying the basic principle that the government could discharge only its "enumerated powers."[51] In 1789 Madison had actively worked to prevent the eventual Tenth Amendment from being saddled with the loaded word "explicitly" to describe the powers delegated to Congress. But the obverse possibility—that a declaratory statement of the general purposes of government could be translated into a license for unlimited legislative power that would trump the enumerated objects of Article I, Section 8—was equally dangerous.

These concerns persuaded Madison and Jefferson that the formation of an opposition party was essential. Yet basic questions remained about its purposes and extent. Was it primarily a mechanism for coordinating opposition within Congress by mobilizing public opinion "out-of-doors"? Would it require forging coalitions with political interests in the states? Would its success depend on capturing the presidency, whenever the incumbent retired to his vines and figs at Mount Vernon, which would in turn require figuring out how to manipulate the untested system of presidential electors? Perhaps most important, would the initial cluster of domestic controversies driven by the Hamiltonian program retain the staying power to provide a durable framework for party competition? Or might Hamilton's very success obviate the need for party competition?

The untested variable in this matrix was the effect that issues of foreign policy might exert in reinforcing the original basis for party conflict. The framers of the Constitution had correctly estimated that the United States would not live blissfully isolated from the imperial conflicts of the Atlantic world. Americans expected Old World conflicts to have New World reverberations. The influence that Britain and Spain could respectively exert along the nation's northern and southwestern borders would obviously affect the expansion of American settlement. Hamilton's financial program depended on maintaining amicable relations with Britain.

These were important issues of public policy. But did they also have the potential to promote the development of national political parties? The party press essays contain only a few casual references to the French Revolution. Not that affairs in France were wholly absent from Madison's thinking. He was an early enthusiast of the French constitution of 1791 and a congressional resolution congratulating "the French Nation" on its adoption. He celebrated the early course of the French Revolution "because it has grown as it were out of the American revolution."[52] He was pleased to receive honorary citizenship in the French republic, joining Washington and Hamilton as the three Americans so recognized.[53]

As Washington began his second term, however, the political calculus of foreign relations shifted dramatically. America's

wartime ally, King Louis XVI, had lost his head to that pur-
portedly merciful mode of execution, the guillotine; Britain had
entered the counter-revolutionary war against France; and the
administration had to consider whether the United States was
bound to support its French ally under the treaty of alliance of
1778. The discussion of the last point took place in mid-April and
early May 1793, well after Madison left Philadelphia for Virginia.
To guide these discussions, Washington sent a memorandum of
thirteen questions to his cabinet, most of it prepared, Jefferson
quickly surmised, by Hamilton.[54] The cabinet quickly agreed
on two points. First, the president should issue a proclamation
to prevent American citizens from interfering in the hostilities
between Britain and France. Second, he should officially receive
the new French emissary, *citoyen* Edmond Genet. The cabinet also
unanimously agreed that Congress need not be called into session
to give the president its advice, either as to the meaning of the
treaty of alliance (a senatorial question) or the propriety of going
to war (a matter for both houses). But many of Washington's other
queries, relating to the ongoing nature of the French alliance,
remained subjects of strained debate.

That debate became a matter of open public controversy once
Hamilton began publishing his Pacificus letters favoring an
accommodation with Britain over the alliance with France. The
execution of Louis XVI made it easier to challenge the vitality of
that alliance, but other issues also came into play. Just as Hamilton
was a lawyer's lawyer, so he was also an advocate's advocate, and
no one was better prepared to defend a policy of strict neutrality.
That was what led Jefferson to dragoon Madison into taking up
the pen to oppose Hamilton. "For god's sake, my dear Sir, take up
your pen, select the most striking heresies, and cut him to p[ie]ces
in the face of the public," an agonized Jefferson wrote Madison.
"There is no one else who can & will enter the lists against him."[55]

Madison was not eager to joust. Rebutting Hamilton would
require resources not readily available at Montpelier, as well
as adopting a reasoned tone of address very different from
the concise party essays of 1792. "None but intelligent readers
will enter into such a controversy," Madison replied on July 22,
"and to their minds it ought principally to be accommodated."[56]
Madison unhappily "forced myself into the task of a reply. I can

truly say I find it the most grating one I ever experienced." The sweltering heat of a Virginia drought was one irritant, but more important was "the want of counsel on some points of delicacy as well as of information as to sundry matters of fact."[57] Nevertheless, Madison's first Helvidius essay and the opening essay of Pacificus that it answered constitute a virtual locus classicus of American thinking about the nature of presidential power. Both are powerful theoretical statements, and both continue to echo in a constitutional debate that Americans will never wholly resolve.

In Madison's view, the starting point for this debate was "the extraordinary doctrine, that the power of making war and treaties, are in their nature executive; and therefore comprehended in the general grant of executive power" stated in the opening sentence of Article II, "where not specially and strictly excepted out of the grant."[58] Pacificus had acknowledged several specific exceptions: the advice and consent powers of the Senate in making appointments and treaties, and the authority of Congress to declare war and to issue letters of marque and reprisal (the eighteenth-century equivalent of "low-intensity warfare"). Where Article II mentioned other powers, such as the president's authority as commander-in-chief, or to receive ambassadors, or to take care that the laws be faithfully executed, these clauses were merely clarifying efforts "to specify and regulate the principal articles implied in the definition of Executive Power" while allowing other responsibilities "to flow from the general grant." That responsibility extended, Hamilton argued, to the duty to determine what obligations the nation had to enforce the specific terms of a treaty. Promulgating a neutrality proclamation was thus a specific and completely reasonable application of a general executive duty.[59]

Madison listed three main approaches for assessing these claims: the "authority" of prior writers, "the quality and operation of the power to make war and treaties," and the Constitution itself. The first category he quickly dismissed. Prior authorities, even "the most received jurists," had written "before a critical attention was paid to those objects, and with their eyes too much on monarchical governments." They had written, that is, before the American experiment had shifted the basis of discussion, and without considering how the existence of a republican government would alter the framework of analysis. This criticism explicitly covered Locke and Montesquieu, who were both "evidently warped" by excessive partiality to the British constitution. Madison deemed the whole appeal to prior authorities a fruitless exercise: "Let us quit a field of research which is more likely to perplex than to decide," he concluded, and instead consider "other tests of which it will be more easy to judge."[60]

Those other tests, in the spirit of *Federalist* 37, involved thinking in precise terms about the powers to be analyzed and the actual text of the Constitution. Initially Madison had accepted a definition of executive power similar to Hamilton's. In 1785 he had observed that "all the great powers which are properly executive" had been "transferd to the Fœderal Government." This was a clear reference to war and diplomacy.[61] The last clause of Article VII of the Virginia Plan proposed that the executive should "enjoy the Executive rights vested in Congress by the Confederation," which implicated the same powers. Yet when James Wilson challenged this definition at the Federal Convention, Madison readily accepted his logic. In Wilson's words, "the Prerogatives of the British Monarch" did not provide "a proper guide in defining the Executive powers. Some of these prerogatives were of a Legislative nature. Among others that of war & peace &c." Madison did not record his response to this comment, but Rufus King did. "Mad: agrees wth. Wilson in his definition of executive powers—executive powers ex vi termini [from the force of their ends] do not include the Rights of war & peace &c."[62]

Madison followed this definition in his first positive response to Hamilton's claim. The actual "execution" of treaties and wars presupposed a prior situation in which such decisions were equivalent to a legislative act. Treaties "are confessedly laws," and declarations of war had avowed legal effects. Such acts of state could never be regarded as inherently executive in nature. There was admittedly some ambiguity in the precise delineation of the legislative and executive components of the two powers. Yet even "if these powers be not in their nature purely legislative," they were sufficiently so as to validate claims for the preeminence of the legislature over the rival claims of executive authority.

This analysis is not the smoothest passage of Madisonian prose, and its labored moments illustrate his unhappy task. Yet that same difficulty underlined the essential nature of constitutional inquiry. To Madison's way of thinking, the character of the Constitution had to be determined on its own terms. In the final passage of the first Helvidius essay, he examined various clauses of the Constitution to test whether the powers to make treaties or declare war were primarily executive in nature. With the treaty power, it was the authority of the Supremacy Clause, which made treaties part of the "supreme law of the land," supplemented by the two-thirds vote of the Senate, which compensated for the absence of the House of Representatives. With the power to declare war, it was the "great principle in free government" that "those who are to *conduct a war* cannot in the nature of things, be proper or safe judges, whether *a war ought* to be *commenced, continued,* or *concluded.*" Nor, finally, could one rely on the analogy that might be drawn, under the vesting clause of Article II, with the power of the president to remove subordinate officers—the subject of the first great constitutional debate in the House of Representatives, in June 1789, and still today a source of enormous scholarly controversy.[63] There was no question that depriving the president of the power to remove subordinate officials would undermine his unique responsibility for the entire executive branch. But the legal consequences of making treaties and declaring war were qualitatively different from the strictly administrative duty of removal from office. The power to remove subordinate officers *was* properly executive in nature; the powers over treaties and war were not. That was the truth that Hamilton had confirmed five years earlier, when *Federalist* 75 patiently explained why the authority over treaties had distinctive qualities: "The power in question seems therefore to form a distinct department, and to belong properly neither to the legislative nor to the executive."[64]

What point better confirmed the wisdom of *Federalist* 37, that in the realm of separation of powers "questions daily occur in the course of practice, which prove the obscurity which reigns in these subjects"? The great puzzle that Madison now faced was finally to come to grips with the nature of executive power in a republic. The incumbency of George Washington greatly complicated the task by making it more difficult to imagine how any ordinary president would perform. Rather than face that uncertainty, he, Jefferson, and Hamilton agreed that Washington must remain in office. But Hamilton's claims, with his known admiration for the British constitution, created a fresh basis for measuring the boundaries of executive power. That task became more difficult after issues of foreign relations demonstrated the institutional and political advantages of the presidency.

Madison did not relish his polemical labors as Helvidius. A quarter century later, he closed the document known as his "Detached Memoranda" by "acknowledging" his "consciousness & regret, that it breathes a spirit which was of no advantage either to the subject, or to the Author." If any "apology" was due for its "faults," it must be recognized that he had been writing "in much haste, during an intense heat of the weather, and under an excitement stimulated by friends" reacting to the "intemperance of party" provided in Hamilton's essays, with their "perverted view" of Washington's proclamation and their "dangerous gloss on the Constitution."[65] Nor has Helvidius always received strong praise from later commentators.[66] Yet Helvidius remains significant in at least two respects. First, Madison rejected the idea that one could fix the meaning of a disputed clause by importing definitions and precedents drawn from other regimes and authorities. This constitution had to be understood on its own terms, in conformity with republican principles, without endorsing a conception of inherent executive prerogative derived from British precedent. The authority of the American conventions of 1787–88 mattered in a way that the customary conventions of British governance could not. The Constitution had transferred numerous powers long deemed part of the royal prerogative in Britain into the legislative powers enumerated in Article I, Section 8.

Second, Madison and Jefferson now had to begin reckoning with the political dimensions of executive power. Through 1792 their political struggles with Hamilton had been waged as much *within* the executive branch as *between* the executive and Congress. Hamilton and Jefferson, the rival secretaries, had competed with each other to sway Washington's opinion. So long as domestic affairs dominated the national agenda, their competition had not raised serious questions about the relative authority of the president and Congress. But as the agenda shifted to matters of war and diplomacy, the advantages of the executive came to the fore, under conditions that could hardly have been imagined a few years earlier. This shift in the character of national decision making after 1793 forced Madison to rethink essential elements of national politics.

Yet Madison's thought about this question also depended on other circumstances. Personalities mattered as well as principles, and none more than the president's. Back in May 1792, Washington had pressed Madison "on the *mode* and *time* most proper" for announcing his retirement. He had raised that issue only with a small circle of trusted advisers: Jefferson, Hamilton, Secretary of War Henry Knox, Randolph, and Madison. Washington's personal preferences for retirement were well known. It was his political concerns that needed challenging. Among these was his belief that he was "deficient in many of the essential qualifications, owing to his inexperience in the forms of public business, his unfitness to judge of legal questions, and questions arising out of the Constitution."[67] One can hardly accuse Washington of being disingenuous. Yet he had acquired substantial political experience during the revolutionary war, dealing with the Continental Congress and the state legislatures, and the bank controversy of 1791 demonstrated that he knew how to solicit and evaluate legal and constitutional advice.

Madison answered these concerns at some length. Whatever the president's qualms, no one could prove more adept than Washington "in the great point of conciliating and uniting all parties under a Govt. which had excited such violent controversies." That was "an argument for his remaining, rather than retiring, until the public opinion, the character of the Govt. and the course of its administration should be better decided, which could not fail to happen in a short time." On the other side of the question, what alternative existed? The president had three possible successors. Madison of course preferred Jefferson, but his "extreme repugnance to public life & anxiety to exchange it for his farm & his philosophy" rivaled the president's. Vice President John Adams, whom Madison never trusted, was badly compromised by "his monarchical principles, which he had not concealed." And Chief Justice John Jay, another monarchist, was still roundly "disliked & distrusted" for his role in negotiating the Treaty of Paris in 1782 and his willingness to cede navigation rights on the Mississippi in 1786.[68]

This analysis was politically astute, except in one respect—imagining that the "violent controversies" of the past few years would soon pass. The constitutional dispute over the neutrality proclamation rapidly escalated into a broader disagreement over foreign policy. Whether one was now a proponent or opponent of the French Revolution had a deeper significance than would have been the case before Britain entered the counter-revolutionary alliance and Louis XVI and Marie Antoinette met their fate at the Place de la Révolution (soon to be renamed the Place de la Concorde). Citizen Genet's efforts to mobilize American public opinion to support his country's revolution and his brazen defiance of Washington opened a fissure between the president and his two fellow Virginians, driving Jefferson and Madison to near political distraction.

By September 1793, Madison was actively contemplating how to undo the damage that "the war between the Ex[ecutive] and Genet" was inflicting on all those who favored the French cause. It might well be an uphill struggle, not least because of "the general and habitual veneration" the people felt for Washington. Madison believed that "the genuine sense of the people" remained favorable to France. Yet the question of how to mobilize and express this opinion posed a challenge. One tactic would encourage county meetings to adopt resolutions that disclaimed the conduct of Genet while reiterating why Americans should still support France. "I am not sanguine however that the effort will succeed," he gloomily wrote Jefferson. In that case, "the State Legislatures, and the federal also if possible, must be induced to take up the matter in its true point of view."[69]

Madison's tentative assessment of the possibility of making Congress the locus of opposition reflected the shifting balance of political forces in Philadelphia. The elections of 1792, which produced a House of Representatives enlarged by the first census of 1790, gave Republicans a potential majority in the lower house while the Federalists controlled the Senate.[70] But the idea of maintaining party discipline in a House composed of novice members was itself a novel concept, and one likely to be brought under severe pressure by the flow of unanticipated events. The British seizure of hundreds of American ships in the West Indies in 1793–94 was one such event. It created an entirely new agenda in which Congress concurrently debated Madison's favored scheme of imposing commercial restrictions on Britain, a Federalist plan to enlarge the army in the unlikely event of a foreign invasion, and the administration's preferred alternative of sending an emissary to London to negotiate the outstanding controversies in Anglo-American relations. After a lengthy lame-duck session that kept Congress meeting until early June 1794, the last option prevailed, and John Jay was recalled to diplomatic service.

The whole session was an object lesson in the political advantages the presidency enjoyed. Madison drew the moral as the session closed. "The influence of the Ex. on events, the use made of them, and the public confidence in the P[resident] are an over-match for all the efforts Republicanism can make," he wrote Jefferson on May 25. "The party of that sentiment in the Senate is completely wrecked; and in the H. of Reps. in a much worse condition than at an earlier period of the Session."[71] The one consolation Madison enjoyed at this time came with his courtship of the widow Dolley Payne Todd, a campaign he successfully executed with their marriage in mid-September.

Jay's mission to England imposed a moratorium on the active discussion of foreign policy, but other events further sharpened partisan conflict. Madison scanned the results of the 1794 elections with a keen eye for its implications for the balance of party strength in Congress.[72] Although he showed no sympathy for the Whiskey Rebellion, he viewed Federalist efforts to link that insurgency to the political activities of the "self-created" Democratic-Republican societies as a demagogic "attack on the most sacred principle of our Constitution and of Republicanism."[73] To Madison's way of thinking, the Whiskey rebels, whatever their motives, "were in the most effectual manner, doing the business of Despotism," because it was "the general tendency of insurrections to increase the momentum of power." Had the uprising not been crushed, Federalists would likely have insisted that "a standing army would have been necessary for *enforcing the laws*." Fortunately the American public had shown "a spirit truly republican" in rejecting the insurgents' defiance of duly enacted law.[74]

By mid-February 1795, Americans knew that Jay had indeed negotiated a treaty with Britain. But all they knew of its contents came from scattered hints printed in the British press. The official text arrived just after the Third Congress adjourned in early March. Washington then summoned the Senate to reconvene in June, but the text of the treaty remained confidential. During this interval, Madison anonymously published a pamphlet titled *Political Observations*, which restated the standard Republican complaints about Federalist foreign policies. It was not a noteworthy effort, and the text was muddled with printer's errors. Midway through his argument, however, Madison cautioned his readers that they needed to "distinguish between the respect due to the man" who currently held the presidency "and the functions belonging to the office." In judging the latter, they must "consult the constitution," Madison continued; "they will consider human nature, and, looking beyond the character of the existing magistrate, fix their eyes on the precedent which must descend to his successors."[75]

In late June 1795 the Senate narrowly ratified the treaty with the exact two-thirds vote the Constitution required. Once the treaty was published, the concessions Jay had made produced a potent storm of public protest. Some Republicans thought it might still be possible to convince the president not to sign the treaty. Yet Madison demurred when Robert Livingston of New York urged him to ask Washington to abort the treaty. The president already well knew what he thought, Madison replied. If he seemed unlikely to be swayed by "the state of the public opinion within my sphere of information," nothing Madison could say would have any effect.[76]

So the treaty, duly ratified and signed, was part of the supreme law of the land—or was nearly so, because the Senate had asked that Article 12 of the treaty, relating to the vital question of commercial access to the West Indies, be renegotiated. For the treaty to be implemented, however, the House would need to apportion the requisite funds. In November the Madisons returned to Philadelphia for the opening of the Fourth Congress. The Jay treaty remained in quasi limbo until word arrived that Britain had abandoned the disputed twelfth article. On February 29, 1796, Washington affirmed that the treaty was ratified, and on March 1 he asked the House to appropriate the requisite funds. At this point, the Republican opponents of the treaty finally acted. They appeared to enjoy a majority in the House, subject to the usual uncertainty about the behavior of newcomers. On March 2 the

House approved a resolution proposed by Edward Livingston of New York, asking the president to turn over relevant documents relating to Jay's negotiations. The House could hardly exercise its independent constitutional authority over the appropriation of funds, Livingston argued, without examining the basis on which the administration had acted.

Madison had deep misgivings about Livingston's stratagem, which risked a direct confrontation with the president. He tried to amend the resolution to concede that Washington could exercise his own discretion in deciding which papers to disclose. That amendment lost.[77] Even then he hoped that the House would not pursue this gambit. "The policy of hazarding it is so questionable," he wrote Jefferson, that Livingston "will probably let it sleep or withdraw it."[78] Madison preferred to oppose the treaty on other grounds. Popular sentiment within the Republican party had grown much more critical of the president's unique public character. Yet for personal and political reasons alike, Madison remained reluctant to challenge Washington directly.[79]

Still, there seemed to be *some* constitutional basis for challenging the enforcement of the Jay treaty—some, but not much. By the early fall of 1795, Madison had drafted a petition to the Virginia legislature protesting the treaty's terms. In the manuscript drafts of this petition, Madison omitted the objection that the commercial clauses of the treaty might trench upon the congressional power to regulate foreign commerce and thereby pose a constitutional problem. But such a claim was added to the printed petition that the legislature received in October, before Madison went to Philadelphia. He had discussed the issue with Jefferson and Joseph Jones, who both supported this challenge. True, the language of the petition was hardly capacious on this point: "The President and Senate by ratifying this Treaty, usurp the powers of regulating commerce, of making rules with respect to aliens, of establishing tribunals of justice, and of defining piracy. A formal demonstration of every part of this complex proposition is not requisite." The assembly advanced this claim by proposing a short set of constitutional amendments, the first of which held that "no treaty containing any stipulation upon the powers vested in Congress" should become national law without the approval of the House. The act of proposing such an amendment indicated that the "formal demonstration" earlier deemed "not requisite" was in fact sorely needed. The lackluster reception the Virginia proposals received in other states only confirmed that point.[80]

Even so, Madison knowingly clung to this tenuous position. In a lengthy speech on March 10, he "regretted" that "on a question of such magnitude as the present, there should be any apparent inconsistency or inexplicitness in the Constitution." When such an inconsistency appeared, however, there was no alternative but "to examine the different constructions with accuracy & fairness, according to the rules established therefor, and to adhere to that which should be found most rational, consistent, and satisfactory." But the question of which "rules" to apply remained a matter of debate. In this speech, and in another given on April 6, Madison attempted to explain which rules he found most compelling. These were, in a sense, typically Madisonian speeches, for they listed, distinguished, and evaluated alternative modes of reasoning constitutionally. The March 10 speech identified five "constructions worthy of notice" as potential paths of congressional interpretation.[81] The April 6 speech pivoted on relying upon historical evidence of the original understandings of the ratifiers of the Constitution while disregarding any knowledge of the original intentions of its framers. In a passage that still resonates deeply among all those who now dispute originalist approaches to the interpretation of the Constitution, Madison proposed a ground rule of interpretation:

> But, after all, whatever veneration might be entertained for the body of men who formed our constitution, the sense of that body could never be regarded as the oracular guide in the expounding the constitution. As the instrument came from them, it was nothing more than the draught of a plan, nothing but a dead letter, until life and validity were breathed into it, by the voice of the people, speaking through the several state conventions. If we were to look therefore, for the meaning of the instrument, beyond the face of the instrument, we must look for it not in the general convention, which proposed, but in the state conventions, which accepted and ratified the constitution.[82]

Here was a theory of interpretation that made the people not only the sovereign fount of the supremacy of the Constitution but also the most authoritative source of its meaning.

Madison's declamation on the right of the House to review papers relating to the negotiations was driven by several urgent concerns. As a distinguished framer of the Constitution, he was hard pressed to explain how he could reconcile the Republican position with the plain text and apparent meaning of the Treaty and Supremacy clauses. His chief foe was William Vans Murray, a young and brash Federalist representative from Maryland. In his own lengthy speech of March 23, Murray complimented Madison for his key role in framing the Constitution. But then, Murray pointedly noted, "If the gentleman [Madison] was the Pythia in the temple, ought he not to explain the ambiguous language of the oracle," that is, the Constitution itself. Murray implicitly reminded Madison of his frustrations when his researches into ancient and modern confederacies encountered the inadequacies of the historical records. Yet Americans need no longer labor under this debility. "One hundred years hence, should a great question arise upon the construction" of the Constitution, Murray mused, would they not appreciate the contributions of someone who could "clear up difficulties by his contemporary knowledge? Such a man would have twice proved a blessing to his country."[83]

There were other problems with Madison's position. In his message of March 30, the president informed the House that the Convention had considered a motion stating "that no Treaty should be binding on the United States which was not ratified by a Law"—that is, approved by both houses of Congress. But that "proposition was explicitly rejected."[84] The president's knowledge of this point did not depend on reading Madison's notes of debates. It came instead from his possession of the Convention's journals, which the framers had instructed him to keep, but which Washington had now deposited in the Department of State. This was not some random archival activity on his part but a move calculated to reinforce his wholesale support of the treaty. Washington was referring to a motion made by Gouverneur Morris on August 23, 1787. That came at a time when Madison's note taking had reached a point of "collapse," as illness and committee duties overwhelmed his efforts to preserve an account of the debates.[85] But the evidence in the journals kept by William Jackson was enough for Washington's purposes. In Madison's view, conveyed privately in a letter to Jefferson, the president had violated his trust by yielding control over the notes. As Madison and other framers recalled it, the journal "was by a vote deposited with the P[resident] to be kept sacred until called for by some competent authority. How can this be reconciled with the use he has made of it?"[86]

Whether the president had violated a "sacred" duty or not, Madison had little incentive to discuss the debates at Philadelphia. Whatever shape his unavailable notes of debates were then in, they would not have supported his current constitutional claims. Equally important, Madison's earlier efforts to appeal to the authority of the Convention had proved unpersuasive. He had made that move during the bank controversy of 1791, only to learn that other members of Congress, including former framers, felt that such appeals were problematic and improper.[87] Rather than rely on evidence of the framers' intentions, Madison instead invoked the understanding of its ratifiers. But this appeal also had its doubtful aspects. In his April 6 speech, for example, Madison relied on material drawn from the North Carolina ratification convention of July 1788, which rejected the Constitution, and the amendments the state proposed when it adopted the Constitution two years later. But what interpretive advantage could be gained from a state that was a latecomer to the consensus of 1788? Moreover, the circumstances of ratification were not wholly conducive to the formation of correct constitutional judgments: "The agitations of the public mind on that occasion, with the hurry and compromise which generally prevailed in settling the amendments to be proposed, would at once explain and apologize for the several apparent inconsistencies which might be discovered."[88]

Madison's speech hardly formed a persuasive case for his theory of constitutional interpretation. Its main political objective may have been to rebut the president's appeal to the Convention.[89] Federalists were openly dismissive of Madison's claims. So was the president. But the critical development in the early spring of 1796 was the success with which Federalists mobilized public opinion in favor of the treaty and the president's position. Federalists and their merchant supporters organized town meetings and the signing of petitions in the nation's leading ports, demonstrating that they had skills of their own in generating popular support for their views.[90] Madison watched anxiously as the Republican majority frittered away in late April. Ultimately a House that the Republicans initially dominated approved the implementation of the treaty by a majority of three. Madison, with his long experience of collective deliberation, complained to Jefferson that "the progress of this business throughout has to me been the most worrying & vexatious that I ever encountered," not least because the outcome owed more to "the unsteadiness, the follies, the perverseness, & the defections among our friends" than to "the strength or dexterity, or malice of our opponents."[91]

The significance of the Jay treaty debate ran well beyond the frustration Madison felt while he was defending a political strategy he privately deemed mistaken. That significance included the obvious consequences that the treaty had for the conduct of American foreign relations, as its Anglophilic aspects pushed the United States into the confrontation with France that led to the Quasi-War of 1798. The prolonged debate of 1794–96 was critical in at least three other respects, each of which reflected profound dimensions of Madison's active political thinking.

First, the claims and counterclaims of the opposing parties revealed just how permeable a boundary divided the realms of constitutional interpretation and political argument. Indeed, this line seemed so permeable that it ceased being a boundary at all. Those claims represented both partisan preferences and institutional commitments. The putative Republican majority in the House was asserting an institutional right to review the administration's diplomatic papers. But the impetus for that claim derived from their political opposition to the Jay treaty. The Federalist minority in the House had no desire to support this claim because its preferences reflected the dominant interests the members represented—that is, Madison chafed, the interests of "the Banks, the British Merchts. [and] the insurance Comps.," all of whom preferred to maintain the steady flow of Anglo-American commerce. There was nothing surprising in this alignment. What was remarkable was the way in which political preferences and constitutional claims naturally reinforced each other. That process of reinforcement was a function in part of ambiguities and silences embedded in the text of the Constitution. If that text was unclear, then a realm of construction lay open in which one could plausibly advance a clarifying claim. But a political incentive also operated. Whenever such conditions of ambiguity or silence existed, the temptation to extend or escalate one's political preferences into claims of constitutional right proved irresistible.

Second, in asserting the problematic claims of the House of Representatives, Madison revealed just how far he had moved from his dominant concerns of the late 1780s. If any one principle guided his thinking in the immediate moment of the framing of the Constitution, it was the idea that the greatest danger of institutional imbalance lay in the legislature. The best-known expression of this thought comes in the "impetuous vortex" statement of *Federalist* 48. But the underlying conception was echoed on all the other occasions when Madison's analysis of the workings of institutions pivoted on his assessment of the political forces to which they were most directly responsive. The same logic operated in *Federalist* 46, when Madison compared the political resources available to the states against those available to the national government; in *Federalist* 49, when he explained why popular conventions called to redress constitutional violations were likely to favor the representative assemblies that would encroach most frequently on the authority of other departments; and in his October 1788 letter to Jefferson, explaining why bills of rights were likely to be inefficacious because "the real power" to do injustice resided in the people, who would act instrumentally through government. As late as 1793, the belief that the lower house of a representative assembly posed the greatest danger to constitutional equilibrium because of its greater intimacy with the people formed the dominant concern guiding Madison's constitutional thinking. The debate over the Necessary and Proper Clause in 1791 was a simple extension of that concern.

After 1793, however, the dominance of the executive in the realm of foreign policy forced Madison to recalibrate his thinking. Madison had used his fourth essay as Helvidius to detail all the adverse consequences that would follow should the president retain "the prerogative of judging and deciding whether there be causes of war or not, in the obligations of treaties." If that sentiment gained "the acquiescence of the public," it would become "morally certain" that a wider array of executive powers would "be deduced and exercised sooner or later by those who may have an interest in so doing."[92] In one sense, this was an entirely conventional claim, consistent with the attack on prerogative that informed seventeenth- and eighteenth-century Whig thinking. But after 1793 these conventional axioms were tried in the new balance of American republican politics and found wanting. Even when the Republicans in the House enjoyed a nominal political advantage, they could not prevail against the executive. The political superiority of the presidency had become the dominant fact of American politics. Washington's unique presence compounded that fact, but it was hardly its sole explanation.

The third finding that followed from this situation was that effective control of the government required more than the capacity to attain a working majority in Congress. The political potency of the presidency had now been discovered. Its influence could never have been adequately tested before 1796. So long as Washington stayed in office, there would be no opportunity to know how the presidential electoral system would work. But both sets of party leaders already grasped how important control of the presidency had become. Even when Washington delayed announcing his anticipated retirement in 1796, both parties were ready to spring into concerted action as soon as the news broke. The resulting contest brought a result that the framers of the Constitution would not have expected a scant decade earlier: a truly national contest between two organized coalitions, with two obvious candidates—Jefferson and Adams—competing in an election that a national popular vote could have decided. When Adams gained a narrow victory by three electoral votes, conditions were instantly created to foresee a rerun four years later. A swing of two votes would have elected Jefferson. Those votes could have been harvested in Virginia, North Carolina, and Pennsylvania, all solidly Republican states, had electors there been chosen at large rather than in districts.

It is the challenge of capturing the presidency, rather than the articulation of the states'-rights doctrine of 1798, that better explains the course of Madison's creative thinking after he and Dolley retired to Montpelier early in 1797. This claim may seem surprising, because the conventional reading of the "Madison problem" still pivots on the disjunction between his advocacy of a national negative on state laws "in all cases whatsoever" in 1787 and the Virginia Resolutions of 1798. Yet all that the Resolutions set out to do was to affirm that the state legislatures retained some residual right to engage in political protest against measures that they deemed unconstitutional—in this case the Alien and Sedition Acts that Congress adopted in the summer of 1798. In the period immediately surrounding their enactment, Madison and Vice President Jefferson relied on personal visits at Montpelier and Monticello rather than correspondence to coordinate their strategy. With the Federalists controlling every branch of the national government, sympathetic state legislatures were the only institutional resource the two Republican leaders had available to challenge measures they deemed not only impolitic and unjust but also unconstitutional.

Yet the idea of drafting the Virginia and Kentucky legislatures for this campaign was no radical innovation. Madison had imagined state assemblies playing just such a role in *Federalist* 46. The Virginia petition of 1795 protesting the Jay treaty had been similarly conceived. Colonial protests against British imperial policy before 1774 had relied on the same tactic. The adoption of the Virginia Resolutions thus marked no real break with ideas Madison had entertained and advocated previously. The real difficulty lay in the gap between his advocacy of a residual role for the legislatures in mobilizing political opposition to the acts and Jefferson's flirtation in the Kentucky Resolutions with allowing the states to prevent national law from being implemented within their boundaries. Jefferson's position verged close to a doctrine of nullification. Once Madison learned how far the Kentucky Resolutions went, he reminded Jefferson of the political danger of allowing the legislature to be left vulnerable to "the charge of Usurpation in the very act of protesting ag[ain]st the usurpations of Congress."[93] Like the Virginia petition of 1795, the Virginia and Kentucky resolutions fell flat in securing the support of other states. Their true legacy came later, by setting foundation stones for the construction of a more robust doctrine of states' rights that contributed to the growth of nullificationist and secessionist sentiment in the slaveholding South.

By contrast, the maneuvers leading to the presidential election of 1800 became a story of political opportunity and entrepreneurship—a demonstration of how tempting it was to manipulate constitutional rules for partisan advantage.[94] Madison received advice on this point from Charles Pinckney of South Carolina, his former colleague at the Federal Convention, first in May and again in September 1799. Pinckney urged him "to Write to & speak to all your Friends in the *republican interest* in the state legislature" to replace the existing scheme of popular election of presidential electors by districts with a legislative appointment conducted by a bicameral joint ballot. "The Constitution of the United States fully warrants it," Pinckney noted, "& remember that Every thing Depends upon it."[95] Jefferson was equally interested in the question. In the abstract, he wrote Governor James Monroe in January 1800, he preferred an election by districts, "but while 10 states chuse either by their legislatures or by a general ticket, it is folly & worse than folly for the other 6 not to do it."[96]

Madison was again a member of the Virginia legislature that revised the state's electoral rules in the winter of 1800. Though his correspondence says little on the subject, he was intensely involved in the discussions that led Virginia to institute a popular, statewide, winner-take-all electoral law.[97] Nor was that the only innovation in the rules for appointing electors that the year brought. Learning what Virginia had done, the Massachusetts congressional delegation, dominated by Federalists, urged its General Court to replace the state's district plan with the appointment of presidential electors by the legislature. In New York, the spring elections gave control of the state legislature to the Republicans—a tribute to Aaron Burr's political skills. Hamilton, as keen a vote counter as Jefferson, then urged Governor John Jay to recall the lame-duck assembly so it could replace the existing procedure of legislative election with a district system that would enable Federalists to capture a few votes. On this occasion "scruples of delicacy and propriety" about altering the rules "ought to yield to the extraordinary nature of the crisis," which pivoted on "prevent[ing] an *Atheist* in Religion and a *Fanatic* in politics from getting possession of the helm of the State." Jay declined to answer Hamilton's plea, but he docketed the letter as "proposing a measure for party purposes wh. I think it wd. not become me to adopt."[98]

Several other states altered their rules, not because they wished to find the one best mode of appointing electors but in response to the same perceptions of urgency and partisan advantage that Hamilton voiced so well. The "scruples" that Hamilton overcame but which Jay followed were not casually dismissed. Even in Virginia, the shift to statewide election carried by only five votes in the lower house. In Maryland, a highly intense campaign pivoted largely on disputes over the mode of appointing electors.[99] Politicians and citizens alike knew that election rules were being adroitly exploited for partisan ends, and that perception evoked some measure of discomfort. For both sides, the political imperatives of the election outweighed any independent commitment to making constitutional propriety and legal continuity the criteria of action.

The presidential election of 1800–1801 is better remembered for the glitch that gave both Republican running mates, Jefferson and Burr, an equal majority of seventy-three votes, producing the tie that threw the final choice into the House of Representatives. That glitch ultimately led to the Twelfth Amendment, requiring electors to vote separately for president and vice president. But the strategic or opportunistic exploitation of the Constitution in setting the mode of appointment for electors was at least as important a development. As a mark of the uncertainty of 1787, the framers left that decision to the state legislatures. "The difficulty of finding an unexceptionable process for appointing the Executive Organ of a Govt. such as that of the U.S. was deeply felt by the Convention," Madison recalled in 1823. The final decision, occurring near the end of the debates, was "not exempt from a degree of the hurrying influence produced by fatigue & impatience in all such bodies."[100] By then Madison understood that the collective movement of the states toward winner-take-all popular election or legislative appointment of electors was a function of the precedent set by those states that first selected these practices. Once some states had adopted one of those rules—as Virginia had in 1800—the dominant partisan interests in other states would follow their example. Madison was thus again reasoning in implicitly game-theoretical terms about the characteristics of federal politics, explaining how the adoption of one set of rules by a set of states would determine the decisions of other "players" in the electoral system.

There was, nevertheless, another view of the Constitution at work in these maneuvers. In 1800, leaders in both parties grasped another important truth: whatever the Constitution did not prohibit it made potentially permissible; the Constitution would operate not only as a set of landmarks erected to guide permissible action but also as an invitation to political entrepreneurship. This, too, was an example of what thinking like a constitution could mean. It opened a path to political experimentation that homage to the ostensible landmarks of the Constitution could never foreclose.

In the final analysis, Madison and Jefferson believed that the election of 1800–1801 vindicated the constitutional principles they wished to preserve against the dangerous innovations of Hamilton's state-building agenda. As Richard Hofstadter shrewdly observed in his wonderful book *The Idea of a Party System*, the Republican leaders retained an underlying confidence in their capacity to build a national political majority, even after the Virginia and Kentucky resolutions received so little support from the other state legislatures.[101] Because the electoral system remained so vulnerable to political manipulation at the state level, there was much to worry about in the actual conduct of the election. Moreover, the glitch in coordination among the Republicans that gave Jefferson and Burr a "perfect parity" of electors deepened the anxiety even after the voting was completed.[102] In the period separating the casting of the electoral vote from the assembling of the lame-duck Congress, there was ample room to speculate about the tricks Federalists might play to keep the executive vacant, or somehow to make an acting president out of John Jay or John Marshall, or to elevate Burr over Jefferson.[103]

Nevertheless, throughout this period Madison and Jefferson retained an abiding confidence in the judgment of the people. They had the electoral results to prove it, not only in the victory margin of the presidential electors but also—and even more powerfully—in the dramatic changes in Congress, where Republican gains effectively reversed the existing Federalist majorities in both houses. If a real "Madison problem" remains in juxtaposing the constitutional framer of the 1780s with the party leader of the 1790s, it may well lie here. The Madison who warned Edmund Randolph about the dependency and fallibility of public opinion in January 1788 had become the Madison who believed that the electorate the Republicans had mobilized would remain faithful in principle and loyal to their cause. Jefferson's election and the Republican victories in Congress were a triumph of popular constitutionalism, and they made Madison a more enthusiastic republican in 1801 than he had been in 1787. This was a remedy very different from the one Jefferson had proposed in his "draught" constitution for Virginia, but it was one that still vindicated the people's right to rule, constitutionally. For James Madison, that great votary of the republican creed, it marked a fitting conclusion to the political enterprises of the past decade and a half, when his creative efforts at constitutional thinking made him the greatest lawgiver of modernity.

EPILOGUE

"I May Be Thought to Have Outlived Myself"

The election of 1800–1801 was both an experiment in constitutional politics and a genuine constitutional crisis, as Americans wondered how, when, or even whether the House of Representatives would resolve the tie between Jefferson and Burr. As often occurs with the creation of new constitutional regimes, this transition in political power from one contentious party to its equally contentious rival marked a significant test of the viability of the American system. Numerous other nations have since failed that test. Thus, however critical we may be about "the failure of the founding fathers" to foresee a situation like 1800–1801, the resolution of that crisis marks a crucial milestone in American constitutionalism.

For James Madison the election marked a different transition. He had spent the first quarter century of his political life primarily in legislative institutions. True, he did serve two years on the Virginia council of state, advising Governor Patrick Henry. And the powers exercised by the Continental Congress were often deemed executive in nature. Yet Congress operated much more like a deliberative legislature than a decisive executive body. It was legislative and deliberative experience that formed the basis for Madison's critique of American republicanism in the 1780s. Only in the 1790s did he begin to focus on the nature of executive power. Yet, from 1801 until his political retirement in 1817, his service was entirely executive in nature, first as secretary of state and then succeeding Jefferson as president.

Madison confronted significant constitutional issues during these years. The Louisiana Purchase need not have become one, except that President Jefferson had idiosyncratic scruples about its constitutional permissibility. The dual cases of *Marbury v.*

Madison and *Stuart v. Laird*, decided a week apart in February 1803, were arguably far more consequential. Jefferson and Madison dismissed William Marbury's demand that the secretary of state deliver his signed commission as a federal magistrate for the District of Columbia. The suit was too trivial even to require a defense, they thought. If Chief Justice John Marshall wanted to use the occasion to embarrass the administration while also asserting the doctrine of judicial review by denying Marbury use of the remedy he sought—an exercise of the writ of mandamus authorized by the Judiciary Act of 1789—well, that was the Supreme Court's judicial privilege. Contrary to the dominant myth of modern scholarship, *Marbury v. Madison* did nothing to establish the existence of judicial review of congressional statutes, an idea that was already well accepted. The real test came in *Stuart v. Laird*, when the Court declined to overturn the constitutional authority of the Judiciary Act of 1802, which abolished the new circuit judgeships that the lame-duck Sixth Congress had created in 1801.

So constitutional questions continued to arise, often involving issues of great moment. Yet after 1801 Madison's career as the nation's leading and most creative constitutional thinker was over. He had just turned fifty when he joined Jefferson's administration, his arrival delayed by the death of his father. Over the next decade and a half, issues of diplomacy and eventually war preoccupied his attention. When constitutional questions did arise, they largely involved matters of interpretation rather than the fundamental challenges that surrounded the adoption of the Constitution or the project of organizing an opposition political party to deal with the Hamiltonian assertion of presidential power.

Yet crucial aspects of Madison's understanding of American constitutionalism in his later years still merit more attention than they have received. Two problems in particular stand out. First, there is no adequate account of the constitutional history of Madison's presidency. The conventional wisdom treats his two terms as a political and governmental failure, aptly symbolized by the burning of the White House by the British as he and Dolley separately fled the capital.[1] Gordon Wood, however, has offered a shrewder assessment of Madison's presidency as an extension of his party's underlying philosophy: "to wage the war that began in

1812 in a manner different from the way monarchies waged war." Madison had no ambition to imitate Napoleon or even Hamilton. "Calm in the conviction that in a republic strong executive leadership could only endanger the principles for which the war was fought, he knowingly accepted the administrative confusion and inefficiencies and the military failures."[2] Yet Wood's comment remains only a keen insight; the full history has yet to be written.

Much more has been said about a second subject that also needs consideration—the substantial amount of constitutional interpretation that Madison did during the decades of his retirement at Montpelier. Numerous commentators have examined this archive to see what Madison had to say about a whole array of topics: the Missouri crisis, internal improvements, the Marshall Court in the heyday of its nationalism, the legacy of the Doctrine of 1798, the heresy of nullification, reform of the electoral college, religious freedom, suffrage, and many other matters. Yet here, too, the scholarly record represents the diffuse range of Madison's concerns and the requests he received. It has yet to yield a comprehensive or integrated account of Madison's mature constitutional views as he reflected on American history since 1787.[3]

There are, however, motifs in Madison's writings that may best indicate what a Madisonian mode of thinking constitutionally continued to mean even into his retirement. If *Federalist* 37 remains the best guide to his epistemology of political reasoning, as this book has argued, its lessons remained relevant to the deteriorating constitutional situation that Madison observed in his final years. One of the striking developments in American political discourse after 1815 was the emergence of a deeply reductionist way of thinking about the essential character of the federal union. In the politically charged atmosphere of the nullification crisis, Madison confronted the monstrous heresies associated with the strange doctrines of John C. Calhoun and his allies. Those heresies did have a partial origin in the Virginia and Kentucky resolutions of 1798, which affirmed that the states, as the original compacting parties of the union, retained some residual right to protest acts they deemed ill advised or even unconstitutional. But the assertion of that essentially political right fell far short of the radical conclusions proposed by the nullifiers of South Carolina, with their wholly specious claim that the states, as

independent sovereignties, had some further power to prevent
the implementation of federal law. When disputes arose over
boundaries of national power—or, more to the point, over the
constitutionality of a national law—the proper forum for their
resolution, Madison argued, was the Supreme Court, acting as
the impartial umpire he had briefly sketched at the conclusion
of *Federalist* 39.[4]

On the other side of this debate lay the argument, notably
propounded by Daniel Webster in the 1830 Webster-Hayne
debate in the Senate, that the "We the People of the United States"
announced in the Preamble was the true source of the supremacy
of the Constitution. Madison was far more sympathetic to Webster's position than he could ever be to Calhoun's. Yet simply
to rely on these formulaic, binary notions of the origins of the
union would neither do justice to the complexity of the federal
system nor temper the urgent situation of American politics. In
the 1820s and 1830s, as in the 1780s, the only way to describe
the constitutional system fairly was to puzzle out its details, not
to invoke pretentious rhetorical statements about the nature of
sovereignty (a word that the Constitution never used).

Madison made these points clear in a letter to his protégé,
William Cabell Rives, written as the nullification controversy
was drawing to its close. "It seems strange that it should be
necessary to disprove this novel and nullifying doctrine" of the
undiminished sovereignty of the states, he wrote,

> and stranger still that those who deny it should be denounced as
> Innovators, heretics & Apostates. Our political system is admitted
> to be a new Creation—a real nondescript. Its character therefore
> must be sought within itself; not in precedents, because there are
> none; not in writers whose comments are guided by precedents.
> Who can tell at present how Vattel and others of that class, would
> have qualified (in the Gallic sense of the term) a Compound &
> peculiar system with such an example of it as ours before them.

The nature and character of the American compound republic
would always have to be derived inductively, relying on the terms
of the Constitution and the actual mode of governance. Nor could
one wave away these problems by magically invoking the idea of
the irreducible sovereignty of the states, when the Constitution
explicitly vested powers of "sovereignty & nationality" in the

federal government. "A dispute about the name, is but a battle of words," Madison concluded. "The practical result is not indeed left to argument or inference."[5] Here, in effect, was a latter-day application of *Federalist* 37, including its Lockean awareness of the ease with which political argument could torture the meaning of complex words like "sovereignty."

If one wanted the union to persist, as Madison certainly did, one could not solve the tensions coursing within the federal system by counterposing reductionist theories of sovereignty based on rival images of the compacting states against the full-throated voice of We the People. A commitment to the union required a patient willingness to master and abide by its complicated networks of governance. Yet there was one issue, he knew, that always carried the potential to disrupt the entire constitutional system. That was, of course, the whole question of slavery, whose concentrated presence in one region and essential absence from another always contradicted Madison's underlying theory of the benefits of a nationally extended republic. Madison was justifiably proud of his formulation of that theory back in 1787, and he continued to think it worthy of further elaboration as a definitive demonstration of how republican principles could safely be applied to truly national levels of governance. Yet he knew all along, again going back to 1787, that the theory had one fatal defect.

Madison developed this point in a lengthy letter to Robert Walsh, written early in the Missouri crisis. "Parties under some denominations or other must always be expected in a Govt. as free as ours," he wrote. Here "party," with its now familiar association with institutions of political mobilization, had replaced "faction," the term used in *Federalist* 10, as the marker of partisan division. "When the individuals belonging to them are intermingled in every part of the whole Country," he continued, "they strengthen the Union of the whole, while they divide every part." Here the citizens' identification with national parties might work to maintain the stability of national politics while weakening the centrifugal tendencies of a federal system. Yet an exceptional danger remained. "Should a State of parties arise, founded on geographical boundaries and other Physical and permanent distinctions which happen to coincide with them, what is to control these great repulsive Masses from awful shocks agst.

each other?"[6] This thought echoed one of Madison's key speeches at the Federal Convention. On June 30, 1787, Madison rightly argued that the real clashes of interest in the union would lie not between small and large states but between the northern and southern states, correlating in part to their differences in climate but more directly to the presence or absence of slave labor systems.[7] In his 1819 restatement of the problem, the image of collective national deliberations gave way to a near-geological confrontation between the regions—a theory of tectonic politics *avant le fait* of modern geology.

Madison had no satisfactory answer to this problem, though he doubtless grasped how deeply it challenged and indeed threatened to undermine his prevailing theory. His moral opposition to slavery offers some consolation to his modern votaries, but it will never satisfy modern critics who believe that the task of history is less to explain the past than to judge it on moral grounds. At least by 1791, Madison understood that the pervasive existence of slavery within a society would sap its republican character. "In proportion as slavery prevails in a State, the Government, however democratic in name, must be aristocratic in fact," he observed, in the notes on government that may have been the basis for the never-written treatise on the spirit of republicanism. "All the antient popular governments, were for this reason aristocracies." So, too, "the Southern States of America, are, on the same principle, aristocracies."[8] Yet to this quintessentially political contradiction Madison could conceive no political solution. A conclusive answer to this central challenge to the federal constitutional republic lay beyond his imagination.[9] All that survived was his heartfelt "Advice to My Country," to "be considered as issuing from the tomb, where truth alone can be respected, and the happiness of man alone consulted," and from the record of four decades of public service devoted to "the cause of its liberty" and spent "in most of the great transactions which will constitute epochs of its destiny." That advice was nothing more than an urgent plea "that the Union of the States be cherished and perpetuated."[10]

But, of course, there proved to be no political answer to the problem of slavery. That was why the nation ended slavery through the Civil War—and a sudden and largely unanticipated revival of the constitutional amendment process that at last offered a decisive solution to the question of emancipation.[11] Even then, however, the adoption of the Fourteenth Amendment (1868) was needed to fulfill that pledge. Its fulfillment marked the final completion of Madison's constitutional thinking, as it had first cohered four score years earlier. Near the end of his life, as he and Charles Carroll of Carrollton were the last surviving founders, Madison mused that, "having outlived so many of my contemporaries, I ought not to forget that I may be thought to have outlived myself." Perhaps he spoke too soon. Section 1 of the Fourteenth Amendment, with its major restrictions on the rights-impairing legislative authority of the states, is arguably the most Madisonian element of our Constitution.[12]

NOTES

ABBREVIATIONS

DHRC Merrill Jensen, John Kaminski et al., eds., *Documentary History of the Ratification of the Constitution* (Madison, Wis., 1976–)

Madison: Writings Jack Rakove, ed., *James Madison: Writings* (New York, 1999)

PJM William Hutchinson, William Rachal et al., eds., *The Papers of James Madison: Congressional Series* (Chicago and Charlottesville, Va., 1961–1991)

PTJ Julian Boyd et al., eds., *The Papers of Thomas Jefferson* (Princeton, 1950–)

RFC Max Farrand, ed., *Records of the Federal Convention of 1787* (New Haven, 1966)

INTRODUCTION

1. Wallace to Madison, July 12, 1785, and Madison to Wallace, August 23, 1785, *PJM*, 8: 320–24, 350–58.

2. There has, however, been a recent surge in Madison biographies, including Lynne Cheney, *James Madison: A Life Reconsidered* (New York, 2014); Richard Brookhiser, *James Madison* (New York, 2011); Jeff Broadwater, *James Madison: A Son of Virginia and a Founder of the Nation* (Chapel Hill, 2012); and Michael Signer, *Becoming Madison: The Extraordinary Origins of the Least Likely Founding Father* (New York, 2015). From the vantage point of serious scholarship, these books have little analytical value; as is often the case with founding-era trade books, they rarely address serious issues of analysis and interpretation in any helpful way. More can be expected of the substantial biography of Madison now being written by the legal scholar Noah Feldman. One can also benefit from several other books that focus more on Madison's personal qualities, including David O. Stewart, *Madison's Gift: Five Partnerships That Built America* (New York, 2015); Ralph Ketcham, *The Madisons at Montpelier: Reflections on the Founding Couple* (Charlottesville, Va., 2009); and Catherine Allgor, *A Perfect Union: Dolley Madison and the Creation of the American Nation* (New York, 2006).

3. The opening chapter of Robert Dahl, *A Preface to Democratic Theory* (Chicago, 1956, 2006) is titled "Madisonian Democracy," and its argument about the tensions between the faction-oriented hypotheses of *Federalist* 10 and the idea of separated powers sketched in the first half of *Federalist* 51 defines the central theoretical problems that engage political scientists who want to engage critically with the Madisonian model on its merits. In appraising Dahl's claims, it is helpful to examine his subsequent "Reflections" in the expanded edition of 2006 at xii–xvi. For a further restatement of the problem, see the excellent essay by Samuel Kernell, "'The True Principles of Republican Government': Reassessing James Madison's Political Science," in Kernell, ed., *James Madison: The Theory and Practice of Republican Government* (Stanford, Ca., 2003), 92–125. For further discussions of the Madisonian model, see George Thomas, *The Madisonian Constitution* (Baltimore, 2008); Jennifer Nadelsky, *Private Property and the Limits of American Constitutionalism: The Madisonian Framework and Its Legacy* (Chicago, 1990); and Eric Posner and Adrian Vermeule, *The Executive Unbound: After the Madisonian Republic* (New York, 2010).

4. These essays figure prominently in the penetrating work of Colleen A. Sheehan, *James Madison and the Spirit of Republican Self-Government* (New York, 2009), which ably traces Madison's dynamic consideration of the problem of public opinion.

5. Colleen A. Sheehan, *The Mind of James Madison: The Legacy of Classical Republicanism* (New York, 2015), 3–24.

6. Jack Rakove, ed., *James Madison: Writings* (New York, 1999) [hereafter, *Madison: Writings*], 745–70, 828–42.

7. John Adams, *Thoughts on Government* (Philadelphia, 1776), in Philip Kurland and Ralph Lerner, eds., *The Founders' Constitution* (Chicago, 1987), 1: 110.

8. I sometimes think that the one figure to whom Madison is most comparable is Samuel Adams, who also seemed to live for politics alone. See Jack N. Rakove, *The Beginnings of National Politics: An Interpretive History of the Continental Congress* (New York, 1979), 225.

9. Jack N. Rakove, *Revolutionaries: A New History of the Invention of America* (Boston, 2010), 341–44. For a brilliant analysis of the ways in which Machiavelli and Madison were contributing, at least latently, to a common project, see Alissa M. Ardito, *Machiavelli and the Modern State: The Prince, the* Discourses on Livy, *and the Extended Territorial Republic* (New York, 2015).

10. On the juxtaposition of these two essays, see Kernell, "'True Principles of Republican Government.'" Though there is no question about the importance that Madison ascribed to the argument of *Federalist* 10, its preeminence as the authoritative guide to his (and arguably the founding era's) political theory was very much a twentieth-century phenomenon, dating to the

emphasis placed on it in Charles Beard, *An Economic Interpretation of the Constitution* (New York, 1913), but really attaining its commanding place only in the 1950s, in works by Douglass Adair, Robert Dahl, and Martin Diamond.

11. The precise timing of the evolution of Madison's ideas about the extended republic has become a subject of serious controversy. In her book on the compilation, composition, and revision of Madison's notes of debates at the Philadelphia Convention, Mary Sarah Bilder boldly hypothesizes that the critical concluding passage of item 11 in the memorandum "The Vices of the Political System of the United States," in which Madison first laid out his analysis of the popular sources of faction, was *not* composed in April 1787 (the dating given by Madison) but at a later point, perhaps even in the summer of 1787. See Mary Sarah Bilder, *Madison's Hand: Revising the Constitutional Convention* (Cambridge, 2015), 44–46, 243–44. For my views of Bilder's book, see Jack N. Rakove, "A Biography of Madison's Notes of Debates," *Constitutional Commentary* 31 (2016), 305–37. Moreover, as Colleen Sheehan notes, Madison continued to think that the propositions of *Federalist* 10 and 51 deserved further development, as the reading notes he compiled in 1791 indicate. Sheehan, *Mind of Madison*, 31–33.

12. That would be Cambridge, England, rather than Cambridge, Massachusetts; yet most scholars would agree that the work on the American Revolution done by Bernard Bailyn and his students, including Gordon Wood, Pauline Maier, and arguably myself, suggests that both universities located in one Cambridge or the other come into play.

13. Madison to Jefferson, October 24, 1787, *PJM*, 10: 209–14.

14. For a close reading of Madison's purposes in *Federalist* 49, focusing especially on his emphasis on the value of preserving popular "veneration" for the Constitution, see Jeremy D. Bailey, *James Madison and Constitutional Imperfection* (New York, 2015), 15–37.

15. Jack N. Rakove, *Original Meanings: Politics and Ideas in the Making of the Constitution* (New York, 1996), 268–75.

16. The great skeptic on the importance of Madison's essay is Larry D. Kramer, "Madison's Audience," *Harvard Law Review* 112 (1998–99), 611–79, which questions how well Madison's contemporaries grasped his argument. Kramer asks fair questions, but they diverge from the emphasis I pursue here, which focuses on the role that these ideas played both in Madison's thinking and in his political calculations. It is worth noting that Kramer's concern lies more with the influence of *Federalist* 10 on modern theories of constitutional interpretation than with assessing the politics of constitution making in 1787–88.

17. This is perhaps my favorite Madisonian phrase, taken from a sentence in *Federalist* 49 where, referring to the first constitutions of 1776, he observes that "the experiments are of too ticklish a nature to be unnecessarily

multiplied." *Madison: Writings*, 288. I take what I hope is a modest and acceptable liberty by reducing Madison's literal expression to the phrase "ticklish experiment."

18. Judith Shklar, "Democracy and the Past: Jefferson and His Heirs," in Stanley Hoffmann and Dennis Thompson, eds., *Redeeming American Political Thought* (Chicago, 1998), 96. Shklar originally presented this talk as the Robert Wesson Lecture in Democracy at Stanford University in April 1988, where I was honored to serve as her commentator.

19. It is worth noting that Princeton University claims Madison as its first graduate student, because after the completion of his undergraduate studies in September 1771 he lingered there some months to work on ancient Hebrew. There is no evidence, however, that he later would jokingly greet friends by asking מה נשמע.

20. *PJM*, 11: 297–99.

21. *PJM*, 10: 206–19.

22. *PJM*, 9: 141.

23. *PJM*, 9: 354. Bilder seems to agree that this key observation was part of the original memorandum, not the later addition. *Madison's Hand*, 243.

24. *PJM*, 9: 351–52.

25. John Dunn, "The Identity of the History of Ideas," *Philosophy* 43 (1968), 87–88.

26. The best introduction to these complicated questions can be found in the essays collected in James Tully, ed., *Meaning and Context: Quentin Skinner and His Critics* (Princeton, 1988).

27. This statement echoes a similar observation by Bernard Bailyn in *The Ideological Origins of the American Revolution* (Cambridge, 1967, 1992), x.

CHAPTER 1. "HOW INDEED COULD IT BE OTHERWISE?"

1. James C. Scott, *Seeing Like a State: How Certain Schemes to Improve the Human Condition Have Failed* (New Haven, 1998).

2. I develop this idea in "Thinking Like a Constitution," *Journal of the Early Republic* 24 (2004), 1–26, which originated as my 2003 presidential address to the Society for the History of the Early American Republic.

3. See, for example, two books by Sanford Levinson: *Our Undemocratic Constitution: Where the Constitution Goes Wrong (and How We the People Can Correct It)* (New York, 2006); and *Framed: America's Fifty-One Constitutions and the Crisis of Governance* (New York, 2012).

4. The various versions of the religion article appear in *PJM*, 1: 172–75.

5. Madison to Caleb Wallace, August 23, 1785, *PJM*, 8: 350–51.

6. *Federalist* 48, *PJM*, 10: 456–57; "Vices of the Political System of the U. States," April 1787, *PJM*, 9: 351.

7. *Federalist* 49, in *PJM*, 10: 462.

8. Madison to Jefferson, March 27, 1780, *PJM*, 2: 6. A letter written immediately after his arrival a week earlier is missing. For further discussion, see Rakove, *Beginnings of National Politics*, 275–96.

9. For a general discussion of the drafting of the Confederation, see Rakove, *Beginnings of National Politics*, 135–91.

10. Proposed Amendment [March 12, 1781], *PJM*, 3: 17–19; Madison to Jefferson, April 16, 1781, *PJM*, 3: 71–72.

11. In my perhaps impressionistic view, Morris in this period was much more Hamilton's mentor than Washington was. See Rakove, *Revolutionaries*, 408–12.

12. This is Madison's note of a motion introduced by James Wilson on January 27, 1783, *PJM*, 6: 135, 138n16 (noting Madison's underlining of "general").

13. Lance Banning, *The Sacred Fire of Liberty: James Madison and the Founding of the Federal Republic* (Ithaca, N.Y., 1995), 29.

14. Madison, "Notes of Debates," January 28, 1783, *PJM*, 6: 144–45.

15. *PJM*, 6: 147.

16. *PJM*, 6: 146.

17. On the congressional reaction against the behavior of Howell, see Rakove, *Beginnings of National Politics*, 313–17, 328.

18. See the helpful editorial note provided in *PJM*, 5: 231–34. For a fuller discussion of Madison's purposes in keeping a "legislative diary," see Bilder, *Madison's Hand*, 19–36.

19. Rakove, *Beginnings of National Politics*, 320–23; for the dinner at the FitzSimons house, see *PJM*, 6: 265–66.

20. "Notes of Debates," February 21, 1783, *PJM*, 6: 270–73.

21. Hamilton to James Duane, September 3, 1780, in Joanne Freeman, ed., *Alexander Hamilton: Writings* (New York, 2001), 70–87. This letter is a virtual state paper.

22. On Hamilton's interest, see Rakove, *Beginnings of National Politics*, 288, 303, 325–29. For a remarkable discussion imagining what such a convention might do, see the letter from the Massachusetts congressional delegate Jonathan Jackson to Benjamin Lincoln, April 19, 1783, Fogg Collection, vol. 19, Maine Historical Society, quoted in ibid., 326–27.

23. Madison to James Madison Sr., August 30, 1783, *PJM*, 7: 294.

24. See the fascinating essay by Mary Sarah Bilder, "James Madison, Law Student and Demi-Lawyer," *Law and History Review* 28 (2010), 389–449.

25. Madison to Jefferson, March 16, 1784, *PJM*, 8: 11.

26. *PJM*, 8: 47–49.

27. Madison, "Notes for a Speech" [June 14 or 21, 1784], and Madison to Jefferson, July 3, 1784, *PJM*, 8: 75–79, 93.

28. Richard Henry Lee to Madison, November 20, 1784, *PJM*, 8:144–45; James Monroe to Thomas Jefferson, November 15, 1784, Julian Boyd et al., eds., *The Papers of Thomas Jefferson* (Princeton, 1950–) [hereafter, *PTJ*], 7:461.

29. John Rhodehamel, ed., *George Washington: Writings* (New York, 1997), 516–26.

30. Lee to Madison, November 26, 1784, *PJM*, 8: 151.

31. Madison to Lee, December 25, 1784, *PJM*, 8: 201.

32. Rakove, *Beginnings of National Politics*, 360–68.

33. Madison to Jefferson, October 3, 1785, *PJM*, 8: 373–75.

34. "Draft of Resolutions on Foreign Trade" [ca. November 12, 1785], *PJM*, 8: 409–10.

35. Madison to Washington, December 9, 1785, *PJM*, 8: 438–39.

36. See note and text, and Madison to Jefferson, January 22, 1786, *PJM*, 8: 470–71, 477.

37. Madison to Monroe, January 22, 1786, *PJM*, 8: 483.

38. Madison to Jefferson, March 18, 1786, *PJM*, 8: 502–3.

39. It was my pleasure to observe this notebook in the company of Justice Antonin Scalia and his wife at the Library of Congress dinner commemorating Madison's 250th birthday in 2001.

40. *PJM*, 9: 6–7. Madison's interest in antiquity is extensively explored in Sheehan, *Mind of James Madison*, pt. 1.

41. Madison to Monroe, March 19, 1786, *PJM*, 8: 505–6.

42. See discussion in Rakove, *Beginnings of National Politics*, 370–72.

43. Madison to Monroe, May 13, 1786, *PJM*, 9: 54–55.

44. Madison to Monroe, October 5, 1786, *PJM*, 9: 140–41.

45. Madison to Ambrose Madison, September 8, 1786, and to Monroe, September 11, 1786, *PJM*, 9: 120, 121.

46. Madison to Jefferson, August 12, 1786, *PJM*, 9: 96–97 (italics indicate cypher). Rufus King, then serving in Congress as a delegate from Massachusetts, made an interesting observation about Madison's plans for Annapolis: "Mr. Madison of Virginia has been here for some Time past, he will attend the convention. He does not discover or propose any other Plan than that of investing congress with full powers for the regulation of commerce Foreign, & domestic. But this power will run deep into the Authorities of the individual States, and can never be well exercised without a federal Judicial—the reform must necessarily be extensive." King to Jonathan Jackson, September 3, 1786, in Paul H. Smith, ed., *Letters of Delegates to Congress* (Washington, D.C., 1976–2000), 23: 543.

47. Samuel Osgood to John Adams, November 14, 1786, quoted in Rakove, *Beginnings of National Politics*, 387–88, and see the larger discussion at 380–88.

48. John Jay to Washington, January 7, 1787; Henry Knox to Washington, January 14, 1787; Washington, Sentiments of Mr Jay—Genl Knox and Mr Madison on a form of Governmt [late April–early May 1787], in W. W. Abbot,

ed., *The Papers of George Washington: Confederation Series* (Charlottesville, Va., 1997), 5: 163–66. In the Prologue to her excellent book on the ratification of the Constitution, my old friend, the late Pauline Maier, takes Washington's view of the Convention as her point of departure, which deviates from the Madisonian emphasis that colors my scholarship. Given Washington's critical importance in the entire process of constitutional formation, this certainly makes sense. Yet, in the end, Madison's role in shaping the agenda at Philadelphia was far more decisive. Pauline Maier, *Ratification: The People Debate the Constitution* (New York, 2010), 1–26.

49. *PJM*, 9: 163–64.

50. Madison to Washington, November 8, 1786, *PJM*, 9: 166

51. *PJM*, 9: 354.

52. This is an idea one occasionally finds mooted in private correspondence, such as the wonderful, prescient, but wholly speculative letter written by Jonathan Jackson to Benjamin Lincoln in April 1783, cited in note 22 of this chapter.

53. Madison to James Madison Sr., April 1, 1787, *PJM*, 9: 359.

54. Mary Bilder suggests that "the Vices" may have been written as the basis for an opening speech at the Convention, but I find that claim unpersuasive. Bilder, *Madison's Hand*, 44–46; Rakove, "Biography of Madison's Notes," 338–45.

55. *PJM*, 9: 348–50.

56. *PJM*, 9: 357.

57. *PJM*, 9: 351–52.

58. Ibid.

59. *PJM*, 6: 144–45.

60. Madison to Washington, April 16, 1787, *PJM*, 9: 383–85. For Washington's thoughts on coercion, see his letter to Madison, March 31, 1787, *PJM*, 9: 343. "But the kind of coercion[,] you may ask? This indeed will require thought," Washington concluded. Like other scholars, I owe a great deal to the seminal article by Charles Hobson, "The Negative on State Laws: James Madison, the Constitution, and the Crisis of Republican Government," *William and Mary Quarterly* 36 (1979), 215–35.

61. Madison to Jefferson, March 19, 1787, *PJM*, 9: 318.

62. Madison to Randolph, April 8, 1787, and to Washington, April 16, 1787, *PJM*, 9: 370, 383.

63. Madison to Jefferson, March 19, 1787, *PJM*, 9: 318.

64. A partial transcript of this letter recorded by Nicholas Trist in 1834 also survives. On it Trist notes, after this sentence: "In reading this Mr. Madison paused here; and said he had subsequently satisfied himself that there would be difficulties, perhaps insuperable, in reducing this idea to practice." *PJM*, 9: 322n4.

CHAPTER 2. "THE PRINCIPAL TASK OF
MODERN LEGISLATION"

1. "Vices of the Political System," *PJM*, 9: 353.

2. Madison to Jefferson, October 24, 1787, *PJM*, 10: 212.

3. *Federalist 10*, *PJM*, 10: 266.

4. Short to Jefferson, May 14 [15], 1784, and Randolph to Jefferson, May 14, 1784, *PTJ*, 7: 257, 260.

5. I discuss these aspects of Jefferson's thinking in *Revolutionaries*, chap. 7.

6. Harry C. Payne, *The Philosophes and the People* (New Haven, 1976), 61–62; and see the comments in Rakove, *Original Meanings*, 56.

7. Madison to Jefferson, July 3, 1784, *PJM*, 8: 95.

8. Madison to James Madison Sr., January 6, 1785, *PJM*, 7: 217. For a general discussion of Madison's actions on the religion question in the mid-1780s, see the fine essay by Lance Banning, "James Madison, the Statute for Religious Freedom, and the Crisis of Republican Convictions," in Merrill D. Peterson and Robert C. Vaughan, eds., *The Virginia Statute for Religious Freedom: Its Evolution and Consequences in American History* (New York, 1988), 109–38. There are numerous other accounts of the Virginia events in the scholarly literature.

9. Madison to Monroe, April 12, 1785, *PJM*, 7: 261.

10. George Nicholas to Madison, April 22, 1785, *PJM*, 7: 264–65, and see the headnote to the *Memorial*, *PJM*, 7: 295.

11. Madison to Jefferson, January 22, 1786, *PJM*, 8: 473.

12. Caleb Wallace to Madison, July 12, 1785, *PJM*, 8: 322–23.

13. Madison to Caleb Wallace, August 23, 1785, *PJM*, 8: 350–51.

14. See especially Gordon Wood, *The Creation of the American Republic, 1776–1787* (Chapel Hill, N.C., 1969), 132–61.

15. Ibid., 568.

16. See ibid., 206–22, which builds in important ways on the penultimate section of the original (non-enlarged) version of Bailyn, *Ideological Origins*, 272–301.

17. *PJM*, 8: 351–52.

18. *PJM*, 8: 352. In treating the Continental Congress as the repository of executive powers—here meaning powers over war and diplomacy—Madison was applying to American usage norms associated with monarchical precedent. He held this view going into the Federal Convention of 1787. Yet when James Wilson challenged this idea on June 1, 1787, Madison quickly agreed that British notions of executive prerogative had no place in an American constitution.

19. *PJM*, 8: 353–54.

20. *PJM*, 8: 355–56. Madison used this passage to make a brief endorsement of Jefferson's proposal to allow two departments of government "to call a

plenipotentiary convention" to deal with possible constitutional violations, a proposal he later went out of his way to criticize, in *Federalist* 49 and 50. See Bailey, *James Madison and Constitutional Imperfection*, 22–24.

21. *PJM*, 8: 299.

22. As his letter to Monroe of October 5, 1786, *PJM*, 9: 140–41, suggests.

23. Madison to Jefferson, January 22, 1786, *PJM*, 8: 477.

24. Madison to Jefferson, August 12, 1786, *PJM*, 9: 93–95.

25. Madison to Washington, November 1, 1786, *PJM*, 9: 155.

26. One of the great if neglected monographs on revolutionary politics in the states is Irwin H. Polishook, *Rhode Island and the Union, 1774–1795* (Evanston, Ill., 1969).

27. Notwithstanding the fact that Jackson Turner Main titled his seminal study of state legislative behavior during this period *Political Parties before the Constitution* (Chapel Hill, N.C., 1972).

28. See Woody Holton, *Unruly Americans and the Origins of the Constitution* (New York, 2007). A better analysis of the public policy aspects of this issue is Roger H. Brown, *Redeeming the Republic: Federalists, Taxation, and the Origins of the Constitution* (Baltimore, 1993). But for a longer-term view, see Max M. Edling and Mark D. Kaplanoff, "Alexander Hamilton's Fiscal Reform: Transforming the Structure of Taxation in the Early Republic," *William and Mary Quarterly* 61 (2004), 713–44.

29. *PJM*, 9: 95.

30. Madison to Washington, November 1, 1786, *PJM*, 9: 154. On the significance of the agrarian laws to republican political theory, see the provocative first book (but all his books are provocations) of Eric Nelson, *The Greek Tradition in Republican Political Thought* (New York, 2004).

31. "Notes of Debates," February 19, 1787, *PJM*, 9: 277. The association of power and right in the majority in this way recurs in "the Vices" and in *Federalist* 42, where it is explicitly linked with the Republican Guarantee Clause of the Constitution, Art. IV, Sect. 4.

32. One interesting aspect of Bilder's *Madison's Hand* is her effort to ascribe emotional valences to various passages in the "legislative diary" that became the notes of debates at the Philadelphia Convention. I find her effort intriguing but problematic.

33. Madison to Pendleton, February 24, 1787, and Madison to Jefferson, March 16, 1787, *PJM*, 9: 294, 318, and see 322n2, recording Nicholas P. Trist's comment that, when he and Madison discussed this letter to Jefferson in 1834, Madison explained that this reference to the "opposite extreme" explicitly meant monarchy. It might push the point to say that Madison's sensitivity to awaiting "the arcana of futurity" illustrates the historicist character of his intellect, with its awareness that future events always retain their capacity for surprise.

34. *PJM*, 9: 318. Here Madison was tacitly confronting the legal maxim *leges posteriores priores, contrarias abrogant*, which made the later statutory action of a legislature superior to prior enactments. Under that doctrine, a constitution approved by a legislature could be violated by a later meeting of the same body; or, to put the point another way, a constitution approved legislatively had only statutory authority. For further discussion of this critical point, see Rakove, *Original Meanings*, 94–130.

35. *PJM*, 9: 354.

36. Here it is essential for critically engaged readers to note that Mary Bilder actively challenges the conventional wisdom on the accepted timing of the formulation of this passage. Relying largely on the paper Madison used to complete this concluding section of item 11, she suggests that Madison did not develop this part of his analysis until some point after the April 1787 compilation of the preceding section of "the Vices." Bilder, *Madison's Hand*, 243–44. This suggestion needs to percolate among scholars for a while, and I do not attempt to resolve it here, though it is discussed with some skepticism in my review of her book in *Constitutional Commentary* (see Introduction, note 8, above). Among other technical points, note the close similarity between the penultimate paragraph of item 11 of "the Vices" and the corresponding paragraph in Madison's letter to Washington of April 16, 1787. *PJM*, 9: 357, 384. When Madison speaks of "interested majorities" in the letter to Washington, I believe he is referring to popular majorities in the body politic, which in turn implies that he was not interested solely in the problem of legislative misbehavior or misrule.

37. *PJM*, 9: 355. The use of the somewhat ambiguous phrase "if not more frequent" leaves me wondering whether Madison meant "and still more" or "although not." I usually incline toward the former reading as being more plausible but cannot wholly exclude the latter.

38. The term has acquired new interpretive meaning through the important book by Larry Kramer, *The People Themselves: Popular Constitutionalism and Judicial Review* (New York, 2004). See Kramer, "Madison's Audience," 611–79.

39. Douglass Adair, "The Tenth Federalist Revisited," and "'That Politics May Be Reduced to a Science': David Hume, James Madison, and the Tenth Federalist," in Trevor Colbourn, ed., *Fame and the Founding Fathers: Essays by Douglass Adair* (Chapel Hill, N.C., 1974), 75–106. In addition to Adair, other important contributors to the revival of deep scholarly interest in *Federalist* 10 include Robert Dahl and (among the Straussians) Martin Diamond. An essential contribution to the historiography of the essay is Paul Bourke, "The Pluralist Reading of James Madison's Tenth Federalist," *Perspectives in American History* 9 (1975), 271–95.

40. Madison to Randolph, April 8, 1787, *PJM*, 9: 369.

41. It is worth noting, however, that in the Continental Congress the states did not vote as delegations; rather, when roll calls were taken, each delegate voted individually, and a state's vote was simply the function of its personal tallies.

42. Madison to Washington, April 16, 1787, *PJM*, 9: 383. On the demographic forecasts for post-revolutionary America, see Drew McCoy, "James Madison and Visions of American Nationality in the Confederation Period," in Richard Beeman, Stephen Botein, and Edward C. Carter II, eds., *Beyond Confederation: Origins of the Constitution and American National Identity* (Chapel Hill, N.C., 1987), 261–94.

43. Madison to Jefferson, October 24, 1787, *PJM*, 10:212.

44. *PJM*, 9: 383.

45. *RFC*, 1: 21.

46. See Rufus King's notes for May 31, which have Madison saying that "he had brought with him a strong prepossession for the defining of the limits and powers of the federal Legislature, but he brought with him some doubts about the practicality of doing it:—at present he was convinced it could not be done." *RFC*, 1: 60. One could interpret "at present" either as a rhetorical hedge against the course of debate or as a confirmation of a substantive point made in his 1785 letter to Caleb Wallace, where he doubted the feasibility of limiting legislative power per se but thought it might be regulated by adopting rights-affirming provisions. *PJM*, 8: 351.

47. This is an admittedly difficult issue to decipher, and one wishes that Articles 2 and 5 of the Virginia Plan had been kinder to scholars by being a shade more explicit. The debate of June 7, 1787, clearly implies that some framers, arguably led by James Wilson, clearly thought that the Senate did not have to represent each state individually. On May 31, according to Madison's notes, Wilson had proposed that the people should elect both houses. "He suggested the mode of chusing the Senate of N. York, to wit of uniting several election districts, for one branch, in chusing members for the other branch, to be a good model." Madison's comments, immediately following Wilson's speech, indicate that the latter's proposal was to combine several states into electoral districts for the appointment of senators. Madison criticized this idea; Charles Pinckney endorsed it. *RFC*, 1: 52, 58–59. The discussion was renewed on June 7. About this occasion, Mary Bilder cites the notes of John Lansing to indicate that Madison endorsed Wilson's proposal ("Mr. Maddison same Opinion" as Wilson). Equally important, Bilder further holds, is that the notes of debates preserved in Madison's papers, which do *not* indicate his support of multistate districts, were "replaced sheets" that he later substituted for his earlier records. See Bilder, *Madison's Hand*, 74–77, 244–45; and James H. Hutson, ed., *Supplement to Max Farrand's Records of the Federal Convention of 1787* (New Haven, 1987), 58–59 (for Lansing's comment and Wilson's draft resolution).

48. *RFC*, 1: 151-52.

49. *RFC*, 1: 154.

50. The council of revision was initially discussed on June 4, but debate was postponed until June 6 after Elbridge Gerry introduced a motion giving the executive a limited negative over legislation. *RFC*, 1: 97-98, 104. There are famous problems with ascertaining the contents of Madison's speeches of June 4 and 6 that I do not deal with here; they seem largely extraneous to my argument; but see Bilder, *Madison's Hand*, 70-74.

51. But, then again, consider John Marshall's role in the run-up to *Marbury v. Madison*, when, as outgoing secretary of state, he failed to deliver Marbury's judicial commission.

52. *RFC*, 2: 73-74.

53. *RFC*, 2: 76.

54. *RFC*, 2: 77.

55. *RFC*, 2: 298.

56. Rakove, *Original Meanings*, 108-10; *DHRC*, 13: 238.

57. *Federalist 62, PJM*, 10: 536 (the interior quote is from Washington's letter of September 17, 1787, to the Continental Congress, enclosing the Constitution).

58. *Federalist 47, PJM*, 10: 448-49.

59. *Federalist 37, PJM*, 10: 362.

60. *Federalist 48, PJM*, 10: 456-57.

61. See the remarkable comment on this argument in his notes on government of 1791 at *PJM*, 15:158-60.

62. *Federalist 10, PJM*, 10: 265-66.

63. Gordon S. Wood, "Is There a 'James Madison Problem'?" in Wood, *Revolutionary Characters: What Made the Founders Different* (New York, 2006), 162-64.

64. *Federalist 52, PJM*, 10: 488-93.

65. *Federalist 55, PJM*, 10: 504-5.

66. *Federalist 58, PJM*, 10: 531.

67. *Federalist 62, PJM*, 10: 537.

68. He could, for example, have developed Oliver Ellsworth's description of the Senate as a confirmation of the "partly federal, partly national" nature of the union to justify either the equal state vote or election of senators by the state legislatures. Instead he borrowed the term and applied it to the complicated task of describing the entire federal system in *Federalist 39*.

69. *Federalist 62, PJM*, 10: 537-38.

70. *Federalist 62, PJM*, 10: 538-40.

71. Jeremy Bailey raises serious questions about just how long Madison continued to believe in this ideal of deliberation. Bailey, *James Madison and Constitutional Imperfection*, 38-58. For some contemporary reflections on

the relation between Madison's ideals and the pathetic state of the Senate today, see Jack Rakove, "A Model for Deliberation or Obstruction: Madison's Thoughts about the Senate," in Benjamin Wittes and Pietro Nivola, eds., *What Would Madison Do? The Father of the Constitution Meets Modern American Politics* (Washington, D.C., 2015), 111–28.

   72. *Federalist* 63, *PJM*, 10: 550.

CHAPTER 3. "WHEREVER THE REAL POWER LIES"

   1. Randolph's letter to the Virginia assembly, October 10, 1787, is reprinted in *DHRC*, 15: 123–35; Randolph to Madison, December 27, 1787, and Madison to Randolph, January 10, 1788, *PJM*, 10: 346–47, 354–56. Madison returned to this theme in *Federalist* 38.
   2. *PJM*, 9: 318, 352.
   3. For a more complete discussion, see Rakove, *Original Meanings*, 96–102.
   4. Maier, *Ratification*, 97–124.
   5. Maier presents a more sympathetic account of the second convention movement, particularly after the idea was endorsed by the New York convention in July 1788. Many of the suggestions to emerge from the ratification debates might not have proved so controversial, she suggests. Yet she also notes that the one provision that struck the greatest accord among the Constitution's opponents—to require the national government to rely on the old method of seeking requisitions from the states before it could resort to direct taxes—struck directly against the Federalist conception of the new federal structure they wished to create. Ibid., 425–29.
   6. *PJM*, 10: 355–56.
   7. *Federalist* 10, *PJM*, 10: 267–68.
   8. Constitutional thinking is obviously only one aspect of political thinking, and some readers might find my attempt to distinguish them arbitrary or problematic. Even so, I find this a useful way not only to distinguish different facets of Madison's thinking but also to sketch a tension within it.
   9. *Federalist* 51, *PJM*, 10: 478.
   10. Banning, "James Madison, the Statute for Religious Freedom," 109.
   11. Committee draft of the article on religion [May 27–28, 1774], *PJM*, 1: 174.
   12. Lest one consider this an eighteenth-century anachronism, consider the difficulties that Jehovah's Witnesses encountered, and the leading constitutional law cases they brought, in their often abrasive efforts to disseminate their views in the late 1930s and early 1940s. See Shawn Francis Peters, *Judging Jehovah's Witnesses: Religious Persecution and the Dawn of the Rights Revolution* (Lawrence, Kans., 2000).
   13. Drafts of Madison's amendment [May 29–June 17, 1776], *PJM*, 1: 174–75.
   14. Madison to William Bradford, January 24, 1774, *PJM*, 1: 106.

15. See, in particular, Chris Beneke, *Beyond Toleration: The Religious Origins of American Pluralism* (New York, 2006), 113–55.

16. It is a profound misunderstanding to presume that bills or declarations of rights had the same constitutional authority in 1776 that they came to acquire by 1789, when Madison compelled a reluctant House of Representatives to take up the subject of amendments. In 1776 such texts operated primarily as statements of principle, supplementing the legal authority of the new constitutions. By 1789 the textual affirmation of a right had become a super-legal constitutional command. This transformation is described at greater length in Jack Rakove, *Declaring Rights: A Brief History with Documents* (Boston, 1997).

17. Madison to Jefferson, January 22, 1786, *PJM*, 8: 474.

18. Banning, *Sacred Fire of Liberty*, 100–102.

19. *PJM*, 8: 299–300.

20. Banning, *Sacred Fire of Liberty*, 100–102.

21. Madison to Caleb Wallace, August 23, 1785, *PJM*, 8: 353.

22. See Madison's speech of August 7, 1787, and his accompanying editorial footnote, *RFC*, 2: 203–4 and n17. Speaking at this point in the debates, Madison's justification was that the less propertied members of society would still enjoy an "indirect share of representation in the national government" through the Senate. Mary Bilder suggests that Madison revised his notes on this point to make his views on the restriction of the suffrage to landholders appear "more tentative" than they had been. Bilder, *Madison's Hand*, 127, 217. One has to be careful about pushing the proto-Malthusian aspects of Madison's thinking too far. On this point, see the insightful essay by Drew McCoy, "Jefferson and Madison on Malthus: Population Growth in Jeffersonian Political Economy," *Virginia Magazine of History and Biography* 88 (1980), 259–76. For further discussion, see Madison's "Observations on the 'Draught of a Constitution for Virginia" [October 1788], *PJM*, 11: 285–86.

23. Again, it is important to note the questions that Bilder (*Madison's Hand*) has raised about the exact timing of the composition of the concluding passages of item 11.

24. *PJM*, 9: 354–57, for this and the following paragraphs.

25. Colleen Sheehan makes the same observation in *James Madison and the Spirit Republican Self-Government*, 87, though she might have some reservations about the extent of the shift in his opinions from the 1780s to the 1790s.

26. Ibid., 57–83.

27. On this point, see as well Banning, *Sacred Fire of Liberty*, 445n52.

28. *PJM*, 9: 357, 384.

29. *PJM*, 9: 357, 10: 268.

30. For anyone trained (as I was) in Harvard's Department of History, it is essential to mention the enormously influential book on this subject

by Oscar Handlin and Mary Handlin, *Commonwealth: A Study of the Role of Government in the American Economy: Massachusetts, 1774–1861* (Cambridge, 1969 [1944]), along with the companion volumes written by Louis Hartz on Pennsylvania, Milton Heath on Georgia, and Harry Scheiber on Ohio.

31. Thus, to take the obvious examples, consider the prohibition on taxes on exports or the denial of preferences to the ports of particular states in Art. I, Sect. 9, or, more important, the clauses prohibiting the states from enacting laws impairing the obligation of contracts or from emitting bills of credit in Art. I, Sect. 10.

32. Madison to Jefferson, September 6, 1787, *PJM*, 10: 163–64 (speaking of "the local mischiefs which every where excite disgusts agst the state governments"); and "Observations on the 'Draught of a Constitution for Virginia,'" *PJM*, 11: 285–86, in which Madison suggests that a six-year Senate, "by correcting the infirmities of popular Government . . . will prevent that disgust agst. that form which may otherwise produce a sudden transition to some very different one."

33. *PJM*, 10: 456 (alluding to articles in the state constitutions affirming the separation of powers, whose chief end, according to Montesquieu, was the protection of liberty).

34. Jefferson to Madison, March 15, 1789, *PJM*, 12: 13.

35. See especially the conclusions drawn by Banning in *Sacred Fire of Liberty*, 190–91, where he notes that "the discontents expressed at the convention's close are not a certain guide to his mature convictions." In the important chapter that follows, which deals primarily with *The Federalist*, Banning explains what those convictions were. In a general sense, I remain somewhat skeptical about Banning's claim. The experience of the Convention certainly inspired Madison to think more deeply about the entire process of forming and adopting a constitution—a topic we examine in the next chapter. But on the issues he had analyzed most closely his essential opinions remained intact. There is a significant difference between adjusting to the new realities that a course of political decision making has created, on the one hand, and rethinking one's preferences and commitments, on the other.

36. Madison to Jefferson, September 6, 1787, *PJM*, 10: 163–64.

37. Madison to Jefferson, October 24, 1787, *PJM*, 10: 209–11.

38. *PJM*, 10: 212–14.

39. Jefferson to Madison, December 20, 1787, *PJM*, 10: 335. It says something about the vagaries of eighteenth-century correspondence that Jefferson reported receiving three Madison letters (written July 18, September 6, and October 24) all within the previous week.

40. Bilder suggests, rather intriguingly, that there was a fundamental difference between Madison and Jefferson in the nature and depth of their attachment to the Constitution. *Madison's Hand*, 202–4.

41. *PJM*, 10: 336–38.

42. Jefferson to Alexander Donald, February 7, 1788, *PTJ*, 12: 571. Jefferson expressed the same sentiments in a letter to Madison written the day before; ibid., 569–70.

43. Madison to Jefferson, August 10, 1788; *PJM*, 11: 226.

44. Madison to Jefferson, August 23, 1788, *PJM*, 11: 238–39.

45. Madison to Jefferson, September 21, 1788, *PJM*, 11: 258.

46. Speech of June 24, 1788, *DHRC*, 10: 1507.

47. See Madison's long speech of June 24, 1788, *PJM*, 11: 172–77.

48. Jefferson to Madison, July 31, 1788, *PJM*, 11: 212–13.

49. "Observations on the 'Draught of a Constitution for Virginia,'" *PJM*, 11: 281–95.

50. Madison to Jefferson, October 17, 1788, *PJM*, 11: 297.

51. Rakove, *Original Meanings*, 323–25.

52. *PJM*, 11: 299–300.

53. It is important to recall that Montesquieu's seminal account of the separation of powers in *The Spirit of the Laws* was tied to the idea that one could exercise one's liberty only when one was confident that authority over the making and enforcement of law would not reside in one set of hands; that is, his conception of the separation of powers was intimately tied to a theory of rights (the right to exercise one's liberty being fundamental to eighteenth-century Anglo-American thinking). This is why Madison's reference to "parchment barriers" in *Federalist* 48, the essay that reformulated his approach to the separation of powers, makes perfect sense as an element in his assessment of the value of bills of rights. It is worth noting that this issue is powerfully echoed in modern debates among republican political theorists, such as Sir Quentin Skinner and Philip Pettit, who define liberty not merely as the absence of restraint but also in terms that emphasize the moral capacity of individuals to exercise their liberty.

54. *The Ratification of the New Fœderal Constitution, Together with the Amendments, Proposed by the Several States* (Richmond, Va., 1788).

55. *DHRC*, 10: 1541.

56. *DHRC*, 9: 818–23, and see headnote, 811–13.

57. Madison to Edmund Randolph, October 17, 1788, *PJM*, 11: 305.

58. Edward Carrington to Madison, October 19, 1788, and Henry Lee to Madison, November 19, 1788, *PJM*, 11: 305–6, 356.

59. Madison to Randolph, November 23, 1788, *PJM*, 11: 362–63.

60. I discuss this at greater length in "The Structure of Politics at the Accession of George Washington," in Beeman et al., *Beyond Confederation*, 261–94.

61. Edward Carrington Madison, November 26, 1788, *PJM*, 11: 369; Madison to Washington, January 14, 1789, *PJM*, 11: 418; Benjamin Johnson to Madison, January 19, 1789, *PJM*, 11: 423–24.

62. Turbeville to Madison, December 14, 1788, *PJM*, 11: 396–97; Hardin Burnley to Madison, December 16, 1788, *PJM*, 11: 398.

63. David Jameson Jr. to Madison, January 14, 1789, *PJM*, 11: 419.

64. Madison to George Eve, January 2, 1789, *PJM*, 11: 404–5.

65. See the remarkably lengthy and detailed discussion of this issue in Madison to George Thompson, January 29, 1789, *PJM*, 11: 433–37.

66. *PJM*, 11: 438–39nn1, 2.

67. Benjamin Johnson to Madison, January 19, 1789, *PJM*, 11: 423–24.

68. On this, see Rakove, *Beginnings of National Politics*, 243–74.

69. Rakove, "Structure of Politics," 290–94.

70. Robert Morris to James Wilson, August 23, 1789, Willing, Morris, and Swanwick Papers, Pennsylvania Historical and Museum Commission, Harrisburg; quoted in Rakove, "Structure of Politics," 256n53.

71. "Notes for Speech in Congress" [pre-June 8, 1789], *PJM*, 12: 193.

72. Speech in Congress, June 8, 1789, *PJM*, 12: 204.

73. Speech of August 8, 1789, *PJM*, 12: 344.

74. *PJM*, 14: 170.

CHAPTER 4. "THE EXPERIMENTS ARE OF TOO TICKLISH A NATURE TO BE UNNECESSARILY MULTIPLIED"

1. Madison to Randolph, January 10, 1788, *PJM*, 10: 354–56.

2. Freeman, *Alexander Hamilton: Writings*, 171.

3. *Federalist* 37, *PJM*, 10: 359–60.

4. *PJM*, 10: 360–61.

5. *PJM*, 10: 361–63.

6. *PJM*, 10: 364.

7. *PJM*, 10: 361–62.

8. *Federalist* 37, *PJM*, 10: 362–63. On Madison's interest in the law as such, see Bilder, "James Madison, Law Student and Demi-Lawyer," 389–449.

9. On this subject, I have learned a great deal from Hannah Dawson, *Locke, Language, and Early-Modern Philosophy* (New York, 2007).

10. Rakove, "Thinking Like a Constitution," 1–26.

11. For a broader discussion of this theme, as it relates to the Federalist cause more generally (but also to Madison), see Bailyn, *Ideological Origins*, 351–75.

12. *PJM*, 10: 362–63.

13. *PJM*, 10: 377–78; Adams, *Thoughts on Government*, in Kurland and Lerner, *Founders' Constitution*, 1: 108.

14. See Rakove, *Original Meanings*, 181–88, for a discussion of the use of the term "consolidation" in the ratification debates.

15. *Federalist* 39, *PJM*, 10: 379–82.

16. *Federalist* 47, *PJM*, 10: 448–54.
17. *Federalist* 48, *PJM*, 10: 456–57.
18. *Federalist* 14, *PJM*, 10: 287–88; cf. Bailey, *James Madison and Constitutional Imperfection*, 15–37, for a more skeptical reading of the value Madison placed on veneration.
19. *Federalist* 49, *PJM*, 10: 461.
20. *PJM*, 10: 461–62.
21. *PJM*, 10: 462.
22. *PJM*, 10: 462–63.
23. Ibid.
24. *PJM*, 10: 268. Wood, *Creation of the American Republic*, 560–61. Though many readers doubtless miss the reference, the phrase "liberal tradition" links Wood's observation to Louis Hartz, *The Liberal Tradition in America: An Interpretation of American Political Thought since the Revolution* (New York, 1955).
25. Here my analysis runs fairly close to, but does not wholly agree with, the important essay by my colleague and friend John Ferejohn, "Madisonian Separation of Powers," in Kernell, *James Madison*, 126–55.
26. The point may seem obvious, but it is important to say 1800–1801 because the election was not completed until the 28th ballot in the House of Representatives finally made Jefferson the new president and his alienated running mate, Aaron Burr, vice president.
27. On this point, we await the publication of Jonathan Gienapp, *Inventing the Fixed Constitution: Language, Justification, and Constitutional Interpretation at the American Founding* (Harvard University Press, forthcoming). In the meantime, Gienapp, "Making Constitutional Meaning: The Removal Debate and the Birth of Constitutional Essentialism," *Journal of the Early Republic* 35 (2015), 375–418, marks a good place to start. See also Ferejohn, "Madisonian Separation of Powers," 144–48.
28. Or, as I argue in the conclusion of *Original Meanings*, 365, the ideal of constitutional neutrality "could rarely be attained when the Constitution was so highly politicized, or when politics was so highly constitutionalized." By this I mean that rival readings of the Constitution inevitably emanated from intense political disputes, and political disputes frequently escalated into constitutional quarrels.
29. Wood, "Is There a 'James Madison Problem'?" esp. 165–72. Our understanding of the nature of the early American nation-state has been enormously enhanced by two works of Max Edling: *A Revolution in Favor of Government: Origins of the U.S. Constitution and the Making of the American State* (New York, 2003); and *A Hercules in the Cradle: War, Money, and the American State* (Chicago, 2014). Edling (a Swedish scholar) offers a badly needed Hamiltonian corrective to the Madisonian emphases that dominate American scholarship, including of course my own approach.

30. That experience included participating in the Fifth Provincial Convention, which drafted the Virginia constitution, and sitting on the congressional committee that was assigned the task of asking how the Articles of Confederation would actually be implemented once they were finally ratified in 1781.

31. Ferejohn, "Madisonian Separation of Powers," 130.

32. Madison to Edmund Randolph, March 1, 1789, *PJM*, 11: 453.

33. Madison to Jefferson, March 29, 1789, *PJM*, 12: 38.

34. *Federalist 44*, *PJM*, 10: 422–24.

35. *PJM*, 10: 424.

36. Hamilton to Edward Carrington, May 26, 1792, in Harold Syrett and Jacob Cooke, eds., *The Papers of Alexander Hamilton* (New York, 1961–87), 11: 426–44, provides a lengthy account of his quarrel with Madison and Jefferson (quotation at 428).

37. Freeman, *Alexander Hamilton: Writings*, 323.

38. I discuss this situation at greater length in *Revolutionaries*, 424–42.

39. Jefferson to Philip Freneau, February 28, 1791, *PTJ*, 19: 351.

40. *PJM*, 14: 137–39.

41. The identification of these essays as Madison's depends on the existence of both a set of reading notes that closely correspond to the published texts and Madison's own initialing of his contributions in a bound volume of the *National Gazette* that can be found in the Library of Congress. See *PJM*, 14: 157–70 and the editorial notes appended to the original essays in the same volume.

42. *PJM*, 14: 170; and 11: 198–99. In his private notes, Madison wrote that "a bill of rights . . . acquires efficacy as time sanctifies and incorporates it with the public sentiment." *PJM*, 14: 162–63.

43. Rakove, *Original Meanings*, 332–36.

44. *PJM*, 14: 170.

45. *PJM*, 14: 179.

46. Charters, *National Gazette*, January 18, 1792, *PJM*, 14: 191–92.

47. Ibid.

48. Colleen Sheehan, *Mind of James Madison*, 13–14.

49. *PJM*, 15: 158–60; and see Sheehan, *Mind of James Madison*, 31–33. Although I do not follow Sheehan in emphasizing the last sentence of this quotation (". . . thorough investigation"), I agree with her sentiment. This is a truly remarkable aside.

50. Madison to Henry Lee, January 1, 1792, *PJM*, 14: 180.

51. Madison to Edmund Pendleton, January 21, 1792, *PJM*, 14: 195–96; and see his similar letter to Henry Lee of the same date, ibid., 193–94.

52. Madison to Edmund Pendleton, December 18, 1791, *PJM*, 14: 157; speech in the House of Representatives, March 10, 1792, ibid., 250–52. Washington

vetoed the resolution after its passage. On the link between revolution and constitution, see Keith Michael Baker, "Fixing the French Constitution," in Baker, *Inventing the French Revolution* (Cambridge, U.K., 1990), 252–305.

53. *PJM*, 14: 381; the resolution of the National Assembly can be found in Syrett and Cooke, *Papers of Alexander Hamilton*, 12: 545–46. Hamilton is misnamed "Jean Hamilton" and Madison appears as "N. Maddison," but other dignitaries include Jeremy Bentham, Joseph Priestley, Thomas Paine, and the two British enemies of the slave trade, William Wilberforce and Thomas Clarkson.

54. Washington, Memorandum to Cabinet, April 18, 1793, in W. W. Abbott and Dorothy Twohig, eds., *The Papers of George Washington: Presidential Series* (Charlottesville, Va., 1987–), 12: 452–53; Jefferson, "Notes on a Cabinet Meeting," May 6, 1793, ibid., 529–30.

55. Jefferson to Madison, July 7, 1793, *PJM*, 15: 43.

56. Madison to Jefferson, July 22, 1793, *PJM*, 15: 46–47.

57. Madison to Jefferson, July 30, 1793, *PJM*, 15: 48.

58. Helvidius I, *PJM*, 15: 67. The relevant sentence: "The executive power of the United States shall be vested in a single individual."

59. Pacificus I can be found in Freeman, *Alexander Hamilton: Writings*, 801–9 (quotation at 805).

60. *PJM*, 15: 68. In my perhaps immodest view, Madison is too harsh on Locke.

61. Madison to Caleb Wallace, August 23, 1785, *Madison: Writings*, 41.

62. June 1, 1787, *RFC*, 1: 21, 65–66, 70. Wilson was no foe of a vigorous executive. He figures prominently in Eric Nelson's account of the "patriot royalist" origins of the presidency, Nelson, *The Royalist Revolution: Monarchy and the American Founding* (Cambridge, 2014), as well as in Ray Raphael, *Mr. President: How and Why the Founders Created a Chief Executive* (New York, 2012).

63. Now known in some circles as "the Decision of 1789." See Saikrishna Prakash, "New Light on the Decision of 1789," *Cornell Law Review* 91 (2006), 1021–78; and Gienapp, "Making Constitutional Meaning."

64. *Federalist 75*, in Freeman, *Alexander Hamilton: Writings*, 403–4.

65. "Detached Memoranda" [1819?], in *Madison: Writings*, 770.

66. Thus, see the comment by Saikrishna Bangalore Prakash, who notes that "many have deemed Helvidius the loser of the debate." Prakash, *Imperial from the Beginning: The Constitution of the Original Executive* (New Haven, 2015), 124–25.

67. "Substance of a Conversation with the President," May 5, 1792, in *Madison: Writings*, 519–21.

68. Ibid., 521–23.

69. Madison to Jefferson, September 2, 1793, *PJM*, 15: 92–93.

70. The editors of *The Papers of James Madison* conclude that the Republicans enjoyed an initial 57–48 advantage in the House and the Federalists a 17–13 margin in the Senate after Albert Gallatin was disqualified over the time since his naturalization. *PJM*, 15: 146. Given the primitive nature of party organization, one should be cautious about assigning a fixed partisan identity to many members.

71. Madison to Jefferson, May 25, 1794, *PJM*, 15: 337–38.

72. Madison to Jefferson, November 16, 1794, *PJM*, 15: 380.

73. Speech in Congress, November 27, 1794, *PJM*, 15: 390–92; Madison to Jefferson, November 30, 1794, ibid., 396–98.

74. Madison to Monroe, December 4, 1794, *PJM*, 15: 405–6. Madison's point on "the general tendency of insurrections" echoes his important October 17, 1788, letter to Jefferson on the advantages of bills of rights.

75. *Political Observations* (Philadelphia, 1795), in *PJM*, 15: 521–22. For Madison's disparaging assessment of this pamphlet, see his letter to Jefferson, June 14, 1795, *PJM*, 16: 20.

76. Livingston to Madison, July 6, 1795, and Madison to Livingston, August 10, 1795, *PJM*, 16: 34–35, 48.

77. Madison credited his defeat on this point to the joint opposition of "the whole Treaty party" (the Federalists) with "the warmer men on the other side" (i.e., the Republicans). Madison to Monroe, April 18, 1796, *PJM*, 16: 333.

78. Madison to Jefferson, March 6, 1796, *PJM*, 16: 247.

79. An essential source here is Jeffrey L. Pasley, *The First Presidential Contest: 1796 and the Founding of American Democracy* (Lawrence, Kans., 2013), 132–48, which fills the proverbial much-needed gap in scholarship by providing a comprehensive study of the first contested presidential election.

80. On the preparation of the petition, see the excellent editorial headnote in *PJM*, 16: 62–69, which is followed by the draft text. The later statement on Art. I, Sec. 8 is ibid., 102. For the proposed constitutional amendments, see Thomas J. Farnham, "The Virginia Amendments of 1795: An Episode in the Opposition to Jay's Treaty," *Virginia Magazine of History and Biography* 75 (1967), 75–88.

81. *PJM*, 16: 255–63.

82. *PJM*, 16: 293–301. See also Rakove, *Original Meanings*, 358–65.

83. Murray, quoted in Rakove, *Original Meanings*, 361–62.

84. Message to the House of Representatives, March 30, 1796, in Rhodehamel, *George Washington: Writings*, 930–32.

85. Bilder, *Madison's Hand*, 141–45. I disagree with Bilder's argument that Madison's conception of his notes as a text to be preserved for history emerged only later.

86. Madison to Jefferson, April 4, 1796, *PJM*, 16: 286. Madison did not have his notes with him when he wrote; instead, he asked Jefferson to check his

copy, which had been made by John Wayles Eppes, and report back to him, which Jefferson did in his reply of April 17, 1796, ibid., 328–29. See Bilder, *Madison's Hand*, 219–20.

87. *PJM*, 16: 294–95.

88. *PJM*, 16: 297.

89. Madison noted that he had "no recollection" of the motion in question, a remark that well supports Bilder's account of Madison in the final weeks of the Convention, when his efforts to cover each day's debate effectively collapsed. *PJM:* 16: 295.

90. There is a nice account of this in Pasley, *First Presidential Contest*, 152–62.

91. Madison to Jefferson, May 1, 1796, *PJM*, 16: 343.

92. Helvidius IV, in *PJM*, 15: 106–7.

93. Madison to Jefferson, December 29, 1798, *PJM*, 17: 191–92. See Ralph Ketcham, *James Madison: A Biography* (Charlottesville, Va., 1971), 393–97.

94. In this paragraph and below, I draw on Rakove, "The Political Presidency: Discovery and Invention," in James Horn, Jan Ellen Lewis, and Peter Onuf, eds., *The Revolution of 1800: Democracy, Race, and the New Republic* (Charlottesville, Va., 2002), esp. 50–56.

95. Charles Pinckney to Madison, May 16, 1799, and September 30, 1799 (for quoted passages), *PJM*, 17: 250–51, 272.

96. Jefferson to Monroe, January 12, 1800, *PTJ*, 31: 300–301. Lest one think that candidate Jefferson was thoroughly detached from election details, the remainder of this letter demonstrates how closely he was following every political twist and turn.

97. Noble Cunningham Jr., *The Jeffersonian Republicans: The Formation of Party Organization, 1789–1801* (Chapel Hill, N.C., 1957), 144–47.

98. Hamilton to Jay, May 7, 1800, in Syrett and Cooke, *Papers of Alexander Hamilton*, 24: 464–66.

99. Cunningham, *Jeffersonian Republicans*, 188–92.

100. Madison to George Hay, August 23, 1823, and see his letter to George McDuffie, January 3, 1824, both accessible at Founders Online, National Archives, http://founders.archives.gov/documents/Madison/99-02-02-0023 and 0127. I owe this reference to Edward B. Foley, and see the discussion in his book, *Ballot Battles: The History of Disputed Elections in the United States* (New York, 2016), 70–74. Madison came to favor the appointment of electors by districts and a contingent election of the president by Congress voting in joint session, which would do away with the still-objectionable principle of the equality of states.

101. Richard Hofstadter, *The Idea of a Party System: The Rise of Legitimate Opposition in the United States, 1780–1840* (Berkeley, Calif., 1969), 111–21. Much more has been written about the rise and evolution of American party systems since, yet there is a concise wisdom to Hofstadter's observations that few other historians have attained.

102. Jefferson to Madison, December 20, 1800, *PJM*, 17: 448.

103. See Madison to Jefferson, January 10, 1801, in *PJM*, 17: 453–54.

EPILOGUE

1. A view ably expressed by that well-known Madisonian Karl Rove, who deems him "a great constitutionalist, a halfway decent secretary of state and a lousy president." Richard Berke, "In the White House, a Sense of What History Can Teach," *New York Times*, January 9, 2002, A18. One might only note that Madison left the White House a popular president, which was not exactly the fate shared by the president Rove advised.

2. Wood, "Is There a 'James Madison Problem'?" 170–71.

3. One noteworthy partial exception here, of course, is the wonderful study of Madison's retirement by Drew McCoy, *The Last of the Fathers: James Madison and the Republican Legacy* (New York, 1989), but McCoy, too, deals with only a limited, though obviously critical, range of issues.

4. In retrospect, one wonders whether Madison wished he could have rewritten *Federalist* 39 to give this point about the judicial role greater emphasis. As his correspondence with Spencer Roane after the Supreme Court's decisions in *McCulloch v. Maryland* (1819) and *Cohens v. Virginia* (1821) makes clear, Madison understood that the Supreme Court remained the best arbiter of the boundaries of federalism. For further discussion, see Jack Rakove, "Judicial Power in the Constitutional Theory of James Madison," *William and Mary Law Review* 43 (2002), 1513–47.

5. Madison to William Cabell Rives, March 12, 1833, in *Madison: Writings*, 864. On Rives, see Barclay Rives, *William Cabell Rives: A Country to Serve* (New York, 2014).

6. Madison to Robert Walsh Jr., November 27, 1819, *PJM: Retirement Series*, 1: 557–58.

7. *RFC*, 1: 486–87, discussed in Rakove, *Original Meanings*, 68–69. Bilder proposes, in one of her characteristically provocative suppositions, that Madison "may have no longer been recording spoken words but writing his developing thoughts." *Madison's Hand*, 108.

8. Sheehan, *Mind of James Madison*, 138–40. Beyond the dominance of slavery, Madison also cites the exclusion of non-freeholders from the suffrage as a further source of aristocracy.

9. McCoy, *Last of the Fathers*, remains the best depiction of Madison's conservatism on the question of slavery.

10. "Advice to My Country," in *Madison: Writings*, 866.

11. A story well told in Michael Vorenberg, *Final Freedom: The Civil War, the Abolition of Slavery, and the Thirteenth Amendment* (New York, 2001).

12. Rakove, *Original Meanings*, 337–38 and note. The quotation comes from Madison's letter to Jared Sparks (that original miscreant of historical editing), June 1, 1831.

INDEX

Adair, Douglass, 74, 107
Adams, Abigail, 4
Adams, John, 3, 4, 7, 58–59, 63, 144, 158, 162, 169, 179
Adams, Samuel, 194n9
agrarian laws, 69, 201n30
Alien and Sedition Acts, 180
American Enlightenment, 58
American Revolution, founders' papers and, 3–4
Anglican Church, legal establishment of, 104
Anti-Federalists, 13, 84, 94, 124, 132–35
Articles of Confederation, 27–28; amendments to, 25, 32, 38, 39; execution of, 28; flaws, underlying, 29; incapacity of, 44; ratification of, 26; state legislatures' acts and, 97; structure of, 22; theory of, 34

Bailyn, Bernard, 18
Banning, Lance, 29, 207n35, 102, 107, 109, 121
Beccaria, Cesare, 62
bicameral legislative systems: criticism of, 63; justification for, 64; representation in, 109
Bilder, Mary Sarah, 195n11, 202n36, 203n47, 206n22, 215n7
bills of rights, 206n16, 208n53; authority of, 131; function of, 120; Madison on, 120–21, 124–28, 103–31, 134, 136, 160
Blackstone, William, 52

Bodin, Jean, 52
Burke, Edmund, 147
Burr, Aaron, 181, 182

Calhoun, John C., 187, 188
Cambridge school, 10, 19
Carroll, Charles, of Carrollton, 191
citizens: as arbiters of constitutional disputes, 146, 147, 149–50; classes of, 110, 111; defining the collective good, 118; equality of, 76; participating in public debate, 100, 139; political concerns of, 77; political intelligence of, 98–102; role of, in maintaining constitutional structure, 160; as source of Constitution's meaning, 174. *See also* public opinion
Clinton, George, 149
Congress. *See* Continental Congress; House of Representatives; Senate; U.S. Congress
constitution, thinking like a, 21–23, 143, 146, 183
Constitution (U.S.), 84; analysis of, 143; character of, 144–45, 167; executive power under, 165–68, 178–79; Fourteenth Amendment of, 191; Guarantee Clause of, 124; Just Compensation Clause of, 119; legal supremacy of, 97; as Madisonian, 84, 194n3; Necessary and Proper Clause of, 155–57, 178; perception of, as

146; on three departments of
government, 62–63; on upper
house, 79–80; view of the future,
111; in Virginia Assembly,
25, 26, 33, 34, 57, 59–62; and
Virginia legal code, 34, 37, 57,
58, 62; on Whiskey Rebellion,
171; writing for *National Gazette*,
159–61; writing included in
The Federalist, 5, 9–11, 19, 85,
133, 138; writings of (private,
unpublished), 5–6, 8–9, 16. *See
also* bill of rights; *Federalist, The*;
game theory
"Madison problem," 153–54,
179–80, 183–84
Maier, Pauline, 98, 199n, 205n5
majorities: formed within society,
113; misrule of, 17, 55, 67–68,
72, 74–75; restraint of, 73; rule
of, 41, 69; size of, 114; violating
minorities' rights, 112. *See also*
factious majorities
Mann's Tavern, 41
Marbury, William, 186
Marbury v. Madison, 185–86
Marie Antoinette, 170
Marquis de Condorcet, 46
Marshall, John, 186
Martin, Luther, 93
Maryland, presidential electors
in, 182
Mason, George, 3, 23, 33, 60, 96, 99,
131–32
Massachusetts: presidential
electors in, 181; Shays's
Rebellion in, 69
*Memorial and Remonstrance against
Religious Assessments* (Madison),
60–61, 67, 107
Mind of James Madison, The
(Sheehan), 161
Mississippi River, navigation
claims to, 40–42, 67, 74, 169
Monroe, James, 34, 40, 132, 133
Montesquieu, 10, 12, 45, 53, 74, 75,
86–87, 113, 141, 145, 166, 208n53

Montpelier, 4, 8, 33, 34, 39, 45, 107,
164, 179, 180, 187
Morris, Gouverneur, 121, 175
Morris, Robert, 3, 28–29, 31–32,
135–36, 197n11
Murray, William Vans, 175

national bank, debate over, 155,
156–59
National Gazette, 159
national government (pre-1789):
counterbalancing states'
deficiencies, 45; financial
stability of, 27; funding of, 30,
31–32; legislative powers of, 77,
78–79; powers of, 22, 24, 28, 49,
51, 56
national politics, 150–51
negative, 64, 71; given to executive,
80; judges involved in, 81;
protecting rights within the
states, 118; on state laws, 116,
121–22, 123–24
neutrality proclamation of 1793,
dispute over, 170
New York: constitution of, 64;
electoral laws in, 181
Nicholas, George, 60
North Carolina, ratification
convention of, 176
Notes on the State of Virginia
(Jefferson), 126
nullification, doctrine of, 180, 188

"Observations on the Draught of
a Constitution for Virginia"
(Madison), 126
office holding, rotation of, 140
Osgood, Samuel, 42–43

"Pacificus" essays (Hamilton), 6,
164, 165. See also *Federalist, The*;
Hamilton, Alexander
paper money, 68–69, 75, 110
Papers of James Madison, The, 3
parchment barriers, 82, 120, 127,
130, 208n53

party politics, discipline in, 170
party press essays, 5–6, 19, 115,
159–61, 163
Paterson, William, 92–93
Payne, Harry C., 58
Pendleton, Edmund, 58, 103
Penn, William, 64
Pennsylvania: internal politics
of, 55; during ratification, 98;
unicameral legislature in, 63–64
personal papers, 4
petitions, 105, 108
Pettit, Philip, 208n53
Philip of Macedon, 39
Pinckney, Charles, 40, 80, 181
Pocock, J. G. A., 10, 18
Political Observations (Madison),
172
political party system, 69;
development of, 151, 152; party
platforms for, 159; promotion
of, 152
political thinking, study of, 18–19
political writing, features of, 11
politics: constitutional
interpretation and, 151–52,
177–78; public interest in, 135
popular opinion, 115, 120
Porter, Charles, 65
Preface to Democratic Theory, A
(Dahl), 5
presidency: and control of
government, 158–59; partisan
competition for, 159; political
advantages of, 171, 179
presidential election of 1800–1801,
181–83, 185
private rights, 11, 16, 70, 72. *See also*
bills of rights
property: constitutional
protections for, 119; state
legislation and, 118; suffrage
and, 65, 109, 111, 206n22
property rights: legislation's effect
on, 119; protection of, 118–19;
security of, 108–11

Protestant culture, divisiveness
in, 117
public credit, 29–30
public good, 16, 70, 72; attention to,
11; pursuit of, 110
public opinion, 18, 19, 22,
114–15, 135; broad conception
of, 160, 161; influence of, 108;
mobilization of, 61, 133, 151,
170, 176–77; in national bank
debate, 159; political parties
and, 152, 153; posing dangers
to rights, 129–30; power of, 130;
and ratification, 98; rights and,
119–20
public policy, justice and, 89

Quasi-War of 1798, 177

Randolph, Edmund, 58, 78–79, 96,
99, 156, 169, 183
ratification conventions, 97–98,
135, 176
ratification debates (1787–88),
records of, 3
*Reflections on the Revolution in
France* (Burke), 147
religion: acting unjustly, 113;
disestablishment of, 104–5, 118;
equality among denominations,
104; freedom of, 24, 60, 78, 102–3,
105–6, 117, 118–19; public aid
for, 59–62; state legislation and,
118. *See also* general assessment
bill; Virginia Bill for Religious
Freedom
"Report on the Alien and Sedition
Acts" (Madison), 6
representation: basis for, 71;
changes in, 75–77; population
changes and, 65–66;
proportional, 79
representative bodies, deliberative
qualities of, 56
republicanism: crisis of,
26, factious evils of, 86;
homogeneity of, 64; language of,

states *(continued)*
  republican governments within,
    55; responsibilities of, under
    Confederation, 28; as rival
    jurisdictions, 49–51; settling
    disputes between, 116; size of,
    76–77, 140; sovereignty of, 45,
    77, 116, 122, 189; trespassing
    on others' rights, 47; voluntary
    compliance of, 17. *See also*
    negative
states' rights, 23, 180
Statute for Religious Freedom, 105
statutes, interpretation of, 142
Stuart v. Laird (1803), 186
suffrage, 109; property ownership
  and, 65, 111

Thomas, Isaiah, 60
Thoughts on Government (Adams),
  144
Tocqueville, Alexis de, 114, 147
treaties, 165, 166–67, 171–79
Treaty of Paris, 35, 169
Turbeville, George Lee, 133
Tyler, John, 38
tyranny, anarchy leading to, 129

United States: economic effects on,
  of war, 110; economic growth
  of, 119; enlargement of, 38, 39;
  foreign relations shifts for,
  163–64; regional divisions in, 76
upper house: character of, 79–80;
  representation in, 109
U.S. Congress (post-1789), relation
  with the executive, 151. *See
  also* House of Representatives;
  Senate

veneration for the government,
  constitutions and, 147–48
veto, presidential. *See* negative
"Vices of the Political System of the
  United States, The" (Madison),

16–17, 45–48, 51, 54, 63, 70, 71–72,
  93, 97, 100, 101, 111, 115–16, 127,
  195n11
Virginia Bill for Religious
  Freedom, 60, 62, 102, 108
Virginia: constitution of,
  34; delegation of, to the
  Constitutional Convention, 44;
  electoral laws in, 181, 182; legal
  code of, 34; planter elite in, 99;
  political turmoil in, 75; as pro-
  federal state, 34–35, 36; religious
  dissenters in, 104, 105
Virginia Declaration of Rights, 60,
  102–4, 132
Virginia House of Delegates, 8, 25,
  37, 48, 55–57
Virginia Plan, 78–80, 166, 203n47
Virginia Resolution of 1798, 180,
  187, 193

Washington, George, 3, 6, 31–32,
  43, 75, 132, 156, 199n; as attendee
  at Constitutional Convention,
  44; foreign relations during
  second presidential term of,
  163–64; Genet's defiance of,
  170; incumbency of, 167; and
  Jay's treaty negotiations with
  England, 172–73, 175; and
  journals from the Federal
  Convention, 176; parting
  address of, 35; retirement of,
  169; successors to, possibilities
  for, 169
Washington administration, 158
Wallace, Caleb, 4, 62, 109
Webster, Daniel, 188
Webster-Hayne debate, 188
Wilson, James, 29, 80–81, 125, 126,
  166, 200n18, 203n47
Witherspoon, John, 84
Wood, Gordon S., 18, 63, 89–90, 150,
  153, 157, 186–87
Wythe, George, 58